The Place of the Mosque

TOPOSOPHIA: SUSTAINABILITY, DWELLING, DESIGN

Toposophia is a book series dedicated to the interdisciplinary and transdisciplinary study of place. Authors in the series attempt to engage a geographical turn in their research, emphasizing the spatial component, as well as the philosophical turn, raising questions both reflectively and critically.

Series Editors:

Jessica Dubow (University of Sheffield) and Jeff Malpas (University of Tasmanua)

Editorial Board:

Edmunds Bunkse, Kim Dovey, Nader El-Bizri, Matti Itkonen, Eduardo Mendieta, John Murungi, John Pickles, Ingrid Leman Stefanovic

Books in the Series:

The Place of the Mosque: Genealogies of Space, Knowledge, and Power, by Akel Isma'il Kahera

Toward a Directionalist Theory of Space: On Going Nowhere, by H. Scott Hestevold

Urbanizing Carescapes of Hong Kong: Two Systems, One City, by Shu-Mei Huang

Mapping and Charting in Early Modern England and France: Power, Patronage, and Production, by Christine Petto

Remembering Places: A Phenomenological Study of the Relationship between Memory and Place, by Janet Donohoe

Spoil Island: Reading the Makeshift Archipelago, by Charlie Hailey

Reading the Islamic City: Discursive Practices and Legal Judgment, by Akel Isma'il Kahera

Metamorphoses of the Zoo: Animal Encounter after Noah, Edited by Ralph R. Acampora

The Timespace of Human Activity: On Performance, Society, and History as Indeterminate Teleological Events, by Theodore R. Schatzki

Environmental Dilemmas: Ethical Decision Making, by Robert Mugerauer and Lynne Manzo

When France Was King of Cartography: The Patronage and Production of Maps in Early Modern France, by Christine Petto

The Place of the Mosque

Genealogies of Space, Knowledge, and Power

Akel Isma'il Kahera

LEXINGTON BOOKS
Lanham • Boulder • New York • London

Published by Lexington Books
An imprint of The Rowman & Littlefield Publishing Group, Inc.
4501 Forbes Boulevard, Suite 200, Lanham, Maryland 20706
www.rowman.com

86-90 Paul Street, London EC2A 4NE

Copyright © 2022 by The Rowman & Littlefield Publishing Group, Inc.

All rights reserved. No part of this book may be reproduced in any form or by any electronic or mechanical means, including information storage and retrieval systems, without written permission from the publisher, except by a reviewer who may quote passages in a review.

British Library Cataloguing in Publication Information Available

Library of Congress Cataloging-in-Publication Data Available

ISBN 978-1-7936-4687-3 (cloth)
ISBN 978-1-7936-4689-7 (paper)
ISBN 978-1-7936-4688-0 (electronic)

In loving memory of Nebert Gaskin Millar (1927–2019)

Figure 0.0 Interior of the Dar al Islam Mosque at Abiquiú, New Mexico. Photograph.
Source: William R. Baker

Contents

List of Figures	ix
Preface	xiii
Acknowledgments	xvii
Introduction	1
Chapter 1: On the Genealogy of Place	13
Chapter 2: Resemblances and Similitudes	47
Chapter 3: Architecture and Ontology	83
Chapter 4: Place, Biopolitics, and Legal Discourses	123
Postscript	173
Appendix	189
Glossary	191
Bibliography	195
Index	213
About the Author	225

List of Figures

0.0 Interior of the Dar al Islam Mosque at Abiquiú, New Mexico. Photograph. Source: William R. Baker.   vi

0.1 The Great Mosque of Córdoba, main prayer space. Photograph. Source: Library of Congress.   3

0.2 The added chapel in the Great Mosque of Córdoba. Photograph. Source: Library of Congress.   4

0.3 The *mihrab* in the Great Mosque of Córdoba. Photograph. Source: Library of Congress.   6

1.1 Interior walls of the Alhambra, decorated with the Nasrid motto, "There is no Victor/Conqueror except God" (*la Ghalib ill-Allah*). Photograph. Source: William R. Baker.   21

1.2 Baghdad University mosque, designed by The Architects Collaborative. Photograph. Source: Ali Ihsan Al-Saqr.   26

1.3 Plan of the Baghdad University mosque. Drawing. Source: Muhammed Madandola.   26

1.4 Building section of the State Mosque of Baghdad, proposed by Venturi, Rauch, and Scott Brown. Drawing. Source: Muhammed Madandola.   28

1.5 Plan of the now-destroyed Babri mosque, Faizabad, Ayodhya, India. Drawing. Source: Muhammad Madandola.   30

1.6 Al-Nuri Mosque, adjacent to a Yazidi shrine, circa 1932. Photograph. Source: G. Eric and Edith Matson Photograph Collection, Library of Congress.   32

2.1 The Alhambra. Photograph. Source: William R. Baker.   50

2.2 The Fox Theatre. Photograph. Source: Georgia State Archives. 51

2.3 The Alhambra, Palacio de Generalife. Photograph. Source: William R. Baker. 52

2.4 Beckford Moorish summerhouse, Bath. Photograph. Source: Dr. Steve Wharton. 54

2.5 The Fox Theatre, elevation from Ponce de Leon Avenue NE. Drawing. Source: Muhamad Madandola. 55

2.6 *The Moorish Chief*, 1878, oil painting by Eduard Charlemont. Source: John G. Johnson Collection, Philadelphia Museum of Art, Cat. 951. 58

2.7 The Mosque Theater. Photograph. Source: Author. 62

2.8 The Mosque Theater, facade details. Photograph. Source: Barry Parham. 64

2.9 Opa-Locka City Hall. Photograph. Source: State Archives of Florida. 69

3.1 The *Ka'ba*, c. 1910. Photograph. Source: Library of Congress. 86

3.2 The Little White Mosque, Abiquiú, New Mexico. The *mihrab* protrudes beyond the *qibla* wall. Photograph. Source: William R. Baker. 89

3.3 Qaytbay complex, Cairo, Egypt. Drawing. Source: Muhammed Madandola. 94

3.4 Street in Cairo Exhibition, World's Columbian Exposition, Chicago, Illinois, 1893. Photograph. Source: Library of Congress. 96

3.5 The entrance to the Street in Cairo Exhibition at the Chicago World's Fair, 1893. Photograph. Source: Library of Congress. 98

3.6 Abdul-Rahman ibn Ibrahim Sori, Muslim ruler and Fula prince. Engraving, c. 1834, originally published in *The Colonizationist and Journal of Freedom*, Boston. Source: Library of Congress. 100

3.7 The Islamic Center of Washington, DC. Photograph. Source: Library of Congress. 103

3.8 Rossi's original drawings for the Islamic Center of Washington, DC. Source: Muhammed Madandola. 106

List of Figures xi

3.9 Drawing of the modified plan. Source: Muhammed Madandola. 107

3.10 The Islamic Center of Washington, DC. The interior court (*sahn*). Photograph. Source: Mark Susman. 108

3.11 Details of the main prayer hall. Photograph. Source: Mark Susman. 109

3.12 The plan for the mosque of Abu al-Abbas al-Mursi (d. 1286, whose tomb it contains), Alexandria, Egypt. Architects Eugenio Valzania and Mario Rossi built it between 1929 and 1945. Drawing. Source: Muhammed Madandola. 111

4.1 The Islamic Center of Murfreesboro, Tennessee. Photograph. Source: Christopher McCoy. 141

4.2 Washington Tavern, Basking Ridge, New Jersey. Photograph. Source: Library of Congress 149

4.3 Frederick Douglass. Photograph. Source: Library of Congress. 160

4.4 Omar ibn Said. Photograph. Source: Beinecke Rare Book and Manuscript Library, Yale University. 161

5.1 The Hagia Sophia, c. 1890–1900. Photograph. Source: Library of Congress. 180

5.2 Brick Lane mosque. Photograph. Source: ©Guy Sinclair, Fabrication Lab, University of Westminster, 2021. 183

5.3 Old Kent Road mosque. Photograph. Source: ©Guy Sinclair, Fabrication Lab, University of Westminster, 2021. 184

5.4 Harrow Central mosque. Photograph. Source: ©Guy Sinclair, Fabrication Lab, University of Westminster, 2021. 184

Preface

It is time that we rethink place and space. The dominant forms of philosophical critique that have long informed modern Western thought no longer sufficiently serve us. French Marxist philosopher Henri Lefebvre "wishes philosophy to overcome its limitations by starting [to undertake] subjects it has always overlooked."[1] This book, in this respect, is a seminal undertaking: it proposes that we renew our discourse and analytical strategies when considering the philosophies of Lefebvre, Hans-Georg Gadamer, Gilles Deleuze, Jean Baudrillard, Michel Foucault, and other great thinkers of the twentieth century.

Specifically, let us consider the mosque.

The place—or *topos*—of the mosque tries to find relevance in Western public spaces, in communal discourses, in scholarly reception, and in biopolitical relations. And how mosques function and in return are received in the Western world—where certain forms of architecture are privileged, and others disadvantaged—reveals certain deep-seated anxieties. By focusing on the place of the mosque and how it has come to be understood in the Western world, I approach this discourse from a *genealogical* position. That is, I look at the mosque, both in the United States and elsewhere, as a *genealogical* position stemming from space, knowledge, and power: How does a mosque sit in its neighborhood? What do the neighborhood's inhabitants think about its relationship to the surrounding area? Who is setting the narrative about mosques, their functions, and their accessibility?

In turn, space, knowledge, and power are themselves construed genealogically, stemming, we might say, from how we think about *place*. Thus we might briefly define this triad of space, knowledge and power. When we think about architecture, we think about *space*. But, as philosopher Jeff Malpas notes, "English translations of Foucault almost always translate *espace* as 'space,' whereas in French *espace* is ambiguous between 'space' and 'place' as they are used in English (*lieu* is sometimes translated as it corresponds just to place but it tends more to the English 'site' or 'location')."[2] Architectural space—or place—is often localized; that is, it is often determined in relationship to its surroundings. And the architect brings power and knowledge to the physical organization of an edifice, and we can say the same of specific spaces and places—for example, the Great Mosque of Córdoba or al-Aqsa Mosque in occupied Jerusalem—where historical features can be used to restate the distinctiveness of place and underscore what the building's genealogy is attempting to communicate to us. This leads us to a fresh discourse about biopolitics in Western space where power and knowledge are omnipresent. On the one hand, knowledge is dialectically related to power. That is to say, the arguments over the place of a mosque point to an important question: *How is place controlled within and through regimes of police power, local zoning boards, neighbors, townsfolk, and opponents?* Furthermore, it is instructive to compare the court rulings on disputes regarding land use (for example, cases concerning exclusionary zoning) as a way to discover knowledge, truths, beliefs, and legal propositions. On the other hand, knowledge influences power, and power draws from knowledge, relies on it, and shapes discursive practice.

And so I propose a new way of critiquing how we physically reside in the world. Moving away from narrow academic constructions of place, I instead reconsider the mosque as an edifice that is knowable to *all*. Through a closer examination of the mosque's function—specifically, how it interplays with the social, cultural, political, and aesthetics of its surroundings—I frame a new discourse to examine how time and space—or place—intersect.

Consider the *Ka'ba*, for example—an excellent example of the physical place of the mosque and the relationship between sites. The *Ka'ba* is the centermost building in Islam's most important mosque, located in Makkah. Every day, the Muslim faithful look to the positioning of their mosque's *mihrab*—the chamber pointing toward Makkah. They use the *mihrab* to orient themselves toward the *Ka'ba*—or along the *qibla* axis—to receive *baraka*—divine renewal, grace, and blessings flowing through a spiritual place. Thus, the *Ka'ba*, the *mihrab*, the *qibla* axis, and *baraka* all hold both architectural *and* ontological meaning. In other words, we are looking at how the mosque has been constructed and how, in return, the physical provides reflection and meaning for the Muslim body. Above all, we are evaluating Islam's practices and traditions and how they are seen by a society.

In order to do this, I rely upon Michel Foucault's discursive strategy to genealogically analyze place and space. By mosques' *genealogy* I refer to the historical precedent for how mosques shape our collective imaginations. Presently, insufficient academic and critical attention has been placed on the mosque—though an overabundance of a certain type of negative scrutiny exists in broadcast news media. Looking at how space, knowledge, and power have historically affected our understanding of the mosque, we can first identify and then critique the struggles and the raw memories of the power holders that have shaped how we think about place and space. Specifically, we can deliberate on the biopolitical significance, the forms of power regimes, the domination, the control, and the dislocation or decentering of a community. By employing the genealogical strategy, as architect Angela D'Ascoli says, "we are about to undertake a fairly important inquiry into facts that philosophy has hitherto overlooked and the social sciences have arbitrarily divided and distributed."[3]

So, in adapting the Foucauldian framework, "we have," as Foucault himself puts it, "the outline of what might be called genealogy or multiple genealogical investigations . . . the meticulous discovery of struggles and the raw memory of fights."[4] Above all, Foucault's framework allows us to examine how the locus of mosques have been contested in America—how their placement, usage, and meaning in a community have been challenged and received. This examination is critical to our genealogical framework: it also lends clarity as we look at the interplay between physical sites, specifically considering the concepts and histories of each. Toward this goal, we consider biopolitical and juridical disputes over land use and zoning and the rhetorical disavowal of antimosque sycophants.

Finally, while our discussion here draws on Foucauldian insights to some degree, this book is primarily an elaboration of a conceptual framework I first developed in 2002 in *Deconstructing the American Mosque: Space, Gender and Aesthetics*.[5] In that work I discuss the Muslim community in the United States and—specifically—the community's critical, redemptive efforts to build a mosque, both where specific aesthetics can be conveyed and where religious identity and meaningful spatial arrangements can be represented. At the conclusion of *Deconstructing the American Mosque*, I suggest several follow-up questions for consideration to improve upon the methodological limitations of deconstruction. Answering these questions is one of this book's objectives.

In the following chapters, I examine the mosque by critiquing the demands and limits imposed upon it by daily religious observances and by exploring how the greater community perceives and uses the mosque. What does it mean today for a Muslim community in the West—specifically, in America and Europe—to live while navigating a multitude of prohibitive, repressive, and problematic power relations and societal forces? In other words, what strategies allow a community to address these forces while having the space and freedom to remain resilient and even to thrive?

My aim here is not merely to define *place*. Rather, in this work I probe how place has been understood historically, geographically, and globally in Islam-West relations.

NOTES

1. Angela D'Ascoli, *Public Space: Henri Lefebvre and Beyond*, Architecture series 3 (Milan: Mimesis International, 2018), 14.
2. From my July 7, 2021, e-mail exchange with Jeff Malpas; emphases and parentheticals original. I am grateful for the critical linguistic insights he shared with me.
3. D'Ascoli, *Public Space*, 14.
4. Michel Foucault, *Society Must Be Defended: Lectures at the Collège de France, 1975–76*, ed. Mauro Bertani, trans. David Macey (New York: Picador, 2003), 8.
5. Akel Ismail Kahera, *Deconstructing the American Mosque: Space, Gender, and Aesthetics* (Austin: University of Texas Press, 2002).

Acknowledgments

This book has evolved out of a series of informal biweekly conversations with a group of literati at Clemson University between 2014 and 2015. I am grateful to Professor Todd May for allowing me to be part of the conversation and for the opportunity to benefit from his knowledge of Michel Foucault and Edmund Husserl, among other great thinkers. Todd's discussion—his lucid understanding and illuminating views of continental philosophy's arguments—helped me to formulate the many questions (some of which remain unanswered) in this book.

The idea of writing *The Place of the Mosque* came to fruition during a visit to a Foyles bookshop while in London in January 2020. My wife and soul mate, Sulafa, read the first draft of the introduction and offered invaluable suggestions, which gave me the confidence to go forward. Sulafa's positive and optimistic demeanor also brought love and inspiration to the project.

I am especially indebted to Jana Hodges-Kluck (senior acquisitions editor) and Sydney Wedbush (associate acquisitions editor) at Rowman & Littlefield, for their initial review of the book proposal and for working actively to provide me with information that proved vital to the completion of the manuscript. I am indebted to Jeff Malpas and Jessica Dubow, the Toposophia series editors, who took time to read the manuscript and offer critical and helpful comments and suggestions for revisions. I thank my colleague Mohamed Ghali Mubarak, senior librarian at Hamad Bin Khalifa University, for his invaluable help acquiring the articles critical to preparing this work.

I am sincerely grateful to Ms. Deborah Justice for editing this manuscript, refining the ideas and philosophical approaches. I also offer a special note of gratitude to Muhammad Madandola, for providing the drawings and to Ron Baker for the photographs that I have adapted throughout the book. Finally, an index provides the reader's initial access point to the book; I am indebted to Victoria George, PhD, for the preparation of the copious index. My thanks go to everyone who believed this project to be a valuable undertaking, whose positive encouragement kept me going through the rough periods so familiar to any academic and writer. This work was supported by Hamad Bin Khalifa University, the College of Islamic Studies, Research Division.

Most importantly, honorable mention goes to my family for their warm and loving care—especially my grandchildren, who always bring us joy and are a source of inspiration. Above all, *Alhamdu-lillah!*—for the blessings to complete this project.

AIK
Atlanta, Georgia

Introduction

THE PLACE OF THE MOSQUE

In October 2010, writing to Spanish daily newspaper *ABC*, Monsignor Demetrio Fernández González pleaded with the people of Córdoba to stop referring to the Great Mosque of Córdoba as a *mosque*. The Mezquita de Córdoba—an iconic edifice built by the Umayyad dynasty between 784 and 786 CE—would be more appropriately identified, the bishop of Córdoba wrote, as the Catedral de Nuestra Señora de la Asunción—the Cathedral of Our Lady of the Assumption.[1] Not surprisingly, the bishop's op-ed snagged the attention of scholars, historians, and citizens of Córdoba , and an intractable debate ensued on social media and in international tabloids. From the contentious exchange emerged myriad contrary views. One group renounced the idea outright, believing Bishop González to have overreached his power; inversion of history, domination over interpretation, and control, they felt, were in evidence in the bishop's hasty language.

The wider significance of the debate remains: *Who defines place?* Who gets to decide whether a building is a cathedral or a mosque? Who gets to define *any* space? Here the differences in meaning that we imbue to a place are thrown into stark relief, based on where the place is located, on the knowledge we have or acknowledge of the place's history, and on the power we either wield or lack. Critical theorist Homi Bhabha writes of powerful disorders that interrupt "our collusive sense" of history and our knowledge of the past, which reveal spatial "discontinuities and inequalities."[2] The victors, they say, write the history books. So we must consider the antecedents, the genealogy, when looking to define this mosque—or, indeed, any place.

Who gets to say whether or not the Great Mosque of Córdoba is a mosque? The building itself tells us. Overwhelming iconographic evidence confirms the place as a mosque and immutably stamps the edifice: the minaret, the *mihrab*, the trabeated plan, and Arabic inscriptions all speak of Islam's history and aesthetic culture. Bishop González, in so thoroughly disregarding the building's history—somehow fragmenting both time and space—asks the people of Córdoba to believe a fairy tale, that the building is merely a curious anomaly. The bishop is attempting to rewrite history, excluding and interrupting any part of the edifice's cultural and historical identity that he finds inconvenient; this alone disqualifies his request.

The conflict in Córdoba shows us how completely language can exclude: if we take the Great Mosque as a point of reference, we must rethink the question, *How can mere opinion unmake the significance of a cultural or religious space?* One thing we can learn from this episode is that public space—locally and globally, to both the people of Córdoba and to the international population watching the drama unfold—can quite easily be disturbed, dislocated, and decentered, even when the history of that public space has been long known and well acknowledged.

But who gets to define a space is not just a local problem. With transnational communities in Europe and America, the influx of refugees and immigrants since the period of the Arab Spring and the desire for individual, communal, and religious identity complicate the issue: Córdoba and its buildings are not solely the estates of the Christian West. And the bishop's appeal isn't meant only for the people of Córdoba; the debate over the Great Mosque transfers globally—most immediately to Europe and America, where there is an ongoing struggle over the locus of the mosque in particular.

Thus how a place can be *dis*placed and how it is contested serve as the basis for our critiquing the place of the mosque specifically, public space generally, and any products of a specific culture. The Great Mosque of Córdoba (see figure 0.1) must be considered just as other forms of iconic architecture are considered: its inimitable condition and the space and place of the mosque—its *stabilitas loci*—cannot, we know, be reversed by one man's impassioned denunciation. The question then becomes, *How do we explain the fragmentation of both time and space?* Who, in other words, gets to define what a place is? Does meaning simply amount to the archdiocese's domination? If so, are we to believe that the Great Mosque is a palimpsest, onto which human and aesthetic meaning can be written and overwritten, that the building is today a "'blank page' upon which a specific [edictal] message can [instantly] be inscribed?"[3]

Let us for a moment step back from the questions of spatial domination, appropriation, and inversion of the mosque's status and consider the bishop's statement once more; the significance of advocating for the cathedral site in this manner bears emphasizing. Bishop González insists "that sharing the cathedral [sic., mosque] with Muslims would not be possible, neither for

Figure 0.1 The Great Mosque of Córdoba, main prayer space. Photograph. Source: Library of Congress.

the Catholics nor for the Muslims."[4] But in saying this, he ignores centuries of history. His contention not only flies in the face of public knowledge but also completely ignores the mosque's iconographic power and haptic spirit—most notably, that the *mihrab* inside continues to indicate the axis of prayer a worshiper would assume when facing Makkah. Perhaps the bishop's intention in altering the appellation from *mosque* to *cathedral* is to erase the site from public memory, putting upon it a new identity entirely. But his colloquy doesn't end there; he "call[s] on the city to refer to the [architectural] masterpiece solely as the 'Cathedral of Córdoba' on street signs and tourist brochures."[5] He seeks to rewrite history.

If the bishop's rechristening is indeed meant to disavow the status of the Great Mosque of Córdoba, at least two points challenge him: First, as Michel Foucault tells us, "historical [contexts] alone allow us to see the dividing line in the confrontations . . . that . . . are designed to mask."[6] In other words, how we interpret history betrays our agenda: in his obstinate rejection of historical accuracy, the bishop repeats claims that the Great Mosque of Córdoba sits on the site of a long-razed Basilica of Saint Vincent of Córdoba—a "fact" far from settled.[7] On the contrary, "according to the present archaeological knowledge," writes archeologist Fernando Arce-Sainz, "no evidence shows that there were previous Christian buildings under the Umayyad mosque."[8]

The second point challenging the bishop is the physical building itself: the Great Mosque of Córdoba has its own specific architectural merit that can be traced back to a specific function and everyday practice for a particular period in history.

Of course, the mosque's intended use was entirely upended in 1236 CE with the siege of Córdoba. After the reconquista, as it is known, everyday practices of adherents of the Muslim faith were fragmented, and they were barred from their place of public worship. This displacement also meant that the *adhan*—the quotidian call to prayer—has been silent in the mosque since the thirteenth century, when Ferdinand III, king of Castile and León, consecrated the Great Mosque as Córdoba's cathedral—all without altering the arboreal hypostyle plan, which physically marks the edifice as a mosque. In the early sixteenth century, the bishop and canons proposed demolishing the mosque in order to build a cathedral on the site. As a compromise, after facing widespread opposition from the townsfolk, Holy Roman Emperor

Figure 0.2 The added chapel in the Great Mosque of Córdoba. Photograph. Source: Library of Congress.

Charles V approved the plan to insert a Gothic "chapel" into the very heart of the mosque's trabeated space.[9] (See figure 0.2.)

Thus we see a centuries-long attempt to control body—in the act of prayer—and space and to emancipate the city of Córdoba from the grip of the memory of five hundred years of Islamic rule. Bishop González's polemic is no less than a continuation of that war today in the form of biopolitics. The biopolitical denaturing of the site has been identified by philosopher Roland Barthes, who noted that "in the Córdoba Mosque, the part now stands for the whole, because it obscures the barbaric side of Christianity that might otherwise be seen in the landscape of southern Spain. . . . Christianity has effaced the earlier achievement of Muslim civilization: the mosque at Córdoba."[10]

Barthes describes the destruction of memory. We see this attempted most familiarly in times of war and changeovers of power. But even the bishop's campaign is an explicit attempt to subjugate knowledge, time, and space according to his own agenda. Even as the controversy has recentered the Great Mosque in the world's attention—despite attempts to denature the site, and despite the silence of the *adhan* and absence of communal worship—the mosque's physical attributes, most notably the *mihrab*, are the main iconographic stimuli that have induced public interest and remembrance.

What then emerges is a reflective interpretation of the edifice that challenges the bishop's politically motivated quarrel. The bishop's argument about the Great Mosque, as we have seen, is unconvincing; he fuses two opposed genres of space and time—rejecting the Moorish in favor of the Western, glossing history with his favored interpretation. This controversy mirrors a similar dichotomy facing us today: the pull between *architecture* and *power*. These are not irreconcilable; they even seem to be linked to other places and spaces and to other relationships that can be further analyzed.

The great poet Sir Allama Muhammad Iqbal (1877–1938) wrote of the Great Mosque in a lyrical style that evokes a meditative impulse while vividly recalling the historical form, function, and meaning of the edifice. In his poem "Masjid-e-Qurtaba" (Córdoba Mosque), written on the occasion of his visit to the mosque in 1933, Iqbal writes of a spiritual tryst in which an eschatological vision emerges. His verse captures an unreserved adoration while weaving affection for the splendor and the grandeur of the edifice into the reader's understanding of the enduring relationship between space, knowledge, and power.

Photographs show Iqbal, the devotee, praying on a modest rug in the mosque, and later standing in the iconographic *mihrab* (see figure 0.3). But his lengthy commemorative poem is meant to stir public affection for the resplendent beauty of the edifice:

Figure 0.3 The *mihrab* in the Great Mosque of Córdoba. Photograph. Source: Library of Congress.

> Oh, sacred site of Córdoba, you exist because of Ishq [love],
> Ishq is the eternal being, which does not come and go.[11]

Here, in this couplet, we see the polyvalent language of space, knowledge, and power. The poem's numerous couplets shape our collective imagination and convey the poet's emotive body/space experience. As for knowledge, it could also be argued that the couplet's hermeneutic appeal exceeds the Kantian duality between subject and object: the poem's language plays an intermediary role that depicts a haptic space and a connection to material and iconographic elements. The poem's descriptive markers suggest a plurality of discursive tropes.

In this poem Iqbal's poetic soul is expressed in human thought, with transcendent resonances, projecting the body/space experience and the nature of the haptic space.[12] As we search for meaning, it could be argued that "the power of subtraction"—referring back to the effacement that Barthes described—consists of a set of mechanisms of control that run through the body/space experience and are ultimately expressed in the configuration of the dominant trabeated space and the crossbreed chapel. Iqbal succinctly captures this hybrid condition in one of his couplets when he alludes to the perennial power of resilience and resistance, as he likely understood that the crossbreed chapel was an aberration.

His poetic spirit unites word, space, and time with the quotidian call to prayer—the *adhan*:

The Muslim is destined to last as
his Azan holds the key to the mysteries of the perennial message of Abraham and Moses.[13]

References to the prophets Abraham and Moses assume abundant importance in Islamic monotheistic belief and the sacred text, the Qur'an. Even today the Muslim body/space experience remains as meaningful and valued as it did in the past; in fact, Muslim tourists and Spain's Muslim devotees who visit the Great Mosque have attempted to perform at least one of the five daily prayers there but they have been discouraged—even being chased away through the trees of the courtyard. On one occasion, a group of tourists attempted to perform the prayer in the Córdoba mosque, and a fight broke out with the security guards. In the end, the tourists were arrested.[14] These strikingly unusual incidents were reported on social media, on television news, and in the tabloids, but reports have entirely missed the body/space experience and the haptic desire that Iqbal shared with us. In this confrontation we get another glimpse at the biopolitical dispute that normally exists sub rosa—hidden from us.

Claire Larsonneur, scholar of language and translation, has written of the long history of conflict between East and West, where the struggle to define the other plays out in our relationship to location.[15] Ultimately, the West seeks to frame itself as the norm and Islam as the "other," unaccepted religion. Three specific historical episodes underscore a Western insistence to reject any manifestation of Islam: the defeat of the crusades in 1291 CE, the conquest of Constantinople in 1453 CE, and the Christian reconquest of the Iberian Peninsula in 1236 (and of Granada in 1492). "It could thus chart the possibilities, past and present, of ethics—the 'reflective practice of freedom'—a domain in which human beings could exercise their power to conceive and test the modes of domination and subjectivation under which they happened to live."[16] Above all, the analysis of power probes the extent to which *place* is grounded in the production of the space—for instance, the space of experience.

In short, the subject of power posits a few points of contention: First, in Foucauldian biopolitics—a polymorph system governing body and space—power does not belong to anyone in the domain of control. As we have seen in our discussion of the Great Mosque of Córdoba, the micro-powers of the archdiocese run parallel to the power and knowledge of the local government and the public. In this particular case, the local government agreed, in essence, that "the very process of identification, through which we project ourselves into our cultural identities, has become more open-ended, variable and problematic."[17]

In fact, the local government rebuffed the archdiocese's request to delete the name of the Great Mosque from the annals of history, refuting the archdiocese's claim of legal ownership: "Religious consecration," they said, "is not the way to acquire property."[18] More importantly, this government response recognizes the mosque's historical past and its global and cultural affiliation to the city: Córdoba is a UNESCO World Heritage Site. Once again, both the archdiocese's attempt to rewrite history and the local authorities' refusal to let them allow us to frame the discourse with insights that foreground meaning, identity, and discursive formations.

Another dimension of the struggle includes the objectification of things that can be altered; the Córdoba mosque's minaret is now a bell tower.

SUMMARY

Here we have raised a number of questions that we will explore in depth in the chapters following. We will consider the question of body and space, sparked by the *place* of the mosque, the appropriation of public spaces, the forms of domination that invert the products of a specific culture, and the histories of cultural differences that reside in the realm of space, knowledge, and power. We will further focus on the discursive formation and the analytical principle that *space takes for us the form of relations among sites*. It is not surprising that in *Of Other Spaces* and his other writings Foucault is largely Eurocentric—for example, when he writes of the birth of the prison, the birth of the clinic, and so on. The Grande Mosquée de Paris—a Moorish-inspired building—was completed in 1926, the year of Foucault's birth. It would have benefitted from his discursive analysis; this oversight is unfortunate, especially given the century and a half of French colonial rule in North and West Africa.

Another example that escaped Foucault's attention is the Missiri of Fréjus—*missiri* being a Bambara word for "mosque." This edifice stands in the southern French port city of Fréjus, between Nice and Saint-Tropez.[19] The Missiri is a bright red building with architecture reminiscent of the vernacular mosques in Mali. But the Missiri of Fréjus does not function as a mosque. At best it is a simulacrum installed at Fréjus in acknowledgement of the Francophone West African soldiers who had served in World War I.

The place of the Missiri of Fréjus—which has been vicariously debated—has raised the question of cultural fragmentation: the structure assumes a heterotopic identity, taking Baudrillard's *Simulacrum and Simulation* to a new category of resemblances, wherein the architect's ideas seep in to disrupt our understanding of the building. Among the most important works that bring several concerns to bear on our analysis of place are the conceptual frameworks Foucault deployed in *Of Other Spaces: Utopias and Heterotopias* (1967), *The Order of Things* (1970), *The Archeology of Knowledge* (1972), and *Discipline and Punish* (1977). These important works and others bring evidence to bear on the discourse of place and space that has sustained interest among architects, planners, geographers, sociologists, anthropologists, historians, researchers, and scholars of other disciplines up to today. Hence, as Foucault has noted, in such a system of spatial dispersion, "wherever, between objects, types of statements, concepts, or thematic choices, one can define a regularity (an order, correlations, positions and functionings, transformations) . . . we are dealing with a discursive formation."[20]

The Book's Plan

In the chapters that follow, we will use the ambit of genealogy as a discursive strategy and a form of analysis for the questions we have raised. In chapter 1, I suggest a discursive analysis of the genealogies of space, knowledge, and power. This triad of subjects deals with the regimes of thought connected to the veracity of texts, to perceptions, to beliefs, and to biopolitical tensions. Even more to the point, in thinking about the unframing and emancipation of place and space, genealogy is deployed to query the genesis, the falsifications, and the tensions associated with the "task of making space in question precise, saying where a certain process stops, and what are the limits beyond which something different happens."[21]

In chapter 2 we take up the subject of *resemblances* and *similitudes*, with a critique of the Fox Theatre, the Mosque Theater, and Opa-Locka city hall as the primary nexus of aesthetic reception and interpretation. The critique is a decisive concertation of spatial treatment evading the *real*—the true origins of Islam's aesthetic tradition. Here we examine the occurrences of the architectural impulse to "copy" the artistic production of Moorish aesthetics in the United States, along with images that it represents or that have gained venerable viewpoints. I've coined the phrase *Ceci n'est pas une mosquee*—"This is not a mosque"—to capture the heterotopic character of the Fox, the Mosque, and Opa-Locka. The neoteric term is an expansion of Foucault's *Ceci n'est pas une pipe*; here it refers to *simulacrum* and *mimesis* within a constellation of paradoxical treatments that mark the production of place and space.

In chapter 3, connotations of thought as praxis emerge in our analysis of *architecture* and *ontology* that are linked to three interrelated topics: the ontological tradition of facing the *Ka'ba* (and Makkah), the burden of the architect, and the birth of an urban mosque. These three topics represent a challenge to finding the discursive formations through which knowledge and cognition stand out and have meaning to the devotee. However, our interest in the effects of architecture and ontology is in finding a direct analogy to human subjects. In this conception, there is the subject of body/space experience and the impulse of a community to self-identify and to benefit from quotidian practices and religious convictions. For it means we are dealing with the mosque to link the experiential effects of piety; therefore, facing Makkah and the *Ka'ba* are inherently symbolic and spiritually relevant to the conversation of space, knowledge, and power.

In chapter 4, we segue into a discourse on biopolitical power. By focusing on the Religious Land Use and Institutionalized Persons Act (RLUIPA), we offer an analysis of the multifaceted impact of police power. As sociologist Paul Hirst has noted, "far from being prohibitive the controls of this new form of power are productive."[22] At the same time, the highly contentious Park51—sometimes referred to as the Ground Zero mosque—is implicated in a new type of rhetoric about place and the limits of public knowledge. As we will see, rhetorical statements ungrounded in knowledge stem from what is emotionally perceived and give birth to the arbitrary use of derogatory appellation. These matters of differentiation, inclusion or exclusion, and disagreement are significant in so far as they play a part in the contestation of sites, the production of space, and the category of "other spaces." It is for this reason that the contentious nature of the Ground Zero mosque could be challenged. Likewise, disciplinary power is implicated in local autonomy, governmentality, and the juridical power of the court in three highly debated cases: *Islamic Center of Mississippi, Inc., et al., Plaintiffs-appellants, v. City of Starkville, Mississippi Defendant-appellee*; *United States v. Rutherford County, Tennessee*, and *The Islamic Society of Basking Ridge et al v. Township of Bernards et al*.

The arguments over the place of a mosque point to two important questions: *How is place controlled within and through regimes of police power, local zoning boards, neighbors, townsfolk, and opponents?* And *Is the dispute driven by xenophobia, or is the litigant's case legitimate?* We can think of how these arguments are codified as a set of discursive statements in any legal dispute by asking yet another question: *What counts as juridical power?* More precisely, these cases suggest several forms of uneven mobility, the forms of relationships among sites, and power relations; they cannot be separated, since they are attendant to race and religious identity.

NOTES

1. See Rachel Donadio, "Name Debate Echoes Old Clash of Faiths," *New York Times*, November 4, 2010, https://www.nytimes.com/2010/11/05/world/europe/05cordoba.html.
Bishop González acknowledged the stir caused by his column, telling the *Diario de Córdoba*, "I knew it would be reported around the world, so that everybody would know that the ancient mosque in Córdoba is today a cathedral. The ones offended are those who think it's wrong to call it a cathedral." See Catholic News Agency, "Bishop Requests Historic Cathedral No Longer Be Referred to as Mosque," November 5, 2010, https://www.catholicnewsagency.com/news/bishop-requests-historic-cathedral-no-longer-be-referred-to-as-mosque.

2. Homi K. Bhabha, *The Location of Culture* (London: Routledge, 2004), 4.

3. D'Ascoli, *Public Space*, 46.

4. Caven and Rouch, "Meet the Bishop"; Catholic News Agency, "Bishop Requests Historic Cathedral."

5. Dale Fuchs, "Mass versus Minarets: The Cordoba Controversy," *The Independent*, October 23, 2011, cached at https://www.independent.co.uk/news/world/europe/mass-versus-minarets-the-cordoba-controversy-2108224.html.

6. Michel Foucault, *Society Must Be Defended: Lectures at the Collège de France, 1975–76*, ed. Mauro Bertani, trans. David Macey (New York: Picador, 2003), 7.

7. For further discussion of the mosque site's archeological history, see Fernando Arce-Sainz, "La supuesta basílica de San Vicente en Córdoba: De mito histórico a obstinación historiográfica/The Alleged Basilica of Saint Vincent of Córdoba: From a Historical Myth to an Obstinacy of Historiography," *Al-Qantara* 36, no. 1 (2015): 11–14, https://al-qantara.revistas.csic.es/index.php/al-qantara/article/view/337/329.

8. Arce-Sainz, "Alleged Basilica of Saint Vincent of Córdoba."

9. According to some disputed accounts, upon visiting the mosque in 1526, three year after the Gothic chapel had been erected inside, Charles V (Carlos Primero) is said to have bemoaned that the canons had taken a building that could have been put anywhere else in the world and placed it precisely so that it disfigured another unique and irreplaceable structure. See J G and Margaret, "Córdoba's Cathedral Is a Mosque!" *Spain Then and Now*, accessed June 7, 2020, http://www.spainthenandnow.com/spanish-architecture/cordobas-cathedral-is-a-mosque.

10. Roland Barthes, *Mythologies* (New York: Noonday Press, 1991), 30.

11. Muhammad Iqbal first published "Masjid-e-Qurtaba" (Mezquita of Córdoba) in *Bāl-e Jibrīl* (*The Wing of Gabriel*) (Lahore: Taj, 1935).

I have taken this particular English translation of the original Urdu from "Muhammad Iqbal: Probably the First and Only Muslim in Eight Centuries to Have Prayed in the Mezquita," Hotel Viento 10 blog, September 20, 2018, https://hotelviento10.es/en/?view=article&id=126:posiblemente-el-unico-musulman-que-ha-rezado-en-la-mezquita-en-los-ultimos-ocho-siglos, emphases and parentheticals mine.

For versions of the entire poem, see *Iqbal Urdu* (blog), "(Bal-e-Jibril-124) Masjid-e-Qurtaba The Mosque of Cordoba," Allama Iqbal Poetry, April 2011, http://iqbalurdu.blogspot.com/2011/04/bal-e-jibril-124-masjid-e-qurtaba.html; and also Syed Wajid Raza and Abdul Baseer, "Iqbal in Masjid-e-Qartaba," *Allama Iqbal* (blog), last modified April 7, 2003, http://www.allamaiqbal.com/webcont/406/web_pages/cordova_mosque.htm.

12. D'Ascoli, *Public Space*, 20. D'Ascoli has lucidly noted how space and place constitute each other; the text does not deal with the relative position of the race and the body/space in Europe and America or what Locke calls "place." For more extensive discussion of Locke and the impact physical space has on the body, see Craig Wilkins, *The Aesthetics of Equity: Notes on Race, Space, Architecture, and Music* (Minneapolis: University of Minnesota Press, 2007), 10–13.

13. Iqbal, "Masjid-e-Qurtaba." The *adhan* is also known as the *azan*.

14. Giles Tremlett, "Two Arrested after Fight in Cordoba's Former Mosque," *The Guardian*, April 1, 2010, https://www.theguardian.com/world/2010/apr/01/muslim-catholic-mosque-fight.

15. Claire Larsonneur, "Location, Location, Location," *Études britanniques contemporaines* 37 (2009): 141–52, text available at https://journals.openedition.org/ebc/3692.

16. James D. Faubion, "Michel Foucault," *Britannica.com*, last modified October 11, 2021, https://www.britannica.com/biography/Michel-Foucault/Foucaults-ideas.

17. Sean P. Hier and B. Singh Bolaria, eds., *Identity and Belonging, Rethinking Race and Ethnicity in Canadian Society* (Toronto: Canadian Scholars Press, 2006), 250.

18. Stephen Burgen, "Córdoba Rejects Catholic Church's Claim to Own Mosque-Cathedral," *The Guardian*, March 13, 2016, https://www.theguardian.com/world/2016/mar/13/cordoba-catholic-churchs-claim-mosque-cathedral.

19. See Christiane Gruber, "The Missiri of Fréjus as Healing Memorial: Mosque Metaphors and the French Colonial Army (1928–64)," *International Journal of Islamic Architecture*, 1:1 (2012): 25–60.

20. Michel Foucault, *The Archeology of Knowledge: And the Discourse on Language*, trans. A. M. Sheridan Smith (New York: Pantheon Books, 1972), 38, parenthetical original.

21. Michel Foucault, *Power/Knowledge: Selected Interviews and Other Writings, 1972–1977*, ed. Colin Gordon, trans. Colin Gordon, Leo Marshall, John Mepham, and Kate Soper (New York: Vintage Books, 1980), 68.

22. Paul Q. Hirst, *Space and Power: Politics, War, and Architecture* (Cambridge, MA: Polity Press, 2005), 167.

Chapter 1

On the Genealogy of Place

Over the course of this chapter and others that follow, we'll explore how "space and place are dependent upon and constitutive of each other."[1] With this in mind, let us begin by probing the genealogical relationship of the space and the place (*topos*) of the mosque. In *Discipline and Punish*, Foucault introduces the interpretive practice of genealogy as an analytical tool, a redemptive and discursive strategy that has proven helpful in clarifying our subject at hand—place and the Muslim body/space experience.

The promise of the Foucauldian approach is important, because most explorations of the interface of geography, sociology, cultural studies, history, architectural theory—and so on—have not ever considered that his way of thinking about Western spaces could be relevant to the place of the mosque. Nevertheless, "Foucault's genealogy is meant to deconstruct the history of occurrences and events," whether Western or Eastern, "by showing the real origin, official meanings, and evaluations involved in society's self-understanding."[2]

Another caveat before we begin our exploration: "Nietzsche's genealogy operates with psychological causes (the pride and ambition of the strong, the resentment of the weak, and the malicious ingenuity of priests), which have little to do with Foucault's history of the body."[3] In other words, Foucault's discourse expands Nietzsche's genealogy, but both writers have paid little or no attention to non-Western spaces. The same would apply to Kenneth Frampton's "genealogy of modern architecture," which regrettably neglects the non-Western world.[4] So, while Foucault and others have not dealt with non-Western spaces explicitly, something very real and specific is entailed in the critique bearing on the understanding of place and the "divergent forms or precedents . . . from within the [genealogical] episteme."[5]

For our purpose, *genealogy of place*, simply put, is a type of history—a specific type of history that shows how subjects are constituted in discourses. As Foucault tells us, "I call genealogy . . . a form of history which can account for the constitution of the subject within a historical framework."[6] We must also remember that "genealogy is gray, meticulous, and patiently . . . it operates on a field of entangled [sites] and confused parchments, on documents that have been scratched over and recopied many times."[7] Foucault reminds us that his genealogical method is a "methodology of suspicion and critique . . . that pertain not just to any object of knowledge but to any procedure of knowledge production."[8] And most importantly, the interpretive practice of genealogy prescribes a certain unmasking of the regimes of thought that can reveal much to us about the place of the mosque, and these are most intimately related to Foucault's triad: space, power, and knowledge.

Furthermore, the triad defines and clears a space for the underlying realities, the ultimate foundation on which the discursive analysis of the subject of space and place can rest. Foucault uses the term *interstice* to define the forces at play; so, with the triad, "we have both the meticulous discovery of struggles and the raw memory of fights . . . these genealogies are the combination of erudite knowledge and what people know."[9] By introducing the genealogy of place, then, I intend to link the spaces and places where communal practices and the Muslim body/space have established a relationship to the space-power-knowledge triad.

We must initiate the discussion with an important question: *In what way does the genealogical framework help us to identify the origins and deeper meanings of space and place?* These brief introductory remarks call for a critical review of the constitutive elements of the genealogical framework, and through this emphasis we can trace the disparate modes of production and the place of the mosque.

To start, the genealogy of *place* points out how historiography and the discursive and nondiscursive conditions have come to describe the mosque (*masjid*) as an important subject of inquiry.[10] This knowledge leads us to deconstruct the conventional historiography to properly grasp what people know—that is, to unmask the disagreement and struggles about *place*, architecture and the built environment, and the production of space. In talking about space/place, historian Gastón R. Gordillo tells us that "humans have been giving form to space [and place] for millennia, in less or more overt ways."[11] In other words, architecture's modus operandi is the *production* of space and place; just so for the design of a mosque, which, like all other buildings, pertains to the realm of knowledge, the rudiments of perception, and our spatial and aesthetic senses.

Above all, the genealogy of place offers fresh analysis of the space-power-knowledge triad and a way to "constitute a historical knowledge of struggles and to make use of that knowledge in contemporary tactics."[12] In the same way, we use this strategy "to undertake a fairly important inquiry into facts that philosophy has hitherto overlooked and the social sciences have arbitrarily divided and distributed."[13] Furthermore, by using the genealogical strategy, we hope to uncover substantial entities that define and clarify our analysis of the space-power-knowledge triad as it relates to place and the mosque—specifically focusing on where the mosque's building tradition has passed through carefully time-tested aesthetic conventions.[14]

But even with such a promising analytical framework, the common occurrences of the real lives of people become visible, become capillary, and impact biopolitics, control, and dislocation and the decentering of place. Such frameworks "may occupy radically different places in different discursive formations."[15]

In using Foucault's genealogical method to examine space, place, and the mosque, we must keep two central points in mind: (1) that a space is defined and used by people with their own prejudices and histories and (2) that Foucault gives us the specific questions to ask in order to construct an effective, accurate genealogy. As for the first point, the genealogy of place emphasizes the setting of recurrent practices in the Western environment, the place where "correlations, positions . . . transformations, [and quotidian practices]" are revealed and where "architecture . . . [opens] up to impulses from other disciplines [that] need not be thought of as an indulgence."[16] As for the second point, Hirst and Leach's remark can be found in Foucault's understanding of "other spaces," which "underlines and governs a disparate complex of discourses, and it is in no sense unitary."[17] In an attempt to develop a discursive way about thinking about Western space, philosopher Gary Gutting explains that "this understanding of [other spaces] is implicit in Foucault's claim that it reveals the contingency of that which was said to be necessary."[18] In other words, thinking about space and place, we must consider both the medium of language and these discursive notions of other spaces if we mean to introduce a genealogical strategy to identify how Foucault has conceptualized space, knowledge, and power. And in so doing, we will find a way to situate the place of the mosque.

With this in mind, we might consider the nexus of space and time, as "it might be said that certain ideological conflicts which underlie the controversies of our day take place between pious descendants of time and tenacious inhabitants of space."[19] Every person occupying a space has a story, an assemblage of prejudices and fears and needs that influence how they see, use, and shape the spaces around them. Thus, physical spaces intersect with timelines and histories to create new meanings.

This takes us to the second central theme we examine in this chapter. Foucault identifies the important questions to be asked when doing a genealogy to find meaning so as to simultaneously provide an analysis of the genealogical method, the method's language, its statements, and its knowledge production. For "genealogy, like other critical research methods, does apply itself to knowledge production and the generation of kinds of 'truth,' or as Foucault might prefer, truth-effects."[20]

Within the ambit of genealogy, the terms *truth-effects*, *effective history*, and *subjugated knowledge* reveal something important about the place of the mosque, "from the consideration of history and from the conditions of possibility that 'underwrite what counts as reasonable knowledge."[21] Above all, Foucault's genealogical analysis, which he describes as "effective history," is also an attempt to gain access to the assumptions underlying conventional historiography, allowing us to pursue a fresh interpretation and to thrash out "facts" rather than taking them for granted or taking them to be facts themselves based on the "will to truth." In addition, the use and origin of the vocabulary of place and space sometimes draws heavily on the classical sources, and the meanings assumed by Foucault, Henri Lefebvre, and other authors writing about architecture, urbanism, geography, and other matters varies greatly. Our great thinkers and historians have their own biases that we cannot forget.

Let's take geographer Fred Lukermann's "Concept of Location in Classical Geography," which emphasizes a classical definition of *place*.[22] In my view, this definition is cumbersome, because it lacks the critical and discursive framework. Lukermann describes modern geography as a "confusion of tongues," which would suggest that the "will to truth" is an epistemic concern—in other words, that perhaps no definitive truth can be grasped at all.

Lukermann's thesis is indicative of the way classical geographers—as opposed to cultural geographers—have tried to develop a clearly differentiated concept of place (*topos*). For Lukermann, place includes the following:

- *location*—"the contiguity of places"
- *topography*—"the order of discrete units, one to the other"
- *chorography*—"the description of given areas"
- and *chorographical location*—"the total relational content within given areas."[23]

But this understanding of place seems insubstantial, in that for Lukermann place is reduced to a relation, quantity, and process. Yet place is much more than an object of conquest, ownership, and displacement. Lukermann's concept of place, it seems to me, is unreliable—the concept disregards the discursive formation of societies. In other words, Lukermann's reckoning—with its emphasis on territory, domain and map—lacks the cultural meanings of real places and spaces—thus, it has little or no value for us. Furthermore, Lukermann's emphasis infers the hegemony and domination well-matched to empire—that is, European colonialism and imperialism. Jean Baudrillard, on the other hand, has described *empire* as "rotting like a carcass," a "territory

[that] is no longer a referential being or a substance ... it is no longer the map ... it is *the real* and not the map."[24] When seen solely from the perspective of the victor, the richness and layeredness of history and context and intention in place is crushed under the foot of the hegemon. It is in this regard that genealogy (as a strategy of resistance) gives birth to the discursive formation of "other spaces/places" that continue to exist—where people dwell, worship, or perform rituals—that have value for us.

But in our attempt here to arrive at an understanding of the Muslim body/space experience, we can hope to sort out the basic facts about place in a way that accounts for a genealogical analysis. In addition, the discursive approach to the production of space must include the dialectics of place—the way we may define the place of the mosque—in such a way that we may unmask the meaning of architecture, sacred and profane spaces, urban and rural spaces, that are protected or open and undefined.

In this regard, philosopher Jeff Malpas tells us that "very little has been done in the way of a detailed analysis of the concept of place itself, of the relations between place and the concepts of space, or indeed the relations among various spatial concepts themselves."[25] I want to argue that both space and place share a critical relationship; I will do this by focusing on an effective critique of the present history of space and the place of the mosque. In *Place and Experience*, Malpas mentions certain Foucauldian references to space, place, experience, and epoch: "The present epoch will perhaps be above all the epoch of space," he writes. "We are in the epoch of simultaneity: we are in the epoch of juxtaposition, the epoch of near and far, of the side-by-side, the dispersed."[26]

Malpas has also noticed that the "concept of space as a system of locations ('a network that connects points') as well as spatial notions ... involves concepts of locality and position ... that might suggest broader notions of place."[27] In "Putting Space in Place," Malpas convincingly suggests that place (*topos*) is adjoined with space *and* time—noting that, while space (as an extension) is *quantitative*, place is always *qualitative* (indeterminate, dynamic, and relational), such that, although one can locate a position in space, place is never merely a location.[28] "The English 'place' carries a variety of senses and stands in close relation to a number of terms that cover a very broad range of concepts," Malpas tells us[29]:

> In broad terms, however, one can treat the noun form of "place" as having five main senses: (i) a definite but open space, particularly a bounded, open space within a city or town; (ii) a more generalised sense of space, extension, dimensionality, or a "room" (and, understood as identical with a certain conception of space, place may, in this sense, be opposed to time); (iii) location or position within some order (whether it be spatial or some other kind of ordering,

hierarchical or not); (iv), a particular locale or environment that has a character of its own; and (v) an abode or that within which something exists or within which it dwells.[30]

Malpas's five senses constitute a relationship that I hope to explore further by approaching time, space, and place relative to the Arabic lexicon. In this lexicon there are hermeneutical relationships that have to do with the meaning of human existence in the temporal world. In describing *place*, twelfth-century theologian Fakhr al-Dīn al-Rāzī writes of space, emptiness, and location (*fada, faragh, hayyiz*) when performing exegesis and undertaking hermeneutical reasoning.

Fakhr al-Dīn al-Rāzī's Exegesis on Place

Fakhr al-Dīn al-Rāzī's polemics of space, place, and time has been considered by Peter Adamson revealing the twelfth-century polymath's lucid analysis that connects the philosophical ideas of Plato, Aristotle, and Ibn Sīnā.[31] Adamson's essay, "Fakhr al-Dīn al-Rāzī on Place," explains al-Rāzī's taxonomy of place "as a self-subsisting extension, an idea explicitly rejected by Aristotle and Avicenna after him . . . including the principle that two indiscernible things (in this case two overlapping extensions) must be identical and the idea that motion and rest are always relative."[32] But of course there are other key differences from the classical principles of time, place, and space: al-Rāzī's exegesis on place is sustained by an eschatological interpretation.

As Adamson notes, in *Keys to the Hidden* [*Unseen*], a highly respected commentary on the Qur'an, al-Rāzī writes that the "Lord of the worlds in the opening *sura* intimates that God is the Lord of Place and time, Creator and giver of existence to both; he adds that God's existence precedes that of the created, and this being the case, His essence exists before the occurrence of space, emptiness, and location (*fada, faragh, hayyiz*), and transcends all location."[33] Adamson goes on to retrieve notions shared by Aristotle's *Physics*, that "time will arise once there are bodies capable of motion . . . again this suggests that place depends on bodies."[34]

Thus we understand that al-Rāzī's reading of time, space, and place differs considerably from Aristotle's—and, as such, from the Western historical tradition's, where our own philosophical interpretations reside and more than likely where Western architectural precedents belong. For example, Sigfried Giedion, author of *Space, Time, and Architecture*, describes the organizing principles of architecture under the rubric of a "space conception."[35] He argues that a "space conception" is the way the spatial forms of an edifice are perceived, realized, and given meaning and that the earliest space conception can be seen in Egypt, Sumer, and Greece, connecting the space conception to pantheistic themes. These themes, Giedion says, are representative of the interior and exterior space of the Greek and Roman temples.[36]

Al-Rāzī powerfully shows that even with the rival accounts of place given by Plato and Aristotle we can still distinguish the essence of place. He argues "that place is the three-dimensional extension that may be occupied by a body . . . place is something in which a thing is from which [the thing] separates through motion . . . and into which moving things can come successfully."[37] In other words, we can distinguish al-Rāzī's approach to place (in contrast to those who deny the existence of space or who debate whether or not space must always be occupied) within the following list of doxographic possibilities:

1. Place is space that can be pervaded by body.
2. Place is space that can be pervaded by body whether as "pure" and nonexistent.
3. Place is space that can be pervaded by body as a self-subsisting extension.
4. Place is the inner surface of the containing body.[38]

Yet there is another aspect of al-Rāzī's argument for space and place—for the tangible possibility that it is real and existent and not a mere accident to overcome. The problem is that Plato confuses *place* with *body*. As Adamson writes, "sometimes [Plato] calls it *form* and sometimes *matter*."[39] In an attempt to resolve this peripatetic condition, Raphael's fresco *The School of Athens* dramatically interprets the life world: in an allegorical trope, the artist frames his composition with two statuettes—Minerva, goddess of the scientific arts, and Apollo, god of the liberal arts—testifying to the primacy of creative and intellectual power and to probe the possibilities of art, philosophy, and architecture.[40] In the image, Aristotle is observed pointing down, indicating his curiosity with the reality of life, the power of observation, and the phenomenon of the natural world. Plato is pointing upward, apparently concerned with phenomena that cannot explain the natural laws of the world or our abstract sense of being.

The fresco evokes a set of metaphors, but its ultimate connotation is of the human ability to acquire earthly power—that is, *a priori* knowledge. Raphael sums up the importance of *a priori* knowledge by placing the assembly in the Lyceum; Aristotle and Plato are shown at the fresco's visual center, engaged in discourse, in true peripatetic manner. Not only this, but also Leonardo, Archimedes, Bramante, Michelangelo, and others are suitably arranged to produce a satisfying and effective whole, from which we must understand that they are in a state of mental and emotional stability, able to make rational judgments. Perhaps this is meant to further interrogate the meaning of body, spirit, action, and emotion.

Similarly, in the rotunda outside of Vicenza and in the church of San Giorgio Maggiore in Venice it is no coincidence that we find reoccurring allegorical themes of circle and square. Medieval scholars before Palladio's time understood these two shapes in symbolic terms, one writer going so far as to declare in neo-Platonic terms that "God is a circle whose center is everywhere and whose circumference is nowhere."[41]

Al-Rāzī's proposition would suggest that we can overcome the allegorical lacuna—*obscurum per obscurius*, explaining the obscure by means of the more obscure, which reflects the tensions and ambiguities of pantheism. "Differentiating *here* and *there* when using the same kind of expression for space that we do for a surface . . . implies that space exists like the surface does."[42] This underscores the notion that *place* is *space* that can be pervaded by the *body* as self-subsisting extension: "motion is from one place to another, so the places must exist and be distinct."[43]

Briefly, with al-Rāzī's Qur'anic exegesis and eschatological interpretation in place, we have an assertion of Islam's episteme of knowledge, which overextends through architecture and the Muslim body/space experience. The critical intent with which al-Rāzī employs the construction of place lends itself to the architecture of a mosque as a key indicator of time, place, and space. Finally, al-Rāzī's premise of time, place, and space is sustained by an eschatological interpretation, so that in offering an exegesis of *God is the Lord of place and time, the creator, and giver of existence*, he contends that God is the absolute creator of all human and animal life, all categories of space, form, time, place, and the natural environment, and, indeed, the entire universe.

To conclude this part of our discussion, let me briefly attempt to identify the deeper ontological meanings of al-Rāzī's time, place, and space. At this juncture, not all architectural critics and historians are likely to agree with the argument I have raised, but regardless, we must ask the deeper genealogical question: *Does the place of the mosque have ontological meaning?* In chapter 3 I approach a fuller discussion of the subject of architecture and ontology, the orientation (*qibla*) of mosque toward the *Ka'ba* and the city of Makkah. So, for example, another way of looking at al-Rāzī's exegesis of time, place, and space is to consider that "the [architectural] work of man [woman] no matter how innovative is engendered in a context already formed and ordered by God. . . . All artistic work or significant human creation [is] conceived in a network of relations with a world already supplied and ordered with meaning *by God*."[44]

This raises a couple of interesting questions in turn: *How is architecture in the modern world related to the notion of time, place, and space described* by *al-Rāzī?* Further, *How does al-Rāzī's premise inform the space/place of a mosque?* If architecture itself must become the means of production and knowledge, then it culminates in the meaning of space/place, and the Alhambra in Andalusia (see figure 1.1) is to be regarded as the "real thing," the "utopian model." Furthermore, if the "model" denotes the desired productive quality, then we must remember that the Alhambra thrives on epigraphy and ontological meaning.

Take the phrase *There is no Victor but God*, repeatedly designed across the palace walls, or consider other verses decorating the space, from renowned poets of the court Ibn al-Jayyab (1274–1349), Ibn al-Khatib (1313–1374), and Ibn Zamrak (1333–1393). If the phrase is a supplication (*du'a*)—or, as art historian Robert Hillenbrand has suggested, "calling down the good wishes on the sultan"—then we might be able to say that epigraphy is a hermeneutical subject.[45] In other words, the spatial language and aesthetics provide a reference to the world, but the aesthetic value is one of analogy: they speak of heaven and earth and the ascendency of belief over imagery, and that falls well within the principle of the oneness of God—*tauhid*—and the aesthetics of monotheism.

Scholars have for some time recognized that the Alhambra's aesthetic themes exhibit a rapport with Arabic poetry and the language of the Qur'an;

Figure 1.1 Interior walls of the Alhambra, decorated with the Nasrid motto, "There is no Victor/Conqueror except God" (*la Ghalib ill-Allah*). Photograph. Source: William R. Baker.

the Arabic phraseology on the palace walls brings ontological meaning and the physiological effect into reality. Consider the analysis found in "The Palace of Blessings and Grace," for example, wherein the author highlights the Alhambra's relationship to language, art, architecture, and belief: "Mystical and cosmological symbolism, whether found in literature, art, or architecture, created a context for understanding and attuning oneself to the spiritual world."[46]

In any case, space, knowledge, and power share the apparatus of meanings with ontology and hermeneutics; together they inform Islam's aesthetic traditions and the architecture of the mosque. In chapter 3, I offer an analysis on the birth of the mosque to expand the ontological discourse and the mosque's aesthetic schema coupled with historiographic bonds. Nevertheless, owing to the importance attached to the architect's desire to establish authorship and originality, two idiosyncratic aspects are likely to emerge in the production of space and place: First, an enigmatic sense of space and place imposes itself, along with a corresponding absence of historical continuity. Second, production and its many forms (complexity, displacement, decentering, destruction, contradiction, etc.) become the dominant operative aesthetic device.

ON THE DECENTERING OF PLACE

In this next section, I hope to demonstrate how the production of architecture can be viewed as having binary attributes: on the one hand, we can understand how the architect's knowledge can mold the sense of space and the related categories of form, function, and perception; on the other hand, in the absence of this type of knowledge, the edifice is subject to a fragile and elusive disposition. We can regard the disposition and the mode of decentering where existing social, architectural and spatial arrangements are misrepresented and inverted.[47] In *Rubble: The Afterlife of Destruction*, anthropologist Gastón R. Gordillo describes it as "destructive production . . . it captures the twofold movement of production and destruction without recoding destruction as creative."[48]

Thus thinking about architecture as having binary attributes requires that we be critical about the role of an architect and about the tensions between the very process of identification, the forms of production, and the inversion of *stabilitas loci*. This basic dilemma is nicely illustrated in *Thinking Space* by cultural geographers Mike Crang and Nigel Thrift: "Thinking about space"—and place, I would add—"occurs through the medium of language. Just as there is no pristine 'thought' about the world that does not require the mediation of language . . . so we need to consider the relationship of space and language" and place.[49]

To this premise I would also add that language is always related to biopolitics, the control of human experiences, and even destructive practices, thus making the claim that decentering is also destructive and creative. In other words, an architect's knowledge gives them power, and this becomes an instrument for exercising authority and control over space and over deportment. Above all, there is an argument that can be made about the "[way] of constituting knowledge, together with the social practices, forms of subjectivity and power relations which inhere in such knowledges and relations between them."[50]

Decentering is evident in the proposal for the mosque at the University of Baghdad put forth by Walter Gropius and his firm The Architects Collaborative. The mosque's design, completed in 1973, privileges modernity. Indeed, "the continuous grasp of modernity is obvious all around us," notes professor Robert Mugerauer.[51] Modernity, this comment suggests, is a way of thinking about the context and the production of architecture. Likewise, the Bauhaus ideology—Gropius being the founder of that school of philosophical thought—was formulated to give ascendancy to modernism over the cultural, the sacred, and the metaphysical, regarding tradition as stagnant and unoriginal. According to the late architect Max Bond Jr., "although there have been enormous changes in the profession of architecture, our perceptions of it and the people who practice it, the architectural curriculum is still based fundamentally on the values that were brought to America by the Bauhaus."[52]

At the same time, such an absolute understanding of modernism (and postmodernism) is certainly not satisfactory to many academics, writers, architects—among them Christopher Alexander, Hassan Fathy, I. M. Pei, and others—because modernism and postmodernism fail to explain the value of cultural spaces and places leading to many forms of decentering. Take for example Pei, who traveled for over six months all over the Middle East and Central Asia in research of Islamic architecture before developing the design proposal for the Museum of Islamic Art in Doha, Qatar.[53] Pei's approach to design production appears to have required a great deal of research (although this was not the first museum he had designed—though it was his first in a Muslim country). Pei would seem to have agreed with Mark Twain that travel is the enemy of ignorance.[54]

Gropius had ample opportunity to do the same in preparation for the mosque in Iraq, but with proponents of modernism, Islam's history and its architecture is somewhat forgotten, because it enumerates culture and tradition. This aspect of cultural knowledge and production is considered difficult for the proponents of modernism; it is believed to have no aesthetic value. In chapter 2 I argue that quite the opposite is true.

In elaborating the values of culture and tradition, sociologist Paul Hirst's "three decisive characteristics, common rules of formation of statements" are instructive[55]:

1. Concepts of resemblance, harmony, sympathy, etc., which postulate analogous modes of existence of objects and of relations between knowledge and the world.
2. A common relation to [tradition] as the authentic source and the prefiguration of knowledge, modern knowledge thus precedes by *recovery*.
3. Knowledge generates practices of transformation, practices which are not "technologies" in the modern sense, but involve a distinct relation between subject and the world, a relation in which the world as spirit-existence and the subject as spirit-intellect are brought into harmony.[56]

Hirst's "articulation of cultural differences"—"these in-between spaces," in other words—first "provide the terrain for elaborating strategies of selfhood—singular or communal—that initiate new signs of identity, and innovative collaboration, and contestation, in the act of defining society itself."[57] Second, this would suggest that the analysis of space and place is of a distinctive order but perhaps not identical to the way that Foucault's space-power-knowledge triad may have intended. In other words, examining space and place broadens and transforms the genealogical discourse, as he posits the notion that "discursive formations are patterns of order in statements, quite distinct from familiar unities of the history of ideas—authors, books, and [intellectual] schools."[58]

On the other hand, Hirst writes, "Foucault's vocabulary and method displaces or transforms much of the intellectual apparatus of the conventional history of ideas."[59] We can also see that "within a Foucauldian conception of divergent forms or precedents . . . within the *episteme*, what are the limits to discursive diversity? How do statements apparently diverse when considered as 'themes' coexist, and in what relations of parallelism, contrariety or combination?"[60] Therefore, these two distinctions posit a set of discursive formations, and, writes Foucault, "it seems to me . . . that [the architect's] knowledge needs to be analyzed."[61]

So, how exactly does Gropius's modernist ideology frame the language of decentering and the space/place relationships that control the body and space? In this way, Gropius's task "is not merely constructing spaces but spaces which have specific expressive experimental [and functional] effects of the [body/space] subject."[62] In this regard, architect and lecturer Sulaiman Ahmed Mustafa informs us, "Gropius's . . . dome, cast in concrete and flying almost like a tent, with the supporting corners set in pools of water to reflect inward on the ceiling . . . was actually built as planned."[63]

The description of the mosque's architecture would suggest that the scheme is estranged from history, local knowledge, and experiential time-tested building that grew out of a worldly aesthetic tradition and the conventions that satisfy the function of a mosque. Since the scheme remains devoid of any local (Iraq) and regional (Syria, Palestine, Iran, etc.) aesthetic features—all meaning that concerns the relationship of symbols to the history of ideas—the process of decentering takes place. In other words, our visual experience has been disturbed and inverted. Relative to this condition, Mustafa informs us that "with the whole boundary open to the outside, it is the exact opposite of the most basic principles of mosque design[;] the circular plan itself does not help indicate the direction for prayers[;] it conflicts with the principle of equal length of the rows of prayers. It is bad acoustically and climatically, and its open boundaries do not provide the privacy and concentration required in mosque."[64]

Given the way the plan is laid, placed, and arranged, we may conclude that it has been inscribed in an incongruous manner. In other words, the incongruity is antithetical to Hirst's "[postulations of] analogous modes of existence of objects [and body/space] . . . relations between knowledge and the world."[65] Lefebvre frames the dilemma another way: "One of the most glaring paradoxes about . . . space is the fact that it can be at once the whole set of locations where contradictions are generated . . . the means whereby they are smothered and replaced by an appearance of consistency."[66] In this case, the boundaries of modernity are summed up by Umberto Eco. "The modern notion of [architecture] as a work of art as irreproducible and unique assigns a special status both to the origin of the work and to its formal and material complexity, which together constitute the concept of authorial authenticity."[67]

Given what we know from Eco, Lefebvre, and Hirst, it seems to me that in designing the mosque for the University of Baghdad, Gropius was driven by a hasty quest for originality (see figures 1.2, and 1.3). Indeed, "Gropius spent a great deal of time researching mosques that had been constructed . . . beginning in the Middle Ages," writes Mustafa. "These structures all varied greatly in size and composition. But after extensive research and discussion, he believed he had identified what he considered the three basic elements present in the composition of any mosque"—*mihrab*, minaret, and prayer space.[68]

It remains unclear how Gropius interpreted the *mihrab* and the arrangement of the communal prayer space, the *mihrab* being most important because it signals the direction of the *Ka'ba* in the city of Makkah. Taking into account the various definitions of the production of space that we have come across thus far—the way the mosque was laid, placed, and arranged—consider Mustafa's one final caveat, that "the design of a mosque represents a unique challenge to an architect."[69]

Figure 1.2 Baghdad University mosque, designed by The Architects Collaborative. Photograph. Source: Ali Ihsan Al-Saqr.

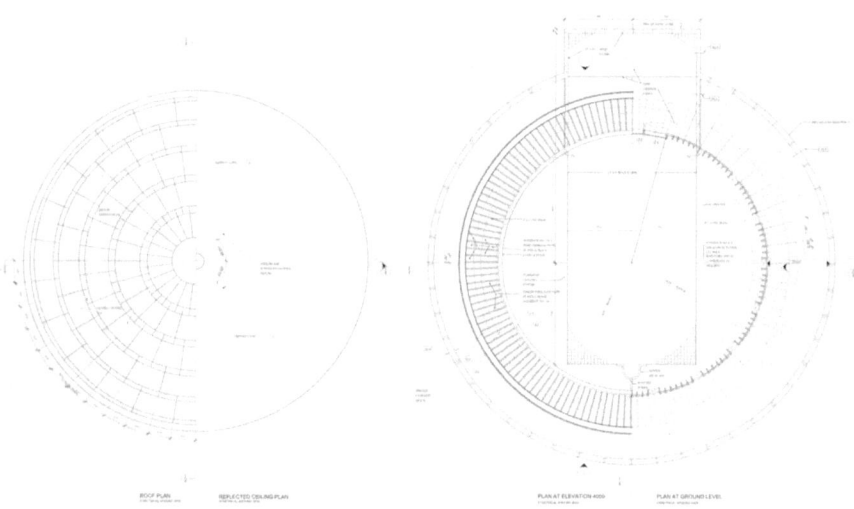

Figure 1.3 Plan of the Baghdad University mosque. Drawing. Source: Muhammed Madandola.

Gropius's production of space reveals his inability or unwillingness to grasp the most import communal function of the mosque and its relation to the quotidian practice. Since the function is so commonplace—it has existed since the seventh century CE—the implicit shift in the way Gropius's scheme is laid, placed, and arranged clearly indicates the condition of decentering. In addition, even though it is commonly understood that the history of the mosque is the subject of a specific culture and the lifeworld, for the individual worshiper it also admits the *stabilitas loci*. In other words, a mosque has typological, cultural, and ontological meaning, but in Gropius's scheme these meanings were overlooked. So, the question remains, why was Gropius unable to give attention to the meaning of place? Furthermore, how did the client overlook these commonplace relationships?

Malpas has noted that even the terms *space* and *place* "may well be thought so commonplace and so much a part of our everyday discourse that [their] transfer to mere theoretical contexts is likely to present an immediate problem."[70] Architect Neil Leach's *Rethinking Architecture* has defined the problem thus: "The indulgence may lie in architecture's failure in the past to engage substantively with other disciplines. Architecture is not the autonomous art it is often held out to be. Buildings are designed and constructed within a complex web of social and political concerns."[71] To add to Leach's point, sociologists Sean Hier and B. Singh Bolaria have noticed that in the present day, "the very process of identification, through which we project ourselves into our cultural identities, has become more open-ended, variable, and problematic."[72]

To conclude this discussion, *decentering* serves as a disclosure of the fragility of an architect's knowledge, although that knowledge is immersed in the lifeworld, where meanings can be retrieved from extant examples, from the texts, and from public knowledge. This helps us avoid the crisis of architecture for which we have no shortage of real-world examples that "engage" a "new" type of enigmatic design language. "This is, in fact, the same common sense disturbed by the notion of the production of space," writes Gordillo, "but this assumption dispels as soon as one stops thinking of space as a disembodied abstraction."[73] His point regarding the disembodied abstraction is another way of describing decentering.

In fact, disembodied abstraction can be found in a few examples where the process of citation makes a tradition unintelligible and imposes the gray area of genealogy on the mosque's historiographic meaning. First, consider architect Robert Venturi's proposal for the Baghdad State Mosque Competition—an example of an aesthetic statement where the unresolved problem of simulacra is quite evident (see figure 1.4). Venturi's postmodern scheme is an aesthetic device meant to assert the degree to which the edifice is possible, plausible, evident, legitimate, prohibitable. In this regard, his

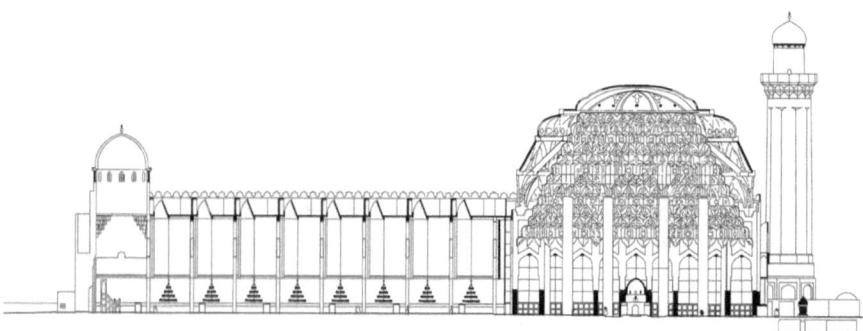

Figure 1.4 Building section of the State Mosque of Baghdad, proposed by Venturi, Rauch, and Scott Brown. Drawing. Source: Muhammed Madandola.

plan for the mosque's "color and signage, with Kufic calligraphic characters, the height of a human being arrayed in a distinct blue external band, [is an attempt to] establish linkages between precedents like the Córdoba Mosque and the legible exteriors familiar from other [Venturi and associates'] projects."[74] Consider the proposal's competing use of camouflage and visual paraphernalia. Frederic Schwartz, former architect with Venturi, Rauch, and Scott Brown, confirmed that "this [mosque] design is a decorated shed on a vast scale."[75]

On the other hand, consider architect Philip Johnson's fascination with the eighth century CE Samarra minaret, which he used as inspiration when designing the chapel in Thanks-Giving Square in Dallas, Texas. In other words, the symbolic order of the minaret and the meanings that reside with the history of its typology has been altered, as such introducing a genealogical gray area. Additionally, the dominant metanarratives and suppositions advanced by Gropius, Johnson, Venturi, and other architects account for dissonance, and that condition is inconsistent with the Muslim body/space, the life of people, and the intrinsic value of the devotee's faith and practice.

These examples and others represent an architectural binary that I spoke about earlier to describe the various facets of *decentering*—where dissonance is revealed and the production of space is created and altered at the same time. The dissonant condition is consistent with Foucault's focus upon how "some [architectural] discourses have shaped and created meaning systems that have gained the status . . . whilst other alternative discourses are marginalized and subjugated."[76] Thinking about the architect's body of knowledge in this way discloses something about Gropius, Venturi, and Johnson's intentions; it uncovers what is hidden about the edifices they designed—about the way they are laid, placed, and arranged—and the conditions that contradict the regime of tradition and the history of ideas.[77] Given this premise, during the architectural production of a mosque or another type of building, it is important to safeguard the community of aesthetic meanings and the ontological conditions that inform how the community defines itself in the world.

The genealogical distinctions that I have just made are important in architect and professor Craig L. Wilkins's view. "It is a fact that the normative view of the world is almost entirely circumscribed by the system of beliefs imbued by the dominant culture, which in the end determines behaviors, actions, and motives," he argues.[78] So, whether we speak of syncretism or the other dimensions of architecture, of modernism, postmodernism, poststructuralism, deconstruction, regionalism, or any other facet of building design, we are faced with a hegemonic discourse itself defined and controlled by those who control the larger cultural narrative.

On the Destruction of Place

While the interpretation of decentering presented here represents various facets of architecture—including heterogeneity, ambiguity, and indeterminacy—my interest is also in considering how deliberate human acts intentionally support the destruction of *place*. In the past two decades we have witnessed an unprecedented scale of devastation because of the war in Syria, Iraq, and Yemen that has targeted the demolition of mosques. In addition, it has been widely reported and documented by human rights agencies that state-sponsored propaganda has led to the destruction of several mosques in China serving the ethnic Uighur Muslim community. *The Guardian* reports that out of ninety-one sites analysed, thirty-one mosques and two major shrines, including the Imam Asim complex and another site, suffered significant structural damage between 2016 and 2018. Of those, fifteen mosques and both shrines appear to have been completely or almost completely razed. The rest of the damaged mosques had gatehouses, domes, and minarets removed.[79]

However, these acts of devastation and ethnic cleansing are not new.[80] We also have reports from Bosnian filmmaker Kemal Pervanić of the devastation of mosques during the Yugoslav Wars in the nineties: "With their mosques, you must not just break the minarets," Pervanić quoted one Serbian police chief saying. "You've got to shake up the foundations because that means they cannot build another. Do that, and they'll want to go. They'll just leave by themselves."[81] In his reportage on the destruction in Bosnia and Herzegovina, journalist Robert Bevan quotes the Serbian mayor of Zvornik as saying "There never were any mosques in Zvornik"—this after the town's Muslim population had been expelled and its mosques destroyed.[82]

As for radical *intergrist* ideology, in one case, power, cognitive authority, and religious ideology became a useful political strategy for the dominant

Hindu society's self-understanding, exacted upon the Babri mosque in the city of Ayodhya, India (see figure 1.5). The mosque was destroyed in 1992 by Hindu fundamentalists who claimed that in 1527 CE a temple built on the fort (hill) of the Hindu god Rama had been removed by Mogul emperor Babur (r. 1526–1530 CE) in order to erect the mosque in its place.[83] Geographer Frédéric Landy has explained the wide-ranging appeal the project to rebuild the Rama temple enjoyed among Hindu nationalists and sympathizers both locally and globally. "Pilgrimage enables a territory to be controlled, both religiously and (geo-)politically," he writes. "On top of the large Hindu nationalist processions that converge toward India's geographical center, we should mention the bricks (flow of products and no longer of men) sent from all over the Hindu world, including from outside India, to contribute to the construction of a temple of Rama in Ayodhya, on the site of the ancient mosque destroyed by Hindu militants in 1992."[84]

In the Ayodhya case, this type of historiography done by tracing the deeper meanings of power, social myth, and religious ritual has been particularly

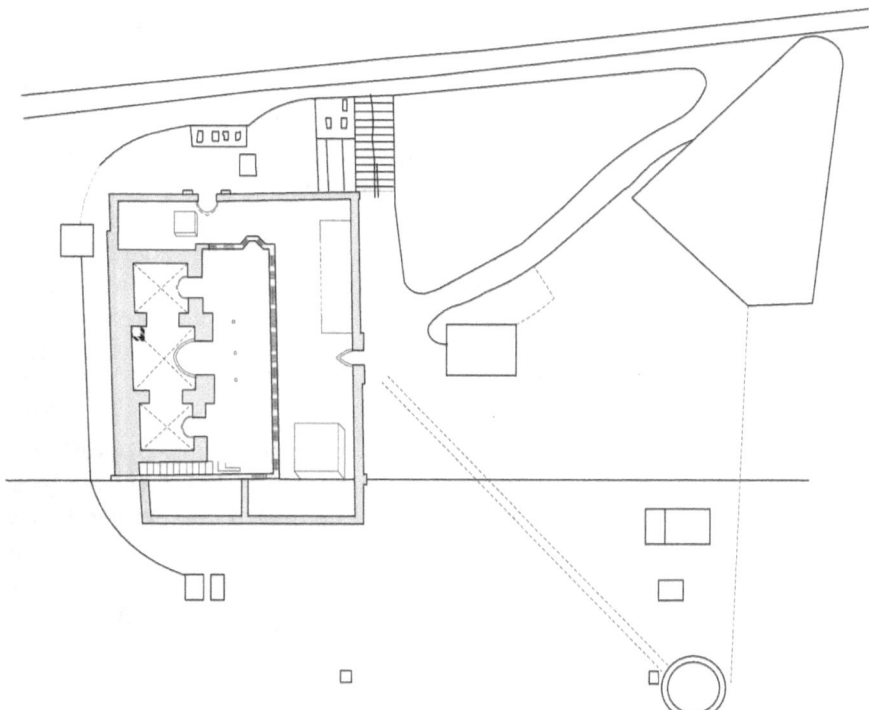

Figure 1.5 Plan of the now-destroyed Babri mosque, Faizabad, Ayodhya, India. Drawing. Source: Muhammad Madandola.

influential and implicitly sympathetic to the valorization of the dominant political ideology and religious belief system.

In our final example of the destruction of place, the anachronistic beliefs of the Islamic State of Iraq and the Levant (ISIL) had postulated the rebirth of the caliphate, which ended in 1924 with the collapse of the Ottoman Empire. In 2014, from the al-Nuri Mosque in the city of Mosul, ISIL announced its campaign to establish power and an extremist religious ideology.[85] Mosul is an import city in Iraq and one of the oldest in the world. For millennia it has been a strategic junction between people, cultures, and trade moving from east to west and north to south. The al-Nuri Mosque's almost-nine hundred-year history dates back to either 1172 or 1173 CE, when it was reportedly constructed by a famous Seljuk sultan, Nūr al-Dīn Maḥmūd Zengī (1118–1174).

Over the centuries, al-Nuri Mosque became recognized as an important historical landmark (see figure 1.6). Its forty-five-meter leaning minaret earned it the popular nickname *al-Hadba*—"the hunchback." Others see in the minaret's posture a person bowing in prayer. But in 2017, during the Battle of Mosul, ISIL lost its control of the city. Just before abandoning their position, militants planted explosives and destroyed the mosque. Most scholars would argue that such extremism is antithetical to Islam's teaching and way of life. Recently, UNESCO launched the campaign 'Revive the Spirit of Mosul' in hopes of rebuilding the city and the Mosque.[86]

Despite ISIL's widespread propaganda and rhetoric, they failed. They spoke as if knowledge were endowed with a guarantee of the establishment of an Islamic State in the modern world, but the destruction of space and place has changed the public sensibility. The claim of "looking for power behind religions and cognitive authority," as the sycophants of ISIL have advocated, or to living in this manner is one of the great contradictions of our time, which may well make radical *intergrist* ideology via the World Wide Web a condition of Foucault's "will to truth." The suffering occasioned by the atrocities, indoctrination, and compulsion was without intelligible cause other than force and brainwashing.[87]

Gutting writes that "brainwashing negates the very possibility of knowledge or the causal production of belief."[88] He describes it as "looking for power behind religions and cognitive authorities that present themselves as grounded in nothing more than the force of disinterested evidence and argument."[89] But Bevan describes it best in *The Destruction of Memory*: "There is both a horror and a fascination at something so apparently permanent as a building, something that one expects to outlast many a human span, meeting an untimely end."[90] What we learn from ISIL's savage acts of destruction is that the meaning in a building is not fixed. Nevertheless, the architectural setting of place has a part to play in establishing our sense of reality—how the building is valued and experienced by many in a cultural setting.

Figure 1.6 Al-Nuri Mosque, adjacent to a Yazidi shrine, circa 1932. Photograph. Source: G. Eric and Edith Matson Photograph Collection, Library of Congress.

All of this may be in keeping with Claude Lévi-Strauss's suggestion that reality is layered whereas history mainly emphasizes conscious actions and events that are individualized according to space and time. To show how historical agency is transformed, by analogy, Lévi-Strauss defines the time-space relationship as "reversible time."[91] Perhaps we can now suggest that the notion of reversible time and space is contingent on a disavowal. The time-space relationship has been noticed by architect and author Angela D'Ascoli, who argues that disavowal (and destruction) is a descriptive marker in Lefebvre's writings and that one of the mechanisms of domination is the "appropriation of space [that] is closely related to another practice[—]that of the diversion (*detournement*) of space occurring when an existing space may outlive its original purpose."[92]

What is just as important is the way we interpret public spaces and places when they are read as an image. In this regard, a palimpsest conveys "the conviction that literary techniques of reading historically, intertextually, constructively, and deconstructively at the same time can be woven into our understanding of urban spaces as lived spaces that shape our collective imaginaries."[93] With these brief accounts, our attention is drawn to the subject of cultural beginnings and the central preoccupation that every society produces its own space—the *stabilitas loci*. Of course, in the sense of selfhood, spatial identities are complex, and the ambivalences are difficult to convey. Once again, Hirst notes that "structures therefore provide a means of knowledge through experience. The structure is an experience-effect."[94] In other words, the mosque's body/space can produce or alter the experience-effect.

So, what happens when that experience is altered, lost, or purposely destroyed? Here I wish to cite Hirst's third rule of experience-effect: "knowledge generates practices of transformation, practices which are not 'technologies' in the modern sense but involve a distinct relation between subject and the world, a relation in which the world as a spirit-existence and the subject as spirit-intellect are brought into harmony."[95] The point to be made is that the actual fabric of Mosul has changed; the al-Nuri Mosque has changed. But does this also mean that the cultural sense of space/place has shifted? What may be less apparent is that the public knowledge that has sustained al-Nuri historical and cultural relationships with the city of Mosul and the significance of the mosque's space/place has been deliberately banished.

Taking into consideration the discursive formations and the emergence of judgments that point to the *decentering* of architecture and *place*, the disavowal has proven that rules may be applied positively and negatively and that these shifts in the place, space, and dimensions of *destruction and dislocation* have profound psychological consequences. Journalist Jenifer Chao, for instance, interprets the Canadian sitcom *Little Mosque on the Prairie*, which ran from 2007 to 2012, as a banal expression in which the Muslim body/space is dislocated. She argues that the television show allows the viewer to focus on the quotidian life of Muslims while simultaneously forcing them to "note the complex background of Islam-West relations that are relevant to the debates concerning Muslim identities . . . assimilation and politics of representation."[96]

Further, the broad nexus that Hier and Bolaria cover in *Identity and Belonging* makes it clear that the fragmenting of ethnicity, race, and nationality, which give us *stabilitas loci*, are now shifting our personal identities and undermining our sense of self: we are no longer seen as integrated subjects. As Hier and Bolaria have pointed, out "this loss of a stable 'sense of self' is sometimes called the dislocation or decentering of the subject. This set of double displacements—decentering individuals both from their place [and space—] . . . constitutes a crisis of identity."[97] In fact, with regard to architecture and power, public place/space is a recurring discourse; Foucault held that "our epoch is one in which space takes for us the form of relations among sites."[98] Foucault uses the term *war* (or *battle*) as an exemplary account for understanding social relations, which connects with his emphasis on the body and space. More importantly, Foucault frames the subjects of space, power, and knowledge within a specified spatial framework: the inversion of space, the otherness of space, the failure of meaning, the plurality of meaning, and the relations among sites.

On the Power/Knowledge Nexus and Place

In my view, Foucault's power/knowledge nexus is a politically constituted biopolitical technique and micro-power phenomenon, because it wields tremendous power on a community's identity, practices, and forms of analysis. This distinction indicates a shift in the power/knowledge nexus as well as signals social and political discontinuities, but it also reveals larger fragmentary changes in the public understanding of Islam. But since Foucault's writings and his discourse analysis do not point to the surveillance of the mosque per se, there is obviously the possibility that we can consider his work on the subject. What happens if we engage these subjects that have historically been excluded from Foucault's positions on Western space so as to invite a fresh discourse? What happens when we realize that the Western space now includes the government's surveillance of communities, male and female bodies, congregants of mosques, and other spaces/places of public assembly?

To illustrate exactly how power/knowledge and biopolitics create a discursive framework for analysis, I offer up two examples for consideration: First, the Moschea della Misericordia, reconsidered from a transglobal perspective, in which we see clearly how an administrative regime (in this case, in the city of Venice) "comes into play" and the condition that corresponds with self-governing principles where "knowledges and the subjects who produce them" relate to forms of power.[99] A very good example of this critique is found in Hirst's assertion that "knowledge is a necessary resource of power. Thus, power needs definite knowledges in order to be productive."[100] In the second example of the power/knowledge nexus and biopolitics, I want to put forth a fresh idea about the 2018 documentary film *The Feeling of Being Watched: Surveillance in a US-Arab Community*.[101]

As for the subject of the body/space that occupy public spaces, the forms of power relations have become problematic, as they are not simply about the place of mosques in America and Europe; they serve as the primary example of interpretive inadequacy, the micropolitics of sites, public space, subjective knowledge, and regimes of power. Luiza Bialasiewicz's "That Which Is Not a Mosque" invites a close rereading of Swiss artist Christoph Büchel's 2015 Venice Biennale exploration of the gray areas connected with knowledge and forms of power where the genealogical analysis is an integral and mutually complementary part of the critique.[102]

The Venice Biennale arts organization has frequently helped the public "engage directly with questions of space, territoriality, borders and the transforming geographies of cities," which is significant within the discursive formation representing the challenge being posed about "spatial" accommodation.[103] To better explore Bialasiewicz's "That Which Is Not a Mosque" and Foucault's power/knowledge claims, I want to probe the Moschea della Misericordia, which Büchel proposed be created within an abandoned church. The artist rented the small Catholic church Santa Maria della Misericordia, which had not been used for worship for more than forty years. In the space, which was owned by a lighting company, Büchel intended "to host the mosque in order to create a quintessentially Venetian layering of cultures" for the project he titled *The Mosque: The First Mosque in the Historic City of Venice*.[104]

Büchel's idea for the place of the mosque introduces a hybrid urban space where Christianity and Islam are connected. Reducing a public space to an object of exclusion or inclusion is ex post facto subsumed by time and space, which enables us to see in Büchel's Moschea della Misericordia a particular set of power relations that appear in opposition. On the one hand, the Moschea della Misericordia was the first urban mosque ever to exist in the historic city of Venice, but by recalling the historical dimensions of Christianity and Islam, Büchel's idea invariably advocated a disparate mode of spatial perception. On the other hand, the creation of the Moschea della Misericordia raised a host of questions from local Venetian authorities. In fact, it could be argued that, while religious, architectural, and culturally based differences can help the public further understand the categories of other spaces, the Moschea became a major problem for Büchel and the Venetian authorities. However, a week after Moschea was opened to the public, the Venice Procura announced that it would be shut down—citing the need to protect the Venetian public—for reasons of health, fire safety, and sanitation.[105]

The Moschea della Misericordia, with all the iconographic elements—*mihrab*, *minbar* (rostrum), and a sanctuary—served as a "temporary" prayer space, but because that place was located in the Santa Maria della Misericordia, this aspect of spatiality had effects on public perception. Furthermore, because the Moschea della Misericordia allowed for the performance of prayer, it was specially configured. This was an obvious marker for the Venice Procura and opponents of the art project; the language of space was therefore interpreted politically and religiously. In short, Büchel's Moschea della Misericordia raised the "political concerns" and the critique of the local authorities to new levels of inquiry and disagreement.[106]

In other words, it is difficult to exclude Büchel's unguarded claims from public knowledge, and therefore the Santa Maria della Misericordia became the epicenter of the political and public reaction. This is perhaps the most provocative challenge emerging from Büchel's proposal; it was widely debated, although it seems that the administrators of the Biennale would have been easily persuaded to allow him to go forward with the project, since Santa Maria della Misericordia was an abandoned building and since the Biennale has always been interested in space, territoriality, and borders.

Bialasiewicz notes that Büchel's Moschea della Misericordia "was merely an analog, an art object, the political and popular reaction it provoked . . . perhaps even more revealing of the ways in which a diffuse fear of anything indicating Muslim presence has become a political obsession."[107]

Of course, the Venice Procura's proclamation is, ex post facto, a category of exclusion, but the horrible mark of this form of exclusion exists in more extreme ways.[108] A central contention of this argument is that the Moschea della Misericordia is a place where the grip of rhetorical exchanges—ignoring the *active* human subject—engage the *production* of space. In this sense, rhetorical exchanges are alien to any objective meaning that could be attached to *place* that may serve as a response to modern-day challenges. The key factor behind the Venice Procura's biopolitical control of human bodies that occupy public spaces—spaces that are supposed to be free, within the interstices of societies social—enables us to ask how our knowledge of spaces of public assembly may differ and how such differences lead to intractable forms of contestation.

Finally, Hirst notes that "this form of power is transformative of those subject to it and it uses knowledge as a resource in the process."[109] It is in this manifold set of power/knowledge relations that we discover the innumerable beginnings or remains of what holds value for society or for others. This is especially true for writers and researchers, as scholar Claire Larsonneur has informed us that "writers of our 21st century, on the lookout for the angle through which they will strive to depict and make sense of society, are thus faced with a double challenge: articulating the local and the global on the one hand, articulating physical and virtual realities on the other hand."[110]

To conclude this section on the power/knowledge nexus, we must discuss the implications of surveillance in today's sociopolitical reality and the prerogatives of spatial justice—the legitimacy of which makes urban life possible—and the result therefrom.

The film *The Feeling of Being Watched* presents countless incidents of encroachment on the individual rights of an Arab and Muslim community in a Chicago suburb and testifies to the long history of government surveillance that consistently views Muslims (and others) as a threat. This, of course, has enormous legal and political implications, aside from the immense psychological damage it inflicts upon the members of the community.

Against this background, the contrived nature and the power of police surveillance have harmful effects in their many unlawful forms. First, police surveillance would suggest that public spaces—especially the mosque—can be perceived to be both illegal and politically motivated. In such cases, surveillance is a means of controlling public space, inserting clandestine activities upon the human experience and the conditions of life with a continuity. Police surveillance, being that it is a recurrent practice, coupled with suspicion and agitation, has resulted in the egregious disturbance of public relations, the freedom of assembly, and quotidian practices, thus constitutively altering their communal character.

The forms of surveillance are also shaped by forces and human bodies subject to biopolitical control. Likewise, the dispute over places of public gathering invites a conversation about spatial ordering that has been intentionally included in the discourse analysis. In doing so the goal has been to emphasize public opposition to the form that the relations take among sites. Islamophobia is omnipresent and persistent; it prevails in matters allowing for subjective decisions to be made about the collective practices of a Muslim community, its cultural difference, and the use of public space.

Undeniably, surveillance is a most egregious form of biopolitics; it entails a fragmentation of the human experience, leading to an attitude of exclusion, public rejection, and censorship. As lawyer and professor Khaled A. Beydoun has noted, "this united fear converges with a competing fear stoked by the state to galvanize hatemongers and mobilize damaging policies targeting Islam and Muslims. That state-stoked fear has a name: Islamophobia."[111] The overwhelming accounts of surveillance have been documented and archived by the Bridge Initiative at Georgetown University, which reports that, from 2001, "under the surveillance program, the NYPD mapped out every mosque within 100 miles of New York" and initially studied "more than 250 mosques in New York and New Jersey." By 2006, the NYPD had also "identified 31 Muslim Student Associations and labeled seven of them 'MSAs of concern.'"[112]

US society is thus self-possessed with race, identity, and power relations and with certain social practices that are constantly examined and reformed or organized for the benefit of some but to the detriment of others. These very practices have constitutively altered the character of our daily lives, our normative beliefs, and other regimes of power that remain. Subjectively, the biopolitical erasure includes Muslim women's clothing (where veiling is banned in public places and spaces), as in France or Quebec, Canada, where Muslim citizens remain alien or are denied the chance to engage in meaningful everyday practices (that are espoused in a liberal democracy) and likewise in public spaces. This also explains why prayers are not allowed in the Great Mosque of Córdoba.

Lastly, we find ourselves once again engaged in new forms of reification, which has given rise to expressions of hate and intolerance; the rhetoric has been anxiously propagated since 2016 with the Trump election, by patriotic zealots and MAGA sycophants (the Ku Klux Klan and the rise of fascist and neo-Nazi ideology), which lays the ground for faith communities to be harassed and attacked and for violence against these communities to follow. The problem of place and space (in Europe and America) permeates today's debate over Critical Race Theory because "we are in the age of simultaneous [access to information via the World Wide Web], of juxtapositions [primitive empiricism, the global war on terror], the near and the far, the side by side and the scattered [global totalitarianism]."[113]

Ultimately, one implication of Foucault's *Archeology of Knowledge* is that he seems to suggest that social life be viewed as being played out in the "spaces of dispersion."[114] This distinction indicates a shift in the power/knowledge nexus, (i.e., surveillance by sectors of the government) as well as social and political discontinuities, but it also reveals larger fragmentary changes in the public understanding of Islam.

Having considered Foucault's power/knowledge nexus, in the foregoing examples from Europe and America, I also want to suggest a valid form of biopolitical analysis that becomes important as we seek to understand and explore the subjects and the forces that drive our history within our societal institutions and how police power operates. Foucault noticed that "the forces that drive our history do not so much operate on our thought, our social institutions or even our environment as our individual bodies."[115] To bring space and place into focus, "Foucault turned his attention to 'governmentality,' the array of political arrangements, past and present, within which individuals have not simply been dominated subjects but have been able in some measure to govern, to be, and to create themselves. He expanded the scope (and lessened the bite) of genealogy."[116]

Building on the foregoing genealogical positions and their relationships to place, I want to briefly comment on the possibility of "knowing" the attributes of place so as to discover the forms of inclusion or exclusion. As we have stated earlier, knowledge shares decisive rules of space/place formation, which means we are not simply dealing with place as an abstract but with an important genealogical subject and its relation to the body/space experience. In this relationship, Hirst has noted that "in the like manner, buildings or a group of structures can be regarded as 'statements' and their relations to discourses specified."[117]

I want to emphasize that the genealogy of place is an important statement. As Hirst has noted, buildings or groups of buildings are typically located in cities (and rural communities) in the United States and Europe as places of public gathering. With the urban mosque in the West, an explanatory force surrounds France's Grande Mosquée de Paris (1926), the Islamic Center of Washington DC (1957), the London Central Mosque and Islamic Center at Regent's Park (1977), New York City's Islamic Center of Manhattan (1991), and Italy's Grand Mosque of Rome and Islamic Center (1995). These examples show us the possibilities each architect thought could emerge by way of the aesthetic features and the way each building is laid, placed, and arranged.

On the one hand, we can regard these examples and their place in the Western urban context as an alternative discourse that circumscribes a new possibility for the architect to think about the use of tradition, the urban condition, and ways that the edifice may engender architectural meaning. On the other hand, the urban mosque is laid, placed, and arranged to accommodate the demands of urban life and its secular forces. This means we are dealing with the building as a quotidian statement and the subject of knowledge. The uniqueness of the urban mosque extends the local and the global frame and this "particular dispersion [is] indebted to other buildings . . . within the network of architecture and related discourses."[118] The distinction is important in terms of the production of space, which, as we have demonstrated, may involve different kinds of actions and the functioning of mental spaces that go beyond the customary accepted attentive forms of a mosque's identity.

In chapter 2, I argue that the exigencies of *place* and the desire for resemblances has resulted in the borrowing of Moorish architectural themes from the Alhambra. I examine how Islam's aesthetic traditions and practices permeate the space-power-knowledge triad. My focus on the latter shifts our attention to the production of space in the United States, which also means addressing another type of dissonance (in many ways related to Johnson's minaret concept) and the lack of hermeneutical understanding on the part of the architect and client.[119] Strangely enough, the Orient—North Africa and the Iberian Peninsula, Egypt, and Palestine—where the history of ideas reside, was the primary source of architectural *fin de siècle* inspiration for North American and European architects seeking to build in the Moorish style, and to discover the ideas, they had to travel east or consult books in search of knowledge.

In any case, well-known historian Robert Hillenbrand has observed that "no sense of historical sequence can be detected [in the work of these architects]. This was, of course a time when Islamic art history had scarcely begun, and thus to its creators this chronological farrago was quite licit."[120] Scholars Diane Long Hoeveler and Jeffrey Cass, for instance, maintain that "British [and French] citizens traveling throughout the Oriental world did so not simply because they were motivated by adventure, economic exploitation, or cultural objectification, but for much more complex and reciprocal reasons. They were not seeking some 'Oriental Other' to appropriate or control (as Edward Said has claimed in *Orientalism*). They were doing something much more interesting and complex."[121] Despite his critics, Said's strategy makes a general reconstruction of Foucault's philosophical thought about the abuse of power and knowledge which runs through the whole of *Orientalism*. Moreover, in chapter 2 I probe the pedagogy of profane spaces—and the cultural objectification that resides in architecture, with the production of Moorish aesthetics—that can be folded into Said's discourse as a genealogical possibility and a historical reality.

NOTES

1. Wilkins, *Aesthetics of Equity*, 11.
2. Gary Gutting, *Foucault: A Very Short Introduction* (Oxford: Oxford University Press, 2005), 49, available online at https://issuu.com/376746/docs/foucault__a_very_short_introduction__very_short_in.
3. Gutting, *Foucault*, 47.
4. See Kenneth Frampton, "Towards a Critical Regionalism: Six Points for an Architecture of Resistance," in *Anti-aesthetic: Essays on Postmodern Culture; A Reader*, ed. and intro. Hal Foster, 16–30 (Seattle: Bay Press, 1983), text available at https://www.modernindenver.com/wp-content/uploads/2015/08/Frampton.pdf.
5. Hirst, *Space and Power*, 163.
6. Michel Foucault, *Power/Knowledge*, 117.
7. Foucault, "Nietzsche, Genealogy, History," trans. Donald F. Bouchard and Sherry Simon, ed. Donald F. Bouchard, in *The Foucault Reader*, comp., ed., and intro. Paul Rabinow (New York: Pantheon Books, 1984), 76.
8. Derek Hook, "Genealogy, Discourse, 'Effective History': Foucault and the Work of Critique," *Qualitative Research in Psychology* 2, no. 1 (2005): 4–5.
9. Foucault, *Society Must Be Defended*, 8.
10. Evangelia Sembou, *Hegel's Phenomenology and Foucault's Genealogy* (Abingdon, UK: Routledge, 2016), 40.
11. Gastón R. Gordillo, *Rubble: The Afterlife of Destruction* (Durham: Duke University Press, 2014), 78.
12. Foucault, *Society Must Be Defended*, 8.
13. D'Ascoli, *Public Space*, 14, drawn from Henri Lefebvre, *Everyday life in the Modern World*, 2nd ed., trans. Sacha Rabinovitch (London: Continuum, 1968), 27.
14. Sembou, *Hegel's Phenomenology*, 34.
15. Neil Leach, ed., *Rethinking Architecture: A Reader in Cultural Theory* (London: Routledge, 1997), xiii.
16. Hirst, *Space and Power*, 163; Leach, *Rethinking Architecture*, xiii.
17. Hirst, *Space and Power*, 163.

18. Gutting, *Foucault*, 50.

19. Foucault, "Des espaces autres," from a talk given at Conférence au Cercle d'études architecturales, Paris, March 14, 1967, published in *Architecture/Mouvement/Continuité*, no. 5 (October 1984): 46, trans. Jay Miskowiec as "Of Other Spaces: Utopias and Heterotopias," and published in English as "Of Other Spaces," *Diacritics* 16, no. 1 (Spring 1986): 22, text available at https://web.mit.edu/allanmc/www/foucault1.pdf.

20. Hook, "Genealogy, Discourse, 'Effective History,'" 8. Fred E. Lukermann, "The Concept of Location in Classical Geography," *Annals of the Association of American Geographers* 51, no. 2 (June 1961): 194.

21. Hook, "Genealogy, Discourse, 'Effective History,'" 4.

22. Lukermann, "The Concept of Location in Classical Geography," 194.

23. Lukermann, "Concept of Location," 194.

24. Jean Baudrillard, *Simulacra and Simulation*, trans. Sheila Faria Glaser (Ann Arbor: University of Michigan Press, 1994), 1, italics mine.

25. Jeff E. Malpas, "Building Memory," *Interstices: Journal of Architecture and Related Arts* 13 (2012): 20.

26. Malpas, *Place and Experience: A Philosophical Topography* (Cambridge: Cambridge University Press, 1999), 19–20, available online at http://assets.cambridge.org/97805216/42170/sample/9780521642170web.pdf.

27. Malpas quoting Foucault, in Malpas, *Place and Experience*, 19–20.

28. See Malpas, "Putting Space in Place: Philosophical Topography and Relational Geography," *Environment and Planning: Society and Space* 30, no. 2 (2012): 226–42.

29. Malpas, *Place and Experience*, 21.

30. Malpas, *Place and Experience*, 21–22.

31. In the West Ibn Sīnā was often known as Avicenna.

32. Peter Adamson, "Fakhr al-Dīn Al-Rāzī on Place," *Arabic Sciences and Philosophy* 27, no. 2 (2017) 205, parenthetical original.

33. Al-Rāzī as quoted in Adamson, "Fakhr al-Dīn Al-Rāzī," 205. Also see Fakhr al-Dīn al-Rāzī, *The Great Exegesis: Vol. 1, The Fātiha*, trans. Sohaib Saeed (Cambridge: The Royal Aal al-Bayt Institute for Islamic Thought and the Islamic Texts Society, 2018), 360–61.

34. Adamson, "Fakhr al-Dīn Al-Rāzī," 206.

35. Sigfried Giedion, *Space, Time and Architecture*, 5th ed. (Cambridge, MA: Harvard University Press, 1967), 124–25. Also see Sigfried Giedion, *The Eternal Present: The Beginnings of Art* (Oxford: Oxford University Press, 1962), 521–26.

36. Giedion, *The Eternal Present*, 521–26.

37. Adamson, "Fakhr al-Dīn Al-Rāzī," 208.

38. Adamson, "Fakhr al-Dīn Al-Rāzī," 210.

39. Adamson, "Fakhr al-Dīn Al-Rāzī," 210, emphasis mine.

40. See the work of Raphael Sanzio da Urbino, *Scuola di Atene* (*The School of Athens*), fresco, 1509–1511, exhibited in the Stanza della Segnatura, Apostolic Palace, Vatican City, Italy. And for more on this discussion, see Rolf Toman, ed., *The Art of the Italian Renaissance: Architecture, Sculpture, Painting, Drawing* (Königswinter, Ger.: Tandem Verlag GmbH, 2005), 335–36.

41. As discussed in Joan Helm, "Erec and Enide: Cosmic Measures in Nature and the Hebrew Heritage," in *Medieval Numerology: A Book of Essays*, ed. Robert Leo Surles (New York: Garland Publishing, 1993), 65.

42. Al-Rāzī in Adamson, "Fakhr al-Dīn Al-Rāzī," 230, emphasis mine.

43. Al-Rāzī in Adamson, "Fakhr al-Dīn Al-Rāzī," 230.

44. Jale Nejdet Erzen, "Aesthetics and Aisthesis in Ottoman Art and Architecture," *Journal of Islamic Studies* 2, no. 1 (1991): 24, italics mine.

45. Robert Hillenbrand, "Occidental Oriental: Islamic Influences in the Art of Britain and America," review of article: John Sweetman, "The Oriental Obsession, Islamic Inspiration in British and American Art and Architecture, 1500–1920," *Oriental Art* 35, no. 4 (Winter 1989–1990): 223, available online at https://www.academia.edu/33212137/Robert_Hillenbrand_Oriental_Occidental_Islamic_influences_in_the_art_of_Britain_and_America_Oriental_Art_N_S_XXXV_4_1989_218_25.

46. Robert Abdul Hayy Darr, "The Palace of Blessing and Grace: Discovering Spiritual Symbolism in the Court of Lions at the Alhambra in Spain," Sufi Garden (website), 2004, http://www.sufigarden.com/images/documents/2004_The-Palace-of-Grace.pdf.

47. Foucault, "Of Other Spaces: Utopias and Heterotopias," 24.

48. Gordillo, *Rubble*, 81.

49. Mike Crang and Nigel Thrift, "Introduction," in *Thinking Space*, ed. Mike Crang and Nigel Thrift (London: Routledge, 2000), 4.

50. Chris Weedon, *Feminist Practice and Poststructuralist Theory* (Oxford: Basil Blackwell, 1987), 108; quoted in Jenny Pinkus, "Foucault," Massey University (website), August 1996, https://www.massey.ac.nz/~alock/theory/foucault.htm.

51. Robert Mugerauer, *Interpreting Environments: Tradition, Deconstruction, Hermeneutics* (Austin: University of Texas Press, 1995), 119.

52. See Akel Ismail Kahera, "Towards an 'Integrated' Design Pedagogy: Exploring Architectural Displacements and the Location of Culture Beyond the Bauhaus Tradition," in *Not White: Proceedings of the 20th National Conference on the Beginning Design Student; April 1–3, 2004, Hampton University Department of Architecture*, ed. Shannon Chance (Hampton, VA: Hampton University Urban Institute, 2006), 109–14, http://ncbds.la-ab.com/20_Proceedings.pdf.

53. Pedro Richardson, "Visiting the Museum of Islamic Art Doha, Qatar," *Travel with Pedro* (blog), accessed October 15, 2021, https://www.travelwithpedro.com/visiting-the-museum-of-islamic-art-doha-qatar/.

54. In *The Innocents Abroad, or The New Pilgrims' Progress*, Twain wrote, "Travel is fatal to prejudice, bigotry and narrow-mindedness, and many of our people need it sorely on these accounts. Broad, wholesome, charitable views of men and things cannot be acquired by vegetating in one little corner of the earth all of one's life." (Hartford, CT: American Publishing Company, 1869).

55. Hirst, *Space and Power*, 164.

56. Hirst, *Space and Power*, 164.

57. Bhabha, *Location of Culture*, 1–2.

58. Hirst, *Space and Power*, 155, See also Paul Q. Hirst, "Foucault and Architecture," *AA Files*, no. 26 (Autumn 1993): 52–60.

59. Hirst, *Space and Power*, 155–56.
60. Hirst, *Space and Power*, 163, emphasis original.
61. Foucault, *Power/Knowledge*, 77.
62. Foucault, *Power/Knowledge*, 162.
63. Sulaiman Ahmed Mustafa, "Baghdad University Design," working paper, South Dakota State University, May 2015, p. 9, https://www.researchgate.net/publication/303868738_Baghdad_University_Design.
64. Mustafa, "Baghdad University Design," 9.
65. Hirst, *Space and Power*, 164–65.
66. Henri Lefebvre, *The Production of Space*, trans. Donald Nicholson-Smith (Oxford: Blackwell, 1991), 363.
67. Umberto Eco, *The Limits of Interpretation* (Bloomington: Indiana University Press, 1990), 179.
68. Mustafa, "Baghdad University Design," 8.
69. Mustafa, "Baghdad University Design," 8.
70. Malpas, *Place and Experience*, 21.
71. Leach, *Rethinking Architecture*, xiii.
72. Hier and Bolaria, *Identity and Belonging*, 250.
73. Gordillo, *Rubble*, 78.
74. Bill Millard, "Mosque that Might Have Been," Center for Architecture (website), May 9, 2012, https://www.centerforarchitecture.org/news/the-mosque-that-might-have-been/. The firm is now known as Venturi, Scott Brown & Associates.
75. Millard, "Mosque that Might Have Been."
76. Pinkus, "Foucault."
77. Dieter Mersch, *Epistemologies of Aesthetics*, trans. Laura Radosh (Zurich and Berlin: diaphanes, 2015), 128.
78. Wilkins, *Aesthetics of Equity*, 11.
79. Lily Kuo, "Revealed: New Evidence of China's Mission to Raze the Mosques of Xinjiang," *The Guardian*, May 6, 2019, https://amp.theguardian.com/world/2019/may/07/revealed-new-evidence-of-chinas-mission-to-raze-the-mosques-of-xinjiang.
80. See, for example, Jasmina Besirevic-Regan, "Yugoslavia," Yale University, Genocide Studies Program, accessed November 18, 2021, https://gsp.yale.edu/case-studies/yugoslavia-former; BBC News, "Who Are the Uyghurs and Why Is China Being Accused of Genocide?" BBC.com, June 21, 2021, https://www.bbc.com/news/world-asia-china-22278037; Al Jazeera, "China Committing Genocide against Uighurs, Says Report," AlJazeera.com, March 10, 2021, https://www.aljazeera.com/news/2021/3/10/china-committed-genocide-against-uighurs-in-xinjiang-says-report; BBC News, "Myanmar Rohingya: What You Need to Know about the Crisis," BBC.com, January 23, 2020, https://www.bbc.com/news/world-asia-41566561.
81. Read Pervanić's tweet in full: "With their mosques, you must not just break the minarets," he said. "You've got to shake up the foundations because that means they cannot build another. Do that, and they'll want to go. They'll just leave by themselves." Simo Drljaca, Prijedor [Serb] police chief, August, 1992 @kemalpervanic, Twitter, June 9, 2020, https://twitter.com/kemalpervanic/status/1270481037286653960, parenthetical in square brackets original.

82. Robert Bevan, *Destruction of Memory: Architecture at War* (London: Reaktion Books, 2006), 7.

83. The case was finally settled in 2019 by the Supreme Court of India, which ruled that a Hindu temple will replace the mosque and that five acres of land elsewhere will be awarded to the Muslim community for the purpose of building a new mosque. See Maria Abi-Habib and Sameer Yasir, "Court Backs Hindus on Ayodhya, Handing Modi Victory in His Bid to Remake India," *New York Times*, November 8, 2019, https://www.nytimes.com/2019/11/08/world/asia/ayodhya-supreme-court-india.html.

84. Frédéric Landy, "Conception of National Territory and Grain Circulation: The Indian Public Distribution System (PDS)," *Annales de géographie* 677, no. 1 (2011): xvii, text available at https://www.cairn-int.info/article-E_AG_677_0026--conception-of-national-territory-and.htm.

85. Mosul, or *mawsil*, means "the linking point" in Arabic.

86. "UNESCO Announces Winning Architectural Design of Competition to Rebuild Al-Nouri Mosque Complex in Mosul," UNESCO.org, April 15, 2021, https://en.unesco.org/news/unesco-announces-winning-architectural-design-competition-rebuild-al-nouri-mosque-complex-mosul.

87. Gutting, *Foucault*, 51–52

88. Gutting, *Foucault*, 53.

89. Gutting, *Foucault*, 51.

90. Bevan, *Destruction of Memory*, 7.

91. See Claude Lévi-Strauss, *Structural Anthropology*, trans. Claire Jacobson and Brooke Grundfest Schoepf (New York: Basic Books Inc., 1963), 301–302. Other descriptions of "reversible space" exist. See, for example, Catherine Gimelli Martin, "Reversible Space, Linear Time: Andrew Marvell's 'Bermudas,'" *Comitatus: A Journal of Medieval and Renaissance Studies*, 21, no. 1 (1990): 72–89, available at https://escholarship.org/uc/item/8k96m653; and also see A. de Ruijter, "The Structuralism of Lévi-Strauss: Problems and Prospects," trans. Jan de Wolf, *JASO—Journal of the Anthropological Society of Oxford* 14, no. 3 (1983): 273–91, available at https://www.anthro.ox.ac.uk/sites/default/files/anthro/documents/media/jaso14_3_1983_273_291.pdf.

92. D'Ascoli, *Public Space*, 48, emphasis original.

93. Andreas Hyussen, *Present Pasts: Urban Palimpsests and the Politics of Memory* (Stanford: Stanford University Press, 2003), 7, as quoted in Christian Gutleben, "'Urban Palimpsests': When Novelistic and Architectural Languages Merge in Penelope Lively's *City of the Mind*," *Études britanniques contemporaines* 52 (2017), 2, https://journals.openedition.org/ebc/3545.

94. Hirst, *Space and Power*, 165.

95. Hirst, *Space and Power*, 164.

96. Jenifer Chao, "Oppositional Banality: Watching Ordinary Muslims in 'Little Mosque on the Prairie,'" *NECSUS/European Journal of Media Studies*, no. 1 (2015): 28, https://necsus-ejms.org/oppositional-banality-watching-ordinary-muslims-in-little-mosque-on-the-prairie/.

97. Hier and Bolaria, *Identity and Belonging*, 275.

98. Foucault, "Des espaces autres," 23.

99. Hirst, *Space and Power*, 157.
100. Hirst, *Space and Power*, 157, and then 167.
101. Assia Boundaoui, dir., *The Feeling of Being Watched: Surveillance in a US-Arab Community*, dist. in the United States by Women Make Movies, 2018.
102. Sembou, *Hegel's Phenomenology*, 40; See Luiza Bialasiewicz, "'That Which Is Not a Mosque': Disturbing Place at the 2015 Venice Biennale," *City* 21, nos. 3–4 (2017): 367–387. https://www.tandfonline.com/doi/pdf/10.1080/13604813.2017.1325221.
103. Luiza Bialasiewicz, "'That Which Is Not a Mosque': 367.
104. Randy Kennedy, "Mosque Installed at Venice Biennale Tests City's Tolerance," *New York Times*, May 6, 2015, https://www.nytimes.com/2015/05/07/arts/design/mosque-installed-at-venice-biennale-tests-citys-tolerance.html.
105. Kennedy, "Mosque Installed at Venice Biennale."
106. Bialasiewicz, "'That Which Is Not a Mosque,'" 367.
107. Bialasiewicz, "'That Which Is Not a Mosque,'" 368.
108. For a broad historical contrast, consider Bevan's *Destruction of Memory*, a well-documented account of the demolition of mosques and minarets and the ethnic cleansing of Bosnian Muslims (the Srebrenica massacre) by the Serbs and Croats and the violent destruction of mosques in the Balkans.
109. Hirst, *Space and Power*, 167.
110. Claire Larsonneur, "Location, Location, Location," *Études britanniques contemporaines* 37 (2009): 3, text available at https://journals.openedition.org/ebc/3692.
111. Khaled A. Beydoun, *American Islamophobia: Understanding the Roots and Rise of Fear* (Oakland: University of California Press, 2013), 6.
112. Bridge Initiative Team, "Factsheet: The NYPD Muslim Surveillance and Mapping Program," Georgetown.edu, May 11, 2020, https://bridge.georgetown.edu/research/factsheet-the-nypd-muslim-surveillance-and-mapping-program/.
113. Foucault, "Des espaces autres," 22.
114. Foucault, *Archeology of Knowledge*; and quotation pulled from Ross King, *Emancipating Space: Geography, Architecture, and Urban Design* (London: Guilford Press, 1996), 219.
115. As discussed in Gutting, *Foucault*, 47.
116. Faubion, "Michel Foucault," parenthetical original
117. Hirst, *Space and Power*, 156.
118. Fontana-Giusti, *Foucault for Architects*, 42.
119. Mersch, *Epistemologies of Aesthetics*, 10.
120. Hillenbrand, "Occidental Oriental," 223.
121. Diane Long Hoeveler and Jeffrey Cass, "Introduction: Mapping Orientalism; Representations and Pedagogies," in *Interrogating Orientalism Contextual Approaches and Pedagogical Practices* (Columbus: The Ohio State University Press, 2015), 2.

Chapter 2

Resemblances and Similitudes

As it is difficult to exclude resemblances and similitudes from the genealogies of space, in this chapter we will try to situate the very fabric of representation to critique a category of subjects forming part of the conditions for a new discourse. By adopting *resemblances* and *similitudes* to address these subjects and forms of representation, this chapter sets up a critical analysis of the Fox Theatre in Atlanta, Georgia; the Mosque Theater in Richmond, Virginia; and the city hall building in Opa-Locka, Florida.

I'm focusing on Foucault's *resemblances* and *similitudes* for three reasons: First, since architectural history, theory, and criticism is wracked by an intractable debate, the critique of the Fox, the Mosque, and Opa-Locka city hall allows for the possibility of a discursive analysis where *resemblance* "presumes a primary reference that prescribes and . . . *similitude* circulates the simulacrum as the indefinite and reversible relation of the similar."[1]

Second, in his essay "From Azulejos to Zaguanes: The Islamic Legacy in the Built Environment of Hispano-America" professor of architecture R. Brooks Jeffery poignantly analyzes ornamentation and architectural form in Hispano-America, taking us back to the apogee of the Nasrid dynasty, Granada, and the Alhambra, between the eleventh and fifteenth centuries, and the legacy of architectural traditions retained by the Moriscos and the Mudejares.[2] As Jeffery notes, Moorish aesthetics, which has its origins in the Ibero-Muslim world, has been adopted into the Hispano-American world since the sixteenth century. In the early twentieth century, the Moorish Revival was adopted by patrons and architects working on the Fox Theatre, the Mosque Theater, and Opa-Locka city hall. However, these individuals were uninterested in Islam's architectural episteme. That is, they were uninterested in understanding the origin and historical and cultural implications of this architectural style and thereby reduced it to a mere aesthetic, losing a great deal of the hermeneutics, truth, and beauty that Islam's architectural episteme encompasses. Their understanding, in other words, was veiled from a reasonable appreciation of the tradition. In this way, the Moorish Revival in America is fragile, ambivalent, and riddled with distortions of the original style and full of aesthetic conjecture. At the same time, in the Hispano-American world the Mudejar style (sic. *Moorish*—that is, craftsmen in the postreconquest era) "developed not in an Islamic context but in a Christian Baroque/neo-Hispanic context." Jeffery notes that "although the influences of the Mudejar continued to be incorporated into the standard repertoire of Hispano-American art and architecture, the original Islamic meaning underlying the artistic expression was lost."[3]

The third reason I'm focusing on Foucault's resemblances and similitudes is that, as methods for assessing Islam and its aesthetic traditions in the United States become increasingly important, we ought to ask how we understand the *original* as a matter of aesthetic value. In this regard, professor Robert Mugerauer, writing of philosopher Hans-Georg Gadamer, has noted how he "powerfully shows how . . . the placement of elements is inverted in a kind of mirroring; in both cases, a prejudgment is made for or against the power of tradition, of authority based on a historical relation to the *original*."[4]

In examining the architectural choices made in designing the Fox, the Mosque, and Opa-Locka, we note a surprising reliance on simulacra themes. In the following, we'll interpret these meanings to examine the polysemic conditions and the ways in which the "Moorish style" was at the time of these buildings' construction "considered appropriate for all manner of buildings, including domestic, commercial and religious structures. But the primary identification of this style was with the architecture of pleasure, exemplified in theatres, clubs, resort hotels, and exhibitions halls."[5] As such, in each of these three cases, the way the edifice is laid, placed, and arranged has resulted in a heterotopic condition, an abnormal placement; thus the true meaning of Ibero-Islamic aesthetic traditions is inverted and distorted.

One final caveat before we delve into our exploration in this chapter: In his review of John Sweetman's 1988 book *The Oriental Obsession*, art historian Robert Hillenbrand poignantly describes the encounter between East and West as an *alternative approach*, "which, because so few are aware of it, is almost entirely ignored: [thus it becomes critical for us] to study the history of Western contacts with the Islamic world in an attempt to better understand modern Western motives and preconceptions—for there is no question but that these color Western attitudes to Islamic society at all levels."[6]

It is this encounter between East and West so described by Hillenbrand that resides in the architectural language of the Fox Theatre, the Mosque Theater, and Opa-Locka city hall: the cultural merger results in a *culture built upon representation*—simulacra, hysteria, and an unmistakable array of resemblances.

The Fox Theatre

We begin our analysis of the Fox Theatre by considering the problem of *resemblances* and *similitudes*; this is because the theater's architectural configuration, intended to reference "Moorish style," renders it a dubious typological reference at best. In short, our primary intent in this examination is "to understand and evaluate the present, particularly with a view to discrediting unjustified claims of authority."[7] For our purpose, this implies that the dubious aesthetic conditions emerging in the Fox—and also in the Mosque Theater and Opa-Locka city hall, as we shall see later—can be tentatively attributed to two agents: (1) the impulse and intent of the architect and (2) the purse of the client or patron. In their pivotal roles as agents of the process of architectural production, architect and client have created a relationship to Moorish aesthetic traditions that is imaginative—not based on reality.

It bears saying that using the term *Moorish* to refer to a particular style is itself inaccurate, not founded in historic reality; usage of the term is part of what I contest here. *Moorish* refers to those people coming from and the culture deriving of *al-Maghrib*, the geographic regions of the western Islamic world (present-day Morocco, Tunisia, Algeria). It refers mostly to the Arab, Muslim, and Berber inhabitants of this part of the world and of residents of Al-Andalus—the Iberian Peninsula—during the Reconquista, in the eighth through fifteenth centuries. The modern European and the American adaption of decorative and architectural forms from *al-Maghrib* and Al-Andalus, which has come to be called "Moorish," had been "stimulated by popular journals, travel books, and novels of Romantic painters and writers."[8] Fin de siècle tourists, artists, and architects were, of course, responding to ideas of the day that were already in vogue and in part to "Romantic" aesthetics idealized in Europe and America. The Moorish episteme, with its diverse styles and forms of representations—"exotic" to the Western-trained eye—has held interest even up to the present day. Since its erection in the ninth century, the Alhambra has been celebrated by architects and patrons as a picture-perfect original (figure 2.1). They have not, however, based their judgments on the structure's "valid" interpretation and on actual historical underpinnings. As such, their omission casts critical light on the discourse.

At the close of the nineteenth century, as all things "Moorish" were coming into vogue across the Western world, American architects were not overly interested in extracting encyclopedic information from the corpus of extant Ibero-Islamic architectural traditions in Hispano-America—which would have revealed rich context to the Alhambra, had they looked, but that instead remained hidden or overlooked. In his own studies of the Ibero-Islamic tradition, R. Brooks Jeffery writes that, back in the period in which the palace was being constructed, "similar to other Islamic architectural expression

Figure 2.1 The Alhambra. Photograph. Source: William R. Baker.

transported to Hispano-America, imported styles and forms developed into a hybrid architectural vocabulary based on the unique needs of the Hispano-American conversion campaign."⁹

A similar claim can be made about the Fox Theatre, its production, its fraternal rumblings, its reception, and its interpretation. For example, at the turn of the twentieth century, Walter Millard Fleming and William S. Paterson—members of the Ancient Arabic Order of the Nobles of the Mystic Shrine—wrote of their fraternity's obsession with all things Moorish in *Mecca Temple*, the history of the order.¹⁰ The Shriners' fixation on these visual themes became standard in other meeting halls they built—including the Mosque Theater (Richmond, 1927) and soon after the Fox Theatre (Atlanta, 1929; pictured in figure 2.2).

In the volume *Mecca Temple*, Shriners Fleming and Paterson gush over the Ponce de Leon Hotel (St. Augustine, Florida, 1887) as one of the "most complete and gorgeous hotels in the world." Their rhapsody evidences their fixation on Eastern aesthetics: "Gazing from the room windows upon the court below one would imagine a scene from *The Arabian Nights*. In the center a large fountain is continuously playing, around about all manner of rich and rare flowers and tropical plants, tastefully arranged, some trained to grow in perfect forms of tables, sofas, chairs, etc. Upon the walls rare and odd creeping vines of moon flowers, morning glories, etc. The building is an architectural beauty, after the *Spanish moresque palaces*, and has about it

Figure 2.2 The Fox Theatre. Photograph. Source: Georgia State Archives.

courts, verandas, plazas, marble mosaics, set in the midst of luxuriant orange, olive, palm."[11] In fact, this passage—especially their reference to *Spanish moresque palaces*—almost echoes praises that had already long been heaped on the Alhambra's Palacio de Generalife (*Jannat al-Arif*, or Garden of the Architect, pictured in figure 2.3) Here we are talking about a *referential simulation*, to use Baudrillard's terminology, which lends itself to our discussion of resemblances and similitudes. But at this point, "it is no longer a question of imitation, nor duplication, nor even parody." Certainly in this passage we find a tentative explanation for the Fox Theatre's production having so heavily borrowed the Alhambra's leitmotifs; the architects and patrons transfer the imaginary—their celebration and re-creation of "all things Moorish"—which loses its meaning in failing to first understand the source material, and the resulting so-called Moorish Revival, grounded in this imaginary style, produces a building that is merely a "simulated generation of differences."[12]

With this we come to our first point in our analysis that confirms Hans-Georg Gadamer's argument: an architectural form that is proper for some groups is not the form desired by others. To gloss Gadamer, "the placement of the elements is inverted in a kind of mirroring: in both cases a prejudgment is made for or against the power of tradition, of authority, based on the *historical* relation to the 'original.'"[13]

In other words, the Moorish Revival has led to various heterotopic distortions in US architecture. And in the face of such forms of heterogeneity it is not surprising to find in the Fox elements belonging to the mosque—most notably, minarets and domes. Likewise, the architect's prejudgment goes

Figure 2.3 The Alhambra, Palacio de Generalife. Photograph. Source: William R. Baker.

against the power of tradition; these architectural elements are sustained not by an authentic tie to history but by a variety of prejudices, values, and interpretations that are largely attributed to the architect's volition.

Consider the Moorish summerhouse of English novelist William Beckford (Bath, c. 1825; pictured in figure 2.4), "a simple domed square with a fair approximation of an Ottoman leaded dome"—which Hillenbrand describes as being more Ottoman than Moorish. "The joggled voussoirs of the entrance arch, on the other hand, are unmistakably Egyptian detail," Hillenbrand continues. "Such charming incongruity is of a piece with freewheeling atmosphere of generalized orientalism."[14] Architects of the Romantic period and their patrons, like Beckford, were divided over the use of images and emblems, reflecting the tensions and the ambiguity of the "Moorish mode." The elementary authority of these images, along with the outer forms of the edifice, were incapable of communicating one specific, cohesive idea and thus are suspect of the central truths of the Moorish mode—being completely pictorial and, moreover, devoid of understanding their intended source.

We begin the second point of our analysis of the Fox Theatre with an account of its history: "In 1927, the Yaarab Temple held a design competition for their new headquarters building . . . a flamboyant interpretation of a mosque with onion domes, towers, horseshoe and lancet arches, and a minaret." The theater "opened on Christmas Day, 1929, near the end of the golden age of the American movie palace."[15] On the one hand, these building features are the hallmark of the Moorish Revival in America, favoring a connection with links to the past. But these buildings are entirely misplaced. Foucault has noted that "heterotopias have the power of juxtaposing in a simple real place different spaces and locations that are incomparable with each other, as in theatres. . . . Significantly these spaces could be linked to different parts of [historical] time."[16]

The Fox is one example where "the truth and beauty are thus only seemingly far apart."[17] Seen in this way, resemblances and similitudes mark the discourse; simultaneously, they trace the production of the edifice.[18] On the other hand, when the Fox Theatre first opened, the local newspaper described it as having a "picturesque and almost disturbing grandeur beyond imagination."[19] The newspaper description is nothing more than rhetoric, but the "deception" is the central perspective to the analysis that we want to pursue. The Fox was chiefly managed by "the architectural firm responsible for the design; it had as its major partners P. Thornton Marye, Richard W. Alger, and Ollivier J. Vinour."[20] Vinour, chief architect and designer, was a native Frenchman, born in Paris, who had studied at the École des Beaux-Arts. His role and designs are important in interpreting the Fox: as Paul Hirst reminds us, "the true architect should therefore be a theorist and adept in order to construct buildings . . . which produce certain direct effects on the human

Figure 2.4 Beckford Moorish summerhouse, Bath. Photograph. Source: Dr. Steve Wharton.

subjects who approach and enter them."²¹ If we recall the Shriners' impression of the Ponce de Leon Hotel, then we might say that Vinour's design is largely reflective of "a sort of place that lies outside all places and yet is actually localizable."²²

The Fox Theatre "was originally planned as part of a large Shrine Temple, as evidenced by its Moorish design. . . . The 4,665-seat auditorium was ultimately developed as a lavish movie theatre in the Fox Theatre. . . . The theater was racially integrated in 1962."²³ Since Vinour can be regarded as a mediator of the Moorish Revival, can we challenge his expertise? Apart from the Fox's destabilizing image, Vinour's composition exemplifies a play of transference on many levels: it demonstrates "how art collecting played an important part not only for architecture and painting but for the decorative arts as well."²⁴ As for Vinour's aggregation of influences, "the Fox includes features and details borrowed from historic mosques" and from the Alhambra. Of course, the allegory explains why "early twentieth-century architectural critics called movie palaces like the Fox a 'prostitution of architecture,' but movie palace builders were not trying to build high-style examples of American architecture. They were trying to construct fantastic, romantic designs that would attract patrons to their movie theaters" (figure 2.5).²⁵

The Fox's surprising combination of architectural themes rework themselves into a complex allegory and end up appearing as something else altogether: the Shriners inaugurated their new "mosque." In other words, while attempting to show a relationship with the customary use of elements originating in a real mosque, Vinour subjectively altered them. His interpretive understanding of resemblances can be traced to travel accounts of Spain, Morocco, Palestine, and the Holy Land, as we have said—for example, to Washington Irving's *Tales of the Alhambra* (1832), Owen Jones's *Plans,*

Figure 2.5 The Fox Theatre, elevation from Ponce de Leon Avenue NE. Drawing. Source: Muhamad Madandola.

Elevations, Sections and Details of the Alhambra (written over the period 1836 to 1845), and Mark Twain's *Innocents Abroad* (1869).[26]

The list of Vinour's influences also would have included "French amateur, draughtsman and photographer" Joseph-Philibert Girault de Prangey (1804–1892), Charles Davillier (1823–1883), Ibero-Islamic ceramics, Henri Regnault (1843–1871), and ceramic producer Théodore Deck (1823–1891). Orientalist painters and travelers who were fascinated with the Orient—for example, Spanish painter José Villegas y Cordero (1844–1921)—add to the reinvention of the Islamic legacy of Al-Andalus and *al-Maghrib*.[27]

Henri Matisse (1869–1954)—like his contemporary Pablo Picasso (1881–1973)—was given over to an enterprise falling well within the program of mimetic overflowing with no real frame of reflection to eschatological understanding of Ibero-Islamic gardens, iconographic themes, and aesthetics. Both artists produced works that bear the mark of consumption, carefully worked to an Orientalist genre that "carried representation into visual expression and a life of its own."[28] Matisse himself visited the Alhambra and the Great Mosque of Córdoba, despite his belief in the ascendancy of art over architecture. After his visits, his paintings became "more heavily decorated and highly reminiscent of the ornate patterning he would have seen in the Alhambra and the Great Mosque in Córdoba. Additionally, his use of Islamic architectural features," the Islamic legacy of Al-Andalus and *al-Maghrib*, "such as miradors and gardens . . . indicates that Matisse may have subconsciously recognized or even possibly understood the paradisiacal symbolism inherent in Islamic architecture."[29]

Thus a decisive focus on aesthetic treatment reflects the way we interpret spatial and visual constructs in our built environment, to interrogate the statements and visual concepts that have the power to influence or transform our understanding and knowledge.[30]

With these observations, we come to the raison d'etre for the flourishing of Moorish influence in the West: obsession with the Alhambra. In the nineteenth century, travelers, writers like American Washington Irving, and painters like Welshman Owen Jones had been dazed by the palace. It was the same several decades later for M. C. Escher, who visited in 1922 and again in 1936—including a visit to the Great Mosque of Córdoba. Escher would later develop a mathematical approach to expressions of symmetry (*Metamorphosis I* and *II*), which had been strongly influenced by the geometric patterns (tessellation) he had found in the palace. But it seems that neither hermeneutics nor truth nor beauty (aniconism) seemed to interest Escher. Instead, he directed his effort to iconism—that is, the union of the tessellation with animal and human imagery. In a 1963 lecture "The Impossible," Escher declared, "If you want to express something impossible, you must keep to certain rules. The element of mystery to which you want to draw attention should be surrounded and veiled by an obvious, readily recognizable commonness."[31]

Escher was right about one thing: rules are important. Nevertheless, he was dismissed by the art world but venerated by mathematicians. Knowing all of this helps us to understand why the Alhambra became the most admired edifice in the West; in the palace complex, mathematics was omnipresent in the plan, the sections, the elevations, on the walls, floors, and ceilings—its composition and métier were knowledge.

There is no doubt that Ollivier J. Vinour's study at the École des Beaux-Arts exposed him to a vast network of writers, painters, travelers, and texts from the Orient. His design for the Fox Theatre was given over to pleasure, and because it was a venue for entertainment, it had to impress the public. Of course, the Fox was built primarily for public entertainment, and this functional relationship has been historically defined by the architect in seeking to indulge the human perceptual and cognitive apparatus. Vinour must be considered one of many transcultural translators in an increasingly globalized world, where the diffusion of the Moorish Revival in the United States (and Europe) was promoted by architects and patrons.

In the nineteenth century, Alexandre de Laborde's (1773–1842) editorial initiative *Voyage historique et pittoresque en Espagne* (1804–1820) "set the frame for future publications on the Alhambra palaces and the mosque-cathedral of Córdoba."[32] A majority of similar editorials and creative works were occupied with the creation of narratives based on Ibero-Islamic representations—even in Edwin Lord Weeks's painting of the Alhambra's Court of the Myrtles. Weeks took poetic license, including fowl uncommon to the Islamic garden.

It is also not coincidental that the misreading of culture and ethnography occurs when traditional aspects of a culture become confused and intertwined with stereotypical perceptions; what "emerges is the potential threat of misunderstanding or misreading of a given culture."[33] Take, for example, *The Moorish Chief*, an oil painting by Viennese artist Eduard Charlemont (1848–1906), depicting a Moorish Chief, exuding power and mystery, and standing in front of an arch that closely resembles the architecture of the Alhambra (figure 2.6). It had been produced for a European audience; the art produced by Eugène Delacroix (1869–1954), Matisse, and other painters of Orientalist subject matter (and Picasso borrowing from African Art) had been made to serve the same audience. In translating this fascination with the Orient "to the public as a whole, swayed by tales, articles and illustrations in popular books and magazines, the Near East as a whole represented an idealized world expressing a multitude of fantasies—the desire for the unusual, for the forbidden, for escape."[34] *The Moorish Chief* "was probably shown at the Paris Salon exhibition of 1878 with the title *Le Gardien du serial* (The harem

Figure 2.6 *The Moorish Chief*, 1878, oil painting by Eduard Charlemont. Source: John G. Johnson Collection, Philadelphia Museum of Art, Cat. 951.

guard). While this subject was unusual for Charlemont, it was very popular in Europe at the time."[35]

What concerns me most in the examination of this Western art are the Orientalist characterizations of the material culture—especially the indebtedness of the art's aesthetic genre to a *doxa* and to sociocultural norms—a culture that the art must expose and deride so that Eurocentric virtues can be implicitly extolled and ultimately reinforced.

Nevertheless, in the lifeworld, the Fox Theatre gained a sense of realism all the while emphasizing the superficiality and insubstantiality of the Moorish Revival. Vinour's production of the Fox—no matter how skillfully done—is not the real thing, because the production precludes the architect's ability to make a compelling case for meaning. Furthermore, Vinour must necessarily exclude the qualitative aspects of tradition from the production. We can further understand how Vinour, like the Orientalist painters and travelers, reposed the rules when we carefully examine the attraction that Matisse, Delacroix, and other Western artists had for the Orient. We are thus talking about an attraction that is immersed in the subject of art and architecture and—as with Vinour's aesthetic imbalance—that offers no thoughtful resolution.

How were Vinour's visual encodings created? Oriental encodings, we must remember, were also used in artworks to further the theme of exoticism.

With regard to the other types of spaces included in the Fox Theatre, "an Egyptian Ballroom is designed after a temple for Ramses II at Karnak, while the mezzanine Ladies Lounge features a replica of the throne chair of King Tut and makeup tables that feature tiny Sphinxes. The Islamic sections feature a number of ablution fountains [normally needed in a mosque], which are currently kept dry."[36] In addition, aside from the auditorium, the building contained "executive offices, a large lounge, a ballroom/banquet hall, kitchen, practice hall, and locker-shower room."[37] "According to A. P. Almond (who had assisted Vinour in researching the design for the Fox Theatre), three large white leather-bound books, one entitled *Nubia* and another *Holy Land*, were the primary reference sources for the design. Another design reference source was the collection of postcards that Mr. Sam Cooper, a local [American] Architect, brought back from a world tour."[38]

This knowledge bears the mark of architectural simulation of materials, of decorative motifs, carefully copied and applied to the building's facade to create the effects of Oriental exoticism, as does Vinour's attempt to copy or reproduce Moorish themes. The same could be said of the work of Owen Jones, British architect, decorator, and art theorist (1809–1874), who in 1842 published *Plans, Elevations, Sections, and Details of the Alhambra* (with M. Jules Goury), though Jones had once cautiously discouraged the impulse to copy, believing that "true beauty results from that repose which the mind feels when the eye, the intellect, and the affections, are satisfied from the absence of any want." In 1856, Jones published *The Grammar of Ornament*, "a remarkable *tour de force* . . . contain[ing] one hundred magnificent and highly detailed color plates of ornaments drawn from architecture, textiles, tiles, rare books, metalwork, stained glass and many other decorative arts."[39]

Similarly, art historians Francine Giese and Ariane Varela Braga note that in the nineteenth-century Western world, from Italy to Russia, architect and antiquarian James Cavanah Murphy's *Arabian Antiquities of Spain* (1813), a compendium of imprecisely depicted Ibero-Islamic architecture, remained a privileged sourcebook, providing a wide range of patterns for architects and decorators, even after the publication of Jones and Goury's *Plans, Elevations, Sections, and Details of the Alhambra*.[40] Jones mentions the forms of nature that provide design motifs for the architect and designer, having himself seen the Alhambra and studied its grammar of ornaments and the language of aesthetics. He recognized that having the impulse to copy signals disengagement.

Vinour's impulse to copy made the Fox Theatre an object of exotic irony and ambiguity. This suggests that the meaning conveyed by Vinour is *resemblance*, where domes, minarets, and all the building's decorative features have been allowed to freely circulate and pass from subject to subject, irrespective of rule or meaning. Escher's advice to stick to the rules was ignored, the rules having undergone hybrid transformations: in other words, Vinour turned to "and borrowed from past civilizations and remote culture; and prominent among these borrowed forms were those from Islam," and in the borrowing was an aesthetic naivete and promotion of exoticism.[41]

Even so, the Fox Theatre operates as a marketable statement with tremendous appeal to public sentiment. The power of the statement—the exotic treatment, despite the heterotopic inferences—reached the observing gaze of a wide audience. But inevitably, the statement has resulted in systematic classification and a particular form of reification: the Fox was listed in the National Register of Historic Places in 1976.

THE MOSQUE THEATER

As we have seen in the forgoing discussion, resemblances and similitudes fuse disparate genres—the historiographic dimension along with the architect's creation of the edifice. As a first point in this discussion, resemblances and similitudes, as outlined above, will help us trace the origins of the Mosque Theater to decipher the architect's and clients' intentions, analyze the resulting architectural configuration, and, finally, uncover the instances of simulacrum.[42] As a second part of our conversation, it is important that we remember all that explorers of the East brought back with them to the West—that it was not only verbal and literary accounts, but the improvisational quality of Moorish aesthetics as well, which were then promoted in design practice. Our discussion of British architect Owen Jones, for example, has centered mainly on Ibero-Islamic design drawn from his documentation of the Alhambra palace.[43] And finally, the third point we must consider in this section is our contention that image can be traced to "precursors and different doctrines current at the time [that] can always be found to locate ideas earlier than proposed by a particular concept or a Zeitgeist."[44] We saw this in the previous section in our analysis of the Fox Theatre as a mirror of the Oriental world.

With these points in mind, let us begin our exploration of the Mosque Theater, built in 1927 in Richmond, Virginia, for the local chapter of the Shriners (figure 2.7).

Of necessity, our critique of the Mosque initiates a discussion about the worst kind of perceptual, intellectual, and social disorder.[45] By 1963, for example, nearly ten years after the US Supreme Court's landmark ruling in *Brown v. Board of Education*, the Mosque had been a theater for public use but was still not fully integrated. And so in *Felix J. Brown, et al. v. City of Richmond, et al.*, a suit was brought against the city by "negro citizens, wishing to attend baseball games at the city's Parker Field and public theatrical and musical performances at the city auditorium known as the Mosque, without being segregated by race as required by sections."[46]

The social turmoil of the era directly impacted even the architecture. "In such a state," Foucault tells us, where there is disorder, "things are 'laid,' 'placed' and 'arranged' in sites so very different from one another that it is impossible to find a common place beneath them all."[47] Indeed, the way the Mosque is laid, placed, and arranged can be seen most clearly in the building's aesthetic language—in the motifs and imagistic facade. Above all, the disorder emerging in the appellation of the building exemplifies a combination of meanings predicated on the word *mosque*.

The edifice began its life known as the ACCA Temple Shrine (1928) and later the Mosque (1940). The name was changed in 1995 to the Landmark Theater and finally to the Altria Theater in 2014. The English word *mosque* (French: *mosquee*; Spanish: *mezquita*) is derived from the Arabic *masjid*, which is a place for the performance of communal worship—in which case the word *masjid* is clearly not suited to describe a secular edifice (a venue for entertainment). Thus we are dealing with a building that serves a function incongruent to its naming.

The Mosque was the "brainchild of Clinton L. Williams, Potentate of the ACCA Temple, Nobles of the Mystic Shrine. Williams felt his fraternal organization had outgrown its meeting place, so he set out to build a venue that

Figure 2.7 The Mosque Theater. Photograph. Source: Author.

would outshine any other Shriner facility, and thus would create an entertainment palace for the City of Richmond."[48] In 1925 the theater was designed in Moorish Revival style by Marcellus E. Wright Sr., in association with Charles M. Robinson and Charles Custer Robinson. The building officially opened in 1927 and was dedicated by the Shriners in 1928. Wright's design for the Mosque—like similar early twentieth-century buildings in Europe and America—generated and communicated images and neoteric meanings. It is this interweaving with the history of Islamic architecture that extolls tradition. We must remember that Islamic architecture is rife with striking examples of decorative brickwork; facades and interiors of mosques, palaces, and tombs and other types of edifices were intricately woven or cloaked in textiles. In tracing the repertoire of visual patterns that were part of the Mosque's architectural scheme, we note the lobbies overlaid with arabesque design, glazed polychromatic terra-cotta, frescoes, and decoration in ornamental plaster.

All these decorative elements are drawn from the full range of images, objects, artifacts, materials, techniques, and ideas taken from the Orient, North African geographic foci, and the Ibero-Islamic world. However, the Mosque's edifice is laid, placed, and arranged with familiar figures and images—domes, arches, and arabesques—part of the fraternity's preoccupation with the Orient.

The building is located in downtown Richmond, Virginia, an urban space, on Laurel Street facing the historic Monroe Park. An array of stylistic elements brings prominence to the building's main facade: on the Laurel Street facade, the dominant entrance bay is designated by a pointed arch the full height of the facade and is decorated with Moorish patterns in terra-cotta, limestone, and bronze. The facade is flanked by two minarets, each with six stories and at least three more soaring beyond the roof of the building.

The minarets are flanked, in turn, by low wings, which designate the position of a former small hotel; the minarets embrace the vertical edges of an arched portal—and an oddly sized dome placed in the corner of the facade at the roof level (figure 2.8). These elements simply *suggest* a visual relationship to an "actual" mosque: once, minarets were used to call the faithful to prayer; today they remain part of the design for a functional mosque but are merely symbolic elements. In other words, the minarets of the Mosque are estranged from their intended purpose, function, and meaning, which makes clear the relationship of the architecture to the source: it is shallow imitation.

At the second floor, the fenestration is comprised of horseshoe-shaped arches decorated with terra-cotta arabesque designs. The upper three floors have simple double-hung window openings with terra-cotta frameworks. Six-story, copper-domed pavilions flank these sections, while the rear elevation has been left without any architectural treatment.

We can't help but once again consider architect Marcellus E. Wright Sr.'s interest in the Orient and can only assume that his impulse was driven by "the emergence of the 'Romantic' point of view during the late eighteenth and early nineteenth centuries which permitted this interest to be expressed by eclectic architects in Europe and America."[49] Similarly, Wright's architectural choices create an important descriptive marker: his concept explains how the mimetic adaption of the edifice is juxtaposed with the genres of visual forms. We could assume that all of these chosen elements had intrinsic value for the fraternal order, the patron, and the architect that could be readily

Figure 2.8 The Mosque Theater, facade details. Photograph. Source: Barry Parham.

understood; the motifs, including the appellation *the Mosque*, were vicariously adapted, then.

These tentative observations are important, because the building follows its own arrangement, only aping an original concept. The end result creates a disorder that distorts the episteme of Ibero-Islamic building traditions. This would suggest differing spheres of resemblances and similitudes, but, more importantly, "with [resemblances and similitudes] the reference anchor is gone."[50] For example, the edifice's discursive formation begins when it is first called "the mosque"—an inescapable etymological and descriptive anchor, and the "image . . . is that thing."[51]

Here I introduce another important consideration: *If the traditional reference anchor of the building is gone, then is the edifice's aesthetic image analogous to Magritte's pipe?* I speak, of course, of Belgian surrealist artist René Magritte's 1929 oil painting depicting a pipe and captioned *Ceci n'est pas une pipe* (This is not a pipe), which set off a firestorm of debate on the questions of meaning, representation, language, and subtext that it raises.[52] Author G. S. Evans sees "the picture of the pipe to be an analogue of a real, *concrete* object," in which case trying to decide what the real thing *is*, is extremely problematic; and he has argued against Foucault's casual dismissal of the possibility that paintings by Magritte—and more directly the drawing and inscription on the pipe or on an object—might effectively function as an analogue of the object.[53]

I would argue that the Mosque Theater is not an analogue, although it displays fragments of the anchor—the simultaneously familiar and nonrepresentational quality: It neglects Escher ("If you want to express something impossible, you must keep to certain rules") and Jones (who maintained that "true beauty" could not be copied) and therefore undermines the effects it draws together.[54]

Furthermore *Ceci n'est pas une pipe* "accounts for the simultaneously familiar and nonrepresentational quality of . . . images by drawing a distinction between *resemblances* and *similitudes*."[55] The architect's creation of the Mosque, like the pipe painting by Magritte, is a "strategy [that] involves deploying largely familiar figures [the architectural elements—dome, minaret, arabesque] whose recognizability is immediately subverted and rendered moot" and impossible to grasp, becoming a senseless *resemblance*.[56]

We see the same confluence of resemblances and similitudes in Foucault's critique of Magritte's painting and the artist's inscription that "this is not a pipe." Just so, the Mosque Theater offers a visually operative *perception* of realism that provides an association to the pipe painting and inscription. I believe that the failing accountability of the appellation—that is, "mosque theater"—like Magritte's pipe could be understood another way: we are talking about the falsity of the architectural composition as both subject and object.

My argument is particularly pertinent to the building's fractured representation, and for that reason I posit *Ceci n'est pas une mosquee* (This is not a mosque) so as to suggest that "*heterotopias* . . . constitute a sort of counter-arrangement of effectively realized utopia, in which all the real arrangements that can be found within society are at one and the same time represented, challenged and overturned."[57]

Ceci n'est pas une mosquee decomplicates the problematic terms *laid*, *placed*, and *arranged*, and the analytical position goes beyond the limits of historiography, architectural reception, and creation. *Ceci n'est pas une mosquee* re-poses the commonly accepted maxim that architecture has its existence primarily in our spatial perception and accordingly appeals to our *a priori* faculty and our aesthetic sensibility; that is to say, a simulacrum labels something incorrectly—for example, the Mosque Theater's two towering minarets.[58] With these conditions in mind, we must also remember that the analysis advocates the search for truth—that is, tradition and its consistent forms—and that this concept "recognizes only that which is formulated without contradiction."[59]

I believe that philosopher Gary Gutting offers a plausible explanation for the reversal of meaning—one that would support our claim that *Ceci n'est pas une mosquee* and the insight underlying the changes from one function to another. He writes that "the spelling changes"—or, in our case, the appellation *mosque theater*—"will deform some familiar words and obfuscate their etymological origins." Another way of putting this is to say that the implied polyvalent meaning of the Arabic term *masjid* can only be applied to the "real thing"—to a building that is in actuality a mosque. In other words, the theater's chosen designation "is likely to obfuscate people's [understanding and perception] rather than enlighten them."[60]

This consideration might reference the very altered way in which a heterotopic image—a thing placed wrongly—drives contradiction that cannot be resolved. This recalls Fontana-Giusti: "Excluding simulacra is a major problem for Western culture, as it is difficult to exclude that structure which is in the very fabric of the culture built upon representation."[61] In this way, the whole construction of the Mosque Theater is built around the demands of the Nobles of the Mystic Shrine and that fraternal order's mimetic and cultural values.

Mimesis—meaning "imitation"—has been so flagrantly used in the Mosque's design that we cannot exclude it from our analysis.[62] The theater's simulacra elements have their origin in the Oriental world while showing a superficial rapport with that world. This is not an authentic building of "the Moorish world" but an inaccurate and puzzlingly placed forgery. I borrow from Baudrillard's analysis of how Western culture and simulacrum operate and agree with him that it is naive for us to look for truth elsewhere: We need not look to "the exotic" for a comparison of cultures, for it is already here, among us, in Richmond, and everywhere, in the Western metropolises, in the white community, in a world completely cataloged and analyzed, then artificially resurrected under the auspices of the real, in a world of *simulation*.[63]

In theory, there are two important analytical observations to be made about simulation: First, the mimetic overflowing of decorative themes we find in Moorish Revival architecture gives us the space to speak about polysemic meanings—the varieties of interpretations, intentions, connotations, and contexts found in the ersatz architecture. The "Moorish style" sought by the Mosque Theater's architect and patrons was an impulsive search to induce effects of the architectural legacy of the Ibero-Islamic foci, born of the widespread interest in the day in Orientalism, Romanticism, and exoticism.

This first point in our analysis, the multiplicities of meanings, is linked to what is known about the Ibero-Islamic world and the convergence of the Moorish architectural traditions already taking shape in the Hispano-American world: these traditions had already been considered relevant in the categories of ornament, space planning, and architecture and also had been playing a role in the production of Christian churches from the sixteenth century onward. For example, in the designs of Christian "Hispano-America, the hypostyle mosque was used in two ways," writes R. Brooks Jeffery: "(1) as a large congregational chapel in direct application of the Islamic form or (2) as a derivative form, in the open-air chapel or *capilla abierta*."[64]

Second, when exploring simulation, we must take note of the diverse range of structures that are for the most part built on a typology that could be influenced by the aesthetic norms and cultural values of Islam. This invites a host of questions about how the Mosque Theater's motifs and imagistic facade are directly linked to resemblances and similitudes. Here we can imagine how the appropriation of the Alhambra's architectural treatments and decorative notions became all the rage in Western design, which led to widespread emulation of the "Moorish style" throughout Europe and the United States. In this way, the Mosque tries to participate in a system of architectural decoration; however, given that the building serves as both the site and the object of the architect's volition, it is disordered, creating a lacuna: something critical is missing from it. And that absence "tends to reduce interpretation to a limited body of discursive knowledge."[65]

As we have noted earlier, the discursive order of the Oriental world also exists in books, poetry, travel accounts, art, and architecture. "The various palatine cultures and their art are potent reminders of the extended and changing character of Islamic hegemony in Spain; they divert us from [American author Washington] Irving's mythic view of the 'Moor'—the monolithic other in brief intense polarity with the Christian west."[66] The US and European fascination with the Orient is deeply imbedded in the body of literature from the beginning of the nineteenth century. Nevertheless, this faddish enchantment discounts the legitimacy of Islam's rich traditions and culture and legal practice, offering in exchange several contentious myths and false interpretations, characterized in an array of literary and visual generalities.[67]

One final consideration in our analysis of the Mosque Theater: the Ibero-Islamic aesthetic "system" was developed within that particular part of Europe, and the best examples can be found in the Alhambra palace, where the style reached its apogee in the fourteenth century CE. Naturally, in the Ibero-Islamic world and the historical epoch, the discursive formations of "Moorish" themes coexist closely to a host of polysemic meanings. And it is this idea that allows us to trace how variations of the system are set free between Orient and Occident. While a full discussion of "the Moorish Revival is a transcultural and transnational phenomenon, [it is] a subject that until recently had received little critical attention."[68]

In summary, we know from Foucault's *Order of Things* that the relationship of language to art, architecture, film, photography, and painting is infinite.[69] This relationship appears within the personal and professional networks of architects, patrons, collectors, painters, travelers, and cultural enthusiasts who have demonstrated interests in Ibero-Islamic architecture.

Examination of the long history of Orientalism raises specific questions about the appropriation and encounters of writers, painters, and travelers to and within the Ibero-Islamic world. Therefore, we can attribute the practice of observing and redocumenting what was undertaken at the site of the Mosque Theater with great suspicion: in his design of the building, Wright has produced an array of visual interpretation allowing the Moorish stereotype to emerge and flourish. More important, Wright—like Jones and Irving—was not privy to the temporal or religious meanings of the Arabic verses written on the walls of the Alhambra insofar as they reflect truth and beauty or the possibility of a hermeneutic recovery.

Taking the influence of other agents into account—and the influence of artists and writers such as Irving (with his exotic propaganda)—artistic expression of the Orient became a commodity associated with the power of the voguish Moorish Revival in the United States, by which the iconoclastic gestures of the Orient were appropriated and directed to the West. In view of these striking observations, "we find that Irving's *The Alhambra*, by supplying a romantic background, had far greater impact on nineteenth-century architecture than the *Alhambra* of Jones."[70] Furthermore, the lack of profound scholarly interest (on the part of Wright) has led to the Mosque Theater's mutations and resemblances. So, despite our best efforts to "presume a primary reference that prescribes" a renewed affirmation, the architect's production of the Mosque Theater is a mimetic structure that is "dominated by [exotic] sensation."[71]

OPA-LOCKA (*OPATISHAWOCKALOCKA*)

Our discussion up to this point has allowed us to understand how the Ibero-Islamic architectural tradition was reinterpreted by architects like Ollivier J. Vinour and Marcellus E. Wright Sr. Similarly, in the 1920s architect Bernhardt E. Muller attempted to engage the public gaze with his *Arabian Nights*–inspired design for the city hall administration building of Opa-Locka, Florida (figure 2.9).[72] Despite the design's attempts at homage, it fares badly with its irruptions; not surprisingly, the heterotopic conditions afflicting the Fox and the Mosque also appear in Opa-Locka. Specifically, the focus on resemblances and similitudes results in an inauthenticity that offers no complete understanding of what makes architecture in a particular form of "otherness," historic times, and places. Critical theorist Homi Bhabha writes that "location and boundary" can help us understand "the way in which [Eurocentric] cultures recognize themselves through the projection of otherness."[73]

Figure 2.9 Opa-Locka City Hall. Photograph. Source: State Archives of Florida.

The interpretive scope of Bhabha's lexical dilemma provides an opportunity to combine Foucault's interpretations of resemblances and similitudes with the analysis of individual architectural works that have adapted the appellation or elements of a mosque. This makes the analysis meaningful, despite the importance given to syncretic language—the mish-mash of terminologies and cultural aesthetics—and disorienting visual effects. Likewise, Fontana-Giusti writes, "Foucault privileges the non-traditional subjects of philosophy such as literature, art and music as liminal domains of life where the new episteme first shows up."[74] In the United States, it shows up in the Opa-Locka scheme, where the town annexed the aesthetic of *The Arabian Nights* to raise its historiographic profile.

By considering resemblances and similitudes, we are offered a critical and discursive approach to studying Opa-Locka's aesthetics language with the hope of learning something important. I would suggest, however, that few arguments if any would seem general enough to support the indeterminate state of the Moorish Revival and its style in the United States. I believe that this debate is an inevitable aspect of heterogeneity, ambiguity, and indeterminacy.

In other words, no single frame of analysis could adequately explain the intention, process, and meaning behind Bernhardt E. Muller's composition for Opa-Locka's city hall, and, as such, interpretive problems remain. Due to Muller's turn against the traditional forms empowered in Moorish buildings such as the Alhambra, Opa-Locka's composition has largely denied the significance of Ibero-Islamic aesthetic practices, which deprivileges the historical and visual meaning of the building. To address these issues and to rethink the validity of historical agency, we must ask how Opa-Locka informs our understanding of history. Is it even possible for us to retrieve meaning from it?

The plot and images of *The Arabian Nights* were enthusiastically mined by Muller and his client, town developer Glenn H. Curtiss, which clarifies the aesthetic realm of Opa-Locka's city hall building. It "is located at the north terminus of Opa-Locka Boulevard at its intersection with Sharazad Avenue. . . . This location in the city plan makes the building highly visible."[75] In 1928, the *Journal of the American Institute of Architects* described the town of Opa-Locka as "pages torn from tales of *The Arabian Nights*."[76] In other words, the town's aesthetic was drawn from fiction. Several reprints of the first edition of the story had been available to Western readers since the eighteenth century, and collections of the tales remained among the most popular books in Europe and the United States for the next hundred years.

Nevertheless, in developing the town of Opa-Locka, American aviator and entrepreneur Glenn H. Curtiss cites the fantasy story to safeguard the mythical meaning of Opa-Locka. It becomes a ready-made synthesis that we may accept and without which "the interplay of resemblances are otherwise difficult to hold."[77] So, once again, the statement extends the discourse in "pursuit of the question of origins [that] has contributed to the understanding of the ontological significance of time . . . the significance and the examination which led to the acknowledgement of space as a relevant intellectual category [of aesthetic meaning]."[78]

Apart from that, paradoxes are omnipresent in the town: its buildings have no typological reference except for the fictitious *The Arabian Nights*. Understood in this way, this unframing of the city hall administration building questions the aesthetic paradoxes and thus accords it with breaking the rules of a tradition. The enjoyment is intentional by means of entropy that takes on the form of an episode introducing a moment in the interior of the great hall of the administration building, the first major structure erected in Opa-Locka. Its walls were adorned with murals depicting scenes from *The Arabian Nights*; it was the most extravagant depiction of the fantasy.[79]

Curtiss intended for the town of Opa-Locka to be more than just another residential development; it was to be a total community and his last and most extravagant real estate venture: "Areas in the plan were to be allotted for industry and business in addition to the residential sections. He envisioned a town where people would have room to grow their own gardens, raise chickens, and possibly generate an income. It was to be a border town, positioned between the rich agricultural mucklands of Dade County and the urbanized and industrial sections of Miami. In such a position, the town could grow with both agriculture and industry and serve as a shipping and receiving station for both."[80] The duplicitous dual meaning of fantasy and reality underlies the architectural language that reveals something about perception, materiality, and disunity.

Put another way, Opa-Locka's architectural *production* inaugurates a play of transferences that clear the way for the paradoxes and contradictions to emerge. In other words, the built form inflects one of the many ways we may interpret the disparate overlaying of materials. Aside from the stucco construction, each building in the city hall complex offers many special features meant to please the eye: The domes, minarets, crenelated parapets, balconies, arches, watchtowers, battered walls, mosaic tile—prematurely aged—were all designed to create an illusion. Alternating voussoirs on central arches extend from horizontal rustication bands, and exterior walls are battered at ends, and stuccoed exterior facades have decorative conical pavilion or onion domes. With this glut of resemblances, the building complex already communicates much more than misleading visual information.

While the resemblances borrow heavily from the Moorish vocabulary, it seems to me that the compositional dilemma demonstrates that the most basic understanding of iconography is absent. At the same time, while we have concentrated on resemblances and similitudes, there are major *differences* between various epochs that have had influence on the development of Muslim architecture, especially in terms of their attachment to local and regional traditions. Muller's design remains tied to domes, arches, and minarets, as perhaps he was unaware that they are common elements in the vocabulary of a traditional mosque.

The importance given to the question of subjectivity and resemblances is one of "analogy rather than significance, or rather, their value as signs, and their duplicating function . . . of which they are the image."[81] Foucault summarizes our dilemma: *How does one banish the resemblance and its implicit burden in the discourse?* It is a question that we may not be able to answer because "it is in vain that we say what we see; what we see never resides in what we say . . . [or] show, by use of images, metaphors, or similes. . . . The space where they achieve their splendor is not that deployed by our eyes but defined by the sequential elements of syntax."[82]

As we recall, the anchor of the new town was the administration building, which was a "dazzling array of domes, minarets, and arches, which combined to create a delightful oriental palace and afforded the appearance of a magical, fantasy city. The building was inspired by the palace of the Emperor Kosroushah from the tale of 'The Talking Bird' and included a courtyard inspired by the 'Garden of the Princess Periezade.'"[83] With this narrative, the building is indebted to the story—the fictional palace of the fictional emperor Kosroushah. Whether or not Muller acknowledged the syncretism when designing the building, the cultural mish-mash makes itself abundantly clear through the mimetic composition.

Indeed, "the whole town was developed in character with the *Arabian Nights* theme. Streets were given names like [Aladdin] Street, Sharazad Avenue, [Sesame] Street, Caliph Street, Ali Baba Avenue and Sinbad Avenue. Curtiss is said to have boasted on occasion that he was creating the 'Baghdad of Dade County.'"[84]

Retrieving meaning—especially from homage, imitation, and counterfeit—is fraught. Consider Picasso: whatever emotion he had at first verbalized toward the underlying premise of African art and "primitivism" or anything connected to it became redundant using sentimental imagery—considering that cultural objects and cultural practices belong to their host society. As you recall, Picasso, the key proponent of Cubism, had confirmed the African mask as the aesthetic source and power behind Cubism.

Primitivism, a viable source of Picasso's creative genius, was resisted by architect and artist John Hejduk, who destroyed the altar but preserved the throne: he proposed instead the *Mask of Medusa*.[85] Hejduk undermined Picasso's fascination with African masks, and ultimately any meaningful appreciation of African architecture and African aesthetics in general. The result of Hejduk's solitary genius, in my view, is nothing but utter confusion, which Francis Bacon correctly identified four centuries ago as the most fatal of errors occurring wherever argument or inference passes from one world experience to another.

Once again, in the design of Opa-Locka's city hall, we see the same inference passing from one world experience to another, with overflowing of resemblances that are "subverted and rendered moot by the 'impossible,' 'irrational' or 'senseless'" consumption of domes, arches and minarets.[86] It would also appear that the choice to use these architectural elements that are traditionally used on a functional mosque adds to the illusion of pleasure and fantasy. And as such, the appropriation posits a mimetic and illusionary relationship, ignoring the traditional uses of Moorish elements; the intent is to conjure up the imaginary *Arabian Nights*.[87]

With this comes a particular set of simulacra: the Moorish themes are repeated throughout, demanding that we ask, *Can we find architectural meaning in the absence of historic agency?* Let us recall Hans-Georg Gadamer's retrieval of meaning, "which enable[s] us to see that meaning is not something that we can produce as we will but rather a dimension of an event within the shared historical realms in which we and our interpretations belong."[88] Yet it is also true that "the death of interpretations is to believe that there are signs, signs that exist primarily, originally, really, as coherent, pertinent, and systematic marks. . . . The life of interpretations, on the contrary, is to believe that there are only interpretations."[89]

And so we interpret the narrative emerging from *The Arabian Nights*: clearly the fantasy was significant enough to the town's developers and the architects to secure a place for the production of space. Despite its being entirely fiction, the tales' visual language is used in the building, privileging ideas that convey meaning to Opa-Locka's visual concept. In this overarching argument, and in view of Curtiss's intention to create the "Baghdad of Dade County," we return to a central difficulty: "Excluding simulacra is a major problem for Western culture," Fontana-Giusti tells us, "as it is difficult to exclude that structure which is in the very fabric of the culture built upon representation."[90]

However, the Opa-Locka scheme is not a unity but a particular dispersion of cultural simulacrum, ideas indebted to make-believe and the genealogy of aesthetic and historical discourses.[91] But the question I want to raise here is about space and time and the motivation for organizing Opa-Locka's town plan around *The Arabian Nights*. Does the narrative fully explain the architect's aleatory impulse for space and time?

Historian Sigfried Giedion, author of *Space, Time and Architecture*, describes this organizing principle under the rubric of a "space conception."[92] None of these subjects has articulated the same field of discourse today as they have in the past—and certainly not at the time of *Space, Time and Architecture*'s publication in 1967. Giedion's designation is therefore limited as a method of analysis for our purposes in discussing Opa-Locka's "space conception." Ultimately, these statements and many others inform several kinds of spatial appropriations that interrogate public sites and public spaces. Here again, Opa-Locka's properties must be accompanied by discursive knowledge as a device to interrogate the notions of exclusion or inclusion and ultimately the architect's production of space. "In this contest (*agon*) between space and time, Foucault deployed a method that took the form of discursive 'geography,' which helped him to challenge the continuities of historiography and its period paradigms."[93]

Above all, such imperceptive attitudes and Bernhardt E. Muller's restaging of space and time in designing Opa-Locka's city hall have led to his inability to understand that Oriental cultures consist of *real* people and *real* places. But more important is the way in which Opa-Locka is laid, placed, or arranged. Could Opa-Locka's pervasive aesthetic reference to *The Arabian Nights* be challenged? What would it mean to assume that Western architecture has always been involved with the permeations of aesthetic meaning? This reflection expands the ethnographic concept, and it explains how Antoine Galland, Sir Richard Burton, and August Müller—each of whom quite eagerly translated, edited, and illustrated editions of *The Arabian Nights* for Western consumption—saw "otherness" in the literary genre. But most importantly, each of the translations was illustrated with architectural images that hadn't been part of the original source manuscript. So to what is the architecture of Opa-Locka aspiring? It is the interpretation of an imaginary drawn from a fiction.

Today there is hardly an issue of political, cultural, or social concern that does not involve complex entanglements with aesthetic irony and ambiguity and the way we use language, which is a categorical manifestation of resemblances and similitudes. Take, for example, the following anecdote: Failing to recognize the two minarets and the dome, while the mosque for Ohio's Islamic Center of Greater Toledo was under construction, one trucker was overheard referring to the building as a new "Mexican restaurant." The trucker's remarks shift the importance given to Opa-Locka's domes, arches, and minarets—although pointedly extravagant—with the elements of Moorish grandeur. However, Opa-Locka lacks any circumstantial meaning, "affirming and representing nothing." Despite the trucker's naivete, his observation has led me to conclude that public knowledge of the American mosque is at best naive and fragmented—as evidenced in the Fox, the Mosque, and Opa-Locka—and as such, subjugated forms of knowing emerge in varying stages and guises.

Ceci n'est pas une mosquee

In this chapter, we have performed a genealogical analysis of space for the purposes of coming to terms with the search for aesthetic meanings. In considering the fictional characters of the Fox Theatre, the Mosque Theater, and Opa-Locka city hall, we were positioned "to identify the accidents, the minute deviations or conversely, the complete reversals—the errors, the false appraisals, and the faulty calculations that gave birth to those things which continue to exist and have value for us."[94] Therefore, resemblances and similitudes are far removed from the gracefulness of Ibero-Islamic traditions, architectural knowledge, and practice. Through examining these three buildings, we learn to better distinguish Ibero-Islamic architecture and practice from the mutant styles that exist in contrariety or combination. For example, the "Moorish style" has resulted in simulacra in the works of artists, painters, travelers, writers, and builders.

Nevertheless, we must be able to understand the effects of simulacra and its polysemic meanings. Therefore, when we talk about meaning, *Ceci n'est pas une pipe* offers an analytical index, within the episteme of statements that coexist in contrariety or combination.[95] *Ceci n'est pas une pipe* allows us to trace the intersections of hybridity and identity and discursive formations. Likewise, *Ceci n'est pas une mosquee* is an analytical index, within the episteme of statements, allowing us to look through the incongruity and the surprising combination of components that exist in the Fox, the Mosque, and Opa-Locka. Of course, the appellation "the Mosque Theater" exemplifies the edifice's simulacra conditions:

> For Foucault, the incongruity between the pipe and its legend illustrates his position, stated in *The Order of Things*, . . . that "[neither words nor the visible] can be reduced to the other's terms: it is in vain that we say what we see; what we see never resides in what we say." . . . In *Ceci n'est pas une pipe* he specifically argues that the drawing (and the series of paintings by Magritte that it inspired) strips us of the certainty that the pipe is a pipe, as it "inaugurates a play of transferences that run, proliferate, propagate, and correspond within the layout of the painting, affirming and representing nothing."[96]

In short, the disorder implied in *Ceci n'est pas une mosquee* could mean that the fascination with the Moorish Revival was awkward but, more importantly, undercut what it posited—affirming and representing nothing. The shallow aesthetic treatment that we observe in the Fox, the Mosque, and Opa-Locka has resulted in a particular understanding "where meaning occurs only within systems of selection and arrangement, which amounts to privileging some possibilities and suppressing or marginalizing others."[97]

With *Ceci n'est pas une mosquee*, something else emerges, because hybridity and identity are categories that are philosophically engaging; "they are also confusing because we are in the midst of pluralistic, skeptical, and radical changes to the assumptions and approaches used for environmental interpretation."[98] The discursive formations of *Ceci n'est pas une mosquee* can be extended further: Within the complex architectural composition of the Fox, the Mosque, and Opa-Locka, while the "Moorish" aesthetic is mimetic, these concept are "not equivalent of the 'spirit of the age.' . . . Such 'spirits' are always ambiguous."[99] Perhaps we can now conclude that the Fox, the Mosque, and Opa-Locka are mere phantasm—apparition or metaphor.

So, according to Gilles Deleuze, a phantasm "falsely presents itself as a centered organism, and that distributes at its periphery the increasing remoteness of things."[100] In like manner, in describing Deleuze's thought, Foucault has noted that in *theatrum philosopicum* (philosophy as theater) "the theatre consists and unfolds into events, the elementary category in the forming of discourses."[101] In other words "phantasms" need to be accepted for what they are . . . they have to function at the limit of bodies . . . and multiply their surfaces . . . laws of which [the architect] remains ignorant"[102] If the properties of space—such as the connectedness to a historical image, the architect's bending and stretching—are based on a deformation (hybridity and identity), then the imaginary domain and the process of simultaneity are extended, and the

Fox, the Mosque, and Opa-Locka thus become a new ground for discursive analysis. If the Deleuzean analysis demonstrates meaning, it can therefore be regarded as a statement that has participated or contributed to aesthetic attribution and signification. This prompts us to ask how Foucauldian theory might update Deleuze's "phantasm" of imaginary meanings and offer a potentially rich field for discursive analysis.

These conditions have been the basis of several attempts to formulate an analysis centered on tradition in the lifeworld where, according to Deleuze's ideas of difference, form and object can create actual spaces and aesthetic sensation. If with *Ceci n'est pas une mosquee* in mind we turn back to Orientalist ideas of architecture, culture, religion, and practices—examples of which reside in art galleries, texts, and museums—we begin to understand the ways in which the destruction of memory can occur and the plundering that took place in the Muslim world before the twentieth century and the fatal attempts to allow it to appear in the West under the hegemonic Moorish Revival. However, culture and tradition are predicated on more that just an impulse or a label; to stimulate our thoughts about culture and tradition, in chapter 3 we explore the genealogical connection to architecture and ontology.

What happens when the mosque is denied its place in the built environment? Is built environment the place where the production of space yields to human agency (to the Muslim body/space experience) and much more than we care to accept? The public understanding of the production of space is the outcome of such conversations; but as Hillenbrand has noted, this is not the purview of one profession: "political analysts, historians, journalists, broadcasters, propagandists from one side or the other . . . are the opinion makers in our society, and far too few of them are aware of the . . . baggage they carry."[103]

For this reason, the inquiry takes us to chapter 3, where the production of space and the discursive formation of urban sites (Chicago and Washington, DC) turn out to be the place where the body/space experience unfolds. The inquiry extends Foucault's *Of Other Spaces* to demark the urban locations through which the analysis of architecture, ontology, and artistic thought takes place.

NOTES

1. Michel Foucault, *This Is Not a Pipe*, illus. and letters René Magritte, trans. and ed. James Harkness (Berkeley: University of California Press, 1982), 9–10.

2. R. Brooks Jeffery, "From Azulejos to Zaguanes: The Islamic Legacy in the Built Environment of Hispano-America," *Journal of the Southwest* 45, nos. 1–2 (Spring–Summer 2003): 289–327.

3. All Jeffery quotations from, "Azulejos to Zaguanes," 294.

4. Mugerauer, *Interpreting Environments*, xxix, emphasis mine.

5. Gerald Steven Bernstein, "In Pursuit of the Exotic: Islamic Forms in Nineteenth-Century American Architecture," PhD diss., University of Pennsylvania, 1968, xxxiv.

6. Hillenbrand, "Occidental Oriental," 218.

7. Gutting, *Foucault*, 50.

8. Bernstein, "In Pursuit of the Exotic," 1.

9. Jeffery, "Azulejos to Zaguanes," 311.

10. See Walter Millard Fleming and William S. Paterson, *Mecca Temple: Ancient Arabic Order of the Nobles of the Mystic Shrine; Its History and Pleasures, Together with the Origin and History of the Order* (New York: Press of Andrew H. Kellogg, 1894). In 1923, the Shriners would open their Moorish Revival meeting place, also called "Mecca Temple," in downtown Manhattan. Today the structure is known as New York City Center.

11. Fleming and Patterson, *Mecca Temple*, 90, emphasis original.

12. Baudrillard, *Simulacra and Simulation*, 3.

13. Interpretation of Gadamer as found in Mugerauer, *Interpreting Environments*, xxix, emphasis original.

14. Hillenbrand, "Occidental Oriental," 220.

15. National Park Service, "Fox Theatre," *Atlanta: A National Register of Historical Places Travel Itinerary* (website), accessed October 27, 2021, https://www.nps.gov/nr/travel/atlanta/fox.htm.

16. Foucault as analyzed in Fontana-Giusti, *Foucault for Architects*, 137.

17. Mersch, *Epistemologies of Aesthetics*, 69.

18. Gutting, *Foucault*, 47.

19. "Fox Theatre Atlanta, " Wikipedia, last modified September 25, 2021, https://en.wikipedia.org/wiki/Fox_Theatre_(Atlanta). The Fox was notable at that time for being the only theater in Atlanta that allowed both white and Black patrons. However, there was a separate Black box office, entrance, and seating; the segregation wall in the middle of the second dress seating still remains, and the "colored" box office window stands unused at the back entrance—left in place for educational and historical purposes.

20. "Fox Theatre," City Planning/Historic Preservation/Property & District Information, City of Atlanta, Georgia (website), Atlanta.gov, accessed October 27, 2021, https://www.atlantaga.gov/government/departments/city-planning/office-of-design/urban-design-commission/fox-theatre. And also see National Park Services, "National Register of Historic Places: Inventory—Nomination Form," listing for Fox Theatre, Atlanta, GA, May 17, 1974, available through the US National Archives Catalog (website), accessed July 1, 2020, https://catalog.archives.gov/id/93208180.

21. Hirst, *Space and Power: Politics*, 162.

22. Fontana-Giusti, *Foucault for Architects*, 137.

23. "Fox Theatre Atlanta," Wikipedia.

24. Francine Giese and Ariane Varela Braga, "The Protagonists of the Moorish Revival: Translating Ibero-Islamic Heritage in Eighteenth- and Nineteenth-Century

Europe," *Art in Translation* 11, no. 2 (2019): 122, https://www.tandfonline.com/doi/epub/10.1080/17561310.2019.1703333.

25. National Park Service, "Fox Theatre Historic District."

26. Washington Irving (1783–1859) was an American historian, biographer, and essayist who also served as ambassador to Spain from 1842 to 1846.

27. Giese and Braga, "Protagonists of the Moorish Revival," 122 and then 120.

28. Edward W. Said, *Orientalism* (New York: Vintage Books, 1979), 118.

29. Bree Midavaine, "Henri Matisse and the Alhambra," term paper for HA 511, "Picasso/Matisse Seminar," Pratt Institute, New York, spring 2014, p. 1, available online at https://www.academia.edu/24561900/Henri_Matisse_and_the_Alhambra.

30. Fontana-Giusti, *Foucault for Architects*, 36.

31. Escher as quoted in Steven Poole, "The Impossible World of M. C. Escher," *The Guardian*, June 20, 2015, https://www.theguardian.com/artanddesign/2015/jun/20/the-impossible-world-of-mc-escher.

32. Giese and Braga, "Protagonists of the Moorish Revival," 121.

33. Isabella Archer, "(Re)Envisioning Orientalist North Africa: Exploring Representations of Maghrebian Identities in Oriental and Occidental Art, Museums, and Markets," *intersections* 11, no. 2, (2010): 106, http://depts.washington.edu/chid/intersections_Autumn_2010/Isabella_Archer_%28Re%29Envisioning_Orientalist_North_Africa.pdf.

34. Bernstein, "In Pursuit of the Exotic," 1.

35. Philadelphia Museum of Art, "*The Moorish Chief*: 1878; Eduard Charlemont, Austrian, 1848–1906," accessed July 6, 2020, https://www.philamuseum.org/collections/permanent/102792.html, text archived at https://www.flickr.com/photos/rverc/38390338456.

36. "Fox Theatre Atlanta," Wikipedia.

37. "Fox Theatre Atlanta," Wikipedia.

38. "Fox Theatre," City of Atlanta, Georgia (website).

39. Fiona Melhuish, "The Grammar of Ornament," featured item, Special Collections Services, University of Reading, February 2009, 5 (quoting Jones), https://www.reading.ac.uk/web/files/special-collections/featurejonesgrammar.pdf.

40. Giese and Braga, "Protagonists of the Moorish Revival," 120.

41. Bernstein, "In Pursuit of the Exotic," 1.

42. Sembou, *Hegel's Phenomenology*, 33–35.

43. Giese and Braga, "Protagonists of the Moorish Revival," 120–21.

44. Hirst, *Space and Power*, 162.

45. See Maurice Merleau-Ponty, *Phenomenology of Perception*, trans. Donald A. Landes, (London: Routledge, 2012), especially p. 132.

46. *Brown v. City of Richmond*, 204 Va. 471 (1963). And also see *Brown v. Board of Education of Topeka*, 347 U.S. 483 (1954).

47. Foucault, *This Is Not a Pipe*, 4.

48. Altria Theater, "History," AltreaTheater.com, accessed June 30, 2020, https://www.altriatheater.com/about-us/history.

49. Bernstein, "In Pursuit of the Exotic," 1.

50. Foucault, *This Is Not a Pipe*, 10.

51. Foucault, *This Is Not a Pipe*, 8.

52. For a brief primer on the dialogue sparked by the painting, see "The Treachery of Images," Wikipedia, last modified September 30, 2021, https://en.wikipedia.org/wiki/The_Treachery_of_Images.

53. G. S. Evans, "This Could Be a Pipe: Foucault, Irrealism and *Ceci n'est pas une pipe*," *irreal (re)views*, last modified 2013, http://cafeirreal.alicewhittenburg.com/review5.htm, emphasis original.

54. Peter Johnson, "Foucault and Visual Art's Adventurous Spaces," *Heterotopian Studies* (website), November 2015, http://www.heterotopiastudies.com/wp-content/uploads/2015/06/Foucault-and-art-article-pdf.pdf.

55. Foucault, *This Is Not a Pipe*, 9.

56. Foucault, *This Is Not a Pipe*, 9, emphasis mine, and then 8.

57. Foucault quoted in Fontana-Giusti, *Foucault for Architects*, 137, emphasis mine.

58. See "Simulacrum," Merriam-Webster.com, accessed May 21, 2020, https://www.merriam-webster.com/dictionary/simulacrum.

59. Mersch, *Epistemologies of Aesthetics*, 37.

60. Gutting, *Foucault*, 50.

61. Fontana-Giusti, *Foucault for Architects*, 153.

62. "Mimesis," Merriam-Webster.com, accessed May 21, 2020, https://www.merriam-webster.com/dictionary/mimesis.

63. Baudrillard's full passage and original wording follow: We have all become living specimens in the spectral light of ethnology, or of antiethnology, which is nothing but the pure form of triumphal ethnology, under the sign of dead differences, and of the resurrection of differences. It is thus very naive to look for ethnology in the Savages or in some Third World—it is here, everywhere, in the metropolises, in the white community, in a world completely cataloged and analyzed, then artificially resurrected under the auspices of the real, in a world of simulation, of the hallucination of truth, of the blackmail of the real, of the murder of every symbolic form and of its hysterical, historical retrospection—a murder of which the Savages, noblesse oblige, were the first victims, but that for a long time has extended to all Western societies. Baudrillard, *Simulacra and Simulation*, 8.

64. Jeffery, "Azulejos to Zaguanes," 312–13, emphasis original.

65. Johnson, "Foucault and Visual Art."

66. Jerrilynn D. Dodds, ed., *Al-Andalus: The Art of Islamic Spain*, publication issued in conjunction with the exhibition, Metropolitan Museum of Art, New York, July 1–September 27, 1992 (New York: Abrams, 1992), xix, online at https://books.google.com/books?id=lLA-yx8bC8UC&printsec=frontcover#v=onepage&q&f=false.

67. Akel Ismail Kahera, *Reading the Islamic City: Discursive Practices and Legal Judgment* (Lanham, MD: Lexington Books, 2012), xxvii.

68. Kahera, *Reading the Islamic City*, xxvii.

69. *The Order of Things*, published within Foucault, *This Is Not a Pipe*, 9.

70. Bernstein, "In Pursuit of the Exotic," 88.

71. Foucault, *This Is Not a Pipe*, 9–10.

72. The city of Opa-Locka takes its name from the Seminole *Opa-tisha-wocka-locka* (*Opatishawockalocka*), which translates into English as "wooded hummock" or "high, dry hummock." See "Opa-locka, Florida," Wikipedia, last modified October 7, 2021, https://en.wikipedia.org/wiki/Opa-locka,_Florida.

73. Bhabha, *Location of Culture*, 1.

74. Fontana-Giusti, *Foucault for Architects*, 142.

75. National Park Services, "National Register of Historic Places: Inventory—Registration Form," listing for Opa-Locka Thematic Resource Area, Opa-Locka, Florida, March 22, 1982, available through the NP Gallery: Digital Asset Management System (website), US Department of the Interior, accessed August 31, 2020, https://npgallery.nps.gov/NRHP/GetAsset/NRHP/64000117_text.

76. H. Sayre Wheeler, "Opa-Locka, Created from *The Arabian Nights*," *Journal of the American Institute of Architects* (April 1928): 157, 158, as quoted in National Park Services, "National Register of Historic Places: Inventory—Registration Form."

77. Fontana-Giusti, *Foucault for Architects*, 41

78. Fontana-Giusti, *Foucault for Architects*, 41 and then 135.

79. Fontana-Giusti, *Foucault for Architects*, 135.

80. National Park Services, "National Register of Historic Places: Inventory—Nomination Form."

81. Foucault, *The Order of Things*, 37.

82. Foucault, *This Is Not a Pipe*, 8, and quotation drawn from 9.

83. National Park Services, "National Register of Historic Places: Inventory—Nomination Form."

84. National Park Services, "National Register of Historic Places: Inventory—Nomination Form," quoting from Cecil R. Roseberry, *Glenn Curtiss: Pioneer of Flight* (Garden City, NY: Doubleday, 1972), 432.

85. John Hejduk, *Mask of Medusa*, ed. Kim Shkapich (New York: Rizzoli, 1989). *Medusa* means "sovereign female wisdom." The Medusa idea was actually imported into Greece from Libya. Architect John Hejduk resisted all forms of primitivism, especially the African mask (which was a viable source of Picasso's creative genius). He destroyed the altar of Picasso's genius but preserved the throne (read: a Euro-centric *Weltanschauung* or worldview). Hejduk proposed instead the *Mask of Medusa*. (Medusa was beheaded by Perseus, a Greek hero, who used her head as a weapon and its ability to turn spectators to stone). The implication here is that the crisis of architectural history is also a crisis of the *Weltanschauung*. Of course, that same *Weltanschauung* disavows descriptions that reside outside of its epistemological canon. So, to combat the Eurocentric hegemony, it is not surprising that over the last three decades several architectural schools have introduced a broader understanding of architectural history, theory, and criticism. Two notable examples are the Aga Khan Program in Islamic Architecture at the Massachusetts Institute of Technology and the Center for Environmental Design Research at the University of California–Berkeley.

86. Foucault, *This Is Not a Pipe*, 8.

87. National Park Services, "National Register of Historic Places: Inventory—Nomination Form."

88. As interpreted in Mugerauer, *Interpreting Environments*, xxxi–xxxii.

89. Foucault, *This Is Not a Pipe*, 12.
90. Fontana-Giusti, *Foucault for Architects*, 153.
91. Fontana-Giusti, *Foucault for Architects*, 43.
92. Giedion, *Space, Time and Architecture*, 124–25; and also see Giedion, *Eternal Present*, 521–26.
93. Fontana-Giusti, *Foucault for Architects*, 134–35, parenthetical and emphasis original.
94. James D. Faubion, *The Essential Works of Foucault, 1954–1984: Aesthetics, Method, and Epistemology*, vol. 2, trans. Michael Hurley et al. (New York: The New Press, 1994), 374.
95. Hirst, *Space and Power*, 155.
96. Foucault, *This Is Not a Pipe*, 49, as quoted in Evans, "This Could Be a Pipe," emphasis and all parentheticals original.
97. Mugerauer, *Interpreting Environments*, xl.
98. Mugerauer, *Interpreting Environments*, xvi.
99. Hirst, *Space and Power*, 162.
100. As interpreted in Fontana-Giusti, *Foucault for Architects*, 155.
101. As interpreted in Fontana-Giusti, *Foucault for Architects*, 156.
102. Fontana-Giusti, *Foucault for Architects*, 154.
103. Hillenbrand, "Occidental Oriental," 218.

Chapter 3

Architecture and Ontology

As we discovered in our analysis of the previous chapter, with resemblances and similitudes the reference "anchor" is gone, and things are "cast adrift without any of them being able to claim the privileged status of 'model' for the rest."[1] In other words, resemblances and similitudes are the standpoint from which the antinomies of architectural form and content cannot be overcome, and as such the architect's creative volition is cast adrift. Our analysis of the Fox, the Mosque, and Opa-Locka reveals that the buildings' multiple meanings bear no meaningful relationship to Islam's principles of hermeneutics, truth and beauty, and the aesthetics of monotheism (*tauhid*) encapsulated in the formula "No God but God" (*la illaha ill-Allah*). In fact, this is an important distinction, because it is consistent with the absence of sacrilegious representation and syncretism (human, animal, or thing); that disposition is replaced with a corpus of aesthetic themes that privilege the aniconic leitmotif within the visual precepts of the mosque's architectural language.

In this chapter we introduce *architecture and ontology* to study the important discursive elements of the mosque's *place*, orientation, and architectural language. Our aim is twofold: (1) to offer a critical reflection of the formative space of the mosque's (*masjid*) plan and orientation (*qibla*), which is recognizable by the niche (*mihrab*) and its position in the anterior wall facing the *Ka'ba* and the city of Makkah and (2) to critique the idea that the American *masjid* "has its being in the human engagement with place, and more specifically, in the engagement with place as opened up through building."[2]

Alongside these important features, scholar of Islam William C. Chittick contends that "the standard Arabic pairing is *zaman wa makan* . . . time and place . . . [which] implies the fixed and exact locations in which things exist."[3] Drawing on this premise, our discursive analysis of time and place underwrites the impulse of a community to self-identify with "architecture's own discursive self-formation . . . enduring grounds or limits."[4] In this regard, we are led to think of how the facade of architectural knowledge in academic discourses is a fragile and precarious layer, prone to theoretical utterances, statements, and propositions.

Take, for example, *On Adam's House in Paradise*, architectural historian Joseph Rykwert's theoretical account of the first hut, which fails to consider the copious details of Adam's house on earth given by ninth-century Islamic commentator and historian Muhammad ibn 'Abd Allah al-Azraqi. Al-Azraqi's description is a valuable source of knowledge that has profound consequences for the interpretation of architecture and its idiosyncratic and ontological meanings.

In the second section of this chapter, "The Burden of the Architect," I critique the architect's volition—that is, the knowledge of *zaman wa makan*, time and place. This methodological stance shifts the emphasis to the task of seeking to formulate the ideal requirements for the communal space for devotees. Insisting on the relation between the ideal requirements and the users, architectural theorist Christian Norberg-Schulz states, "It is no excuse for the architect that the client and the society confront [the architect] with imprecise and one-sided problems, because it is one of [the architect's] main tasks to *formulate* the problems on the basis of the various and often contradictory needs which are brought forth."[5]

Taking two urban sites as our examples—one in Chicago, Illinois, and one in Washington, DC—we highlight the architect's creative struggle that becomes the catalyst for success or failure. We can well imagine the wealth of meaning lost or never to be retrieved again in architect Max Herz's reconstruction of the Qaytbay mosque complex at the 1893 World's Columbian Exposition in Chicago. That is to say, Herz's restaging of the fifteenth-century Mamluk edifice in Chicago "involves different kinds of correlations, positions, functions and transformations that go beyond the usual expected understanding of [the original edifice and its] identity and proximity."[6] On the other hand, architect Mario Rossi's plan for the Islamic Center of Washington, DC (1957) reveals a different logic: the *masjid* is intended to support the stable dimension of place, to reclaim the expectations of communal existence and the practice of Islam in America.

The *Ka'ba* and Makkah

If we must speak of "architecture and ontology," the significance of time and place—*zaman wa makan*—has the advantage of emphasizing the sense in which the power of the *Ka'ba*, Islam's very center, connects the devotee's quotidian practices from far off and in proximity. Take, for instance, the devotee's daily performance of prayers while facing the *Ka'ba* and the annual pilgrimage (*hajj*) to the *Ka'ba*, located in the sacred mosque, the Masjid al-Haram, in the city of Makkah. The potency of the ritual act of circumambulation around the *Ka'ba* sanctions a hermeneutical reflection on sacred space and time.

Accordingly, during his pilgrimage to Makkah at the turn of the thirteenth century, Muslim scholar and mystic Ibn al-Arabi underwent a theophanic experience while circling the *Ka'ba*, apparently inspired by the perpetual essence of the sacred edifice under its black veil covering—as the following range of his subtle "exegetical illuminations" amply testify:

> The Ka'ba is nothing other than our essence, the essence of curtains of pious fear.
> The True One is not contained by sky nor earth nor any word.[7]

In "Love Letters to the Ka'ba," scholar of Islam Denis Gril explores the constellation of Ibn al-Arabi's exegetical illuminations avowing that the human heart is profoundly strengthened by *patience, love,* and *piety*. Moreover, the subtle implications of the "illuminations," and the affective qualities of presence (*wujud*), simultaneously evoke the *Ka'ba*'s immanence and universal symbolism and, most importantly, the timeless power that operates with the same ontological and universal effect. On the one hand, devotees of spiritual knowledge, wisdom, and perpetual remembrance (*ahl al-Dhikr*; Q.16:43; Q. 21:07) call the theophanic experience *fana*, or "denial" of self—the frontier between the eternal and the contingent—by endorsing God as the only inconceivable but eternal reality (*al-Haqq*). In fact, Ibn al-Arabi's "love letters" "constitute a point in which opposites are resolved and all possibilities meet, on the frontier between the eternal and the contingent . . . the image and the whole."[8]

On the other hand, the *Ka'ba*'s affective qualities are related to the Abrahamic tradition—and thereby with all the monotheist religions (figure 3.1). Taking the timeless principle as the point of departure, the *Ka'ba*'s ontological nature stamps its imprint upon the devotee's consciousness (of temporal existence: *wujud*), and this condition is entwined with the formula *la illaha ill-Allah*, (the dogma of monotheism, the *tauhid*) and the doctrine of faith (*iman*).

In short, the *Ka'ba*'s significance is at the center of our examination of meanings found in temporal elements. Specifically, we are speaking of the *qibla*, the axis between the faithful and the *Ka'ba*; the *mihrab*, the chamber in a mosque indicating the direction of Makkah; and the alignment of the *masjid*, the mosque itself.[9] While these temporal elements embrace art and architecture, they are more than mere aesthetic concepts; they are singularly formulated for another role—drawing the devotee into "ontological" interaction (body in space and time) with the *Ka'ba*. In other words, the methodological and epistemological dimensions of sacred geography—that is, the

Figure 3.1 The *Ka'ba*, c. 1910. Photograph. Source: Library of Congress.

stabiltas loci, or a world centered on the *Ka'ba*—coexists with the conditions of time and space.

In elaborating the *stabiltas loci*, historian David A. King writes of the twofold nature of architecture—time and space—pointing out once more that the Qur'anic injunction is a decisive and integral part of the devotee's knowledge. According to King, "we see in these Muslim responses to the

Qur'anic injunction to face the *Ka'ba* in prayer firstly the ingenuity of the Muslim scientists in deriving sophisticated mathematical solutions to the *qibla* problem, and secondly the ingenuity of the legal scholars in deriving an alternative sacred geography which featured a world centered on the *Ka'ba* and provided a simple practical means for Muslims to know how to pray towards the *Ka'ba*."[10]

So, to return to the *masjid*'s enduring typological traditions and spatial limits, the most rudimentary architectural expression of aniconism is as a "wall facing Makkah." Professor of architecture Jaan Holt describes its conception and primordial elements: "The wall facing [Makkah] is made by each individual placing his *mihrab* of direction next to his neighbor. All in attitude are coincident, but architecturally they become a row, which becomes a wall facing [Makkah] marked by one *mihrab* of common agreement."[11]

Holt invites us to speak once again of the aesthetic effect, the inner experience of the devotional space; we can see that the *mihrab* trope entails the attitude of contemplation and the orientation (*qibla*) that is particularly evident with "one *mihrab* of common agreement." In other words, the *mihrab* and the *qibla* trope evoke the human engagement with time and space that adds to our understanding of architecture and ontology.

Gary Gutting sums up the value of orientation: "It is a history of the present," he writes. "The primary intent is not to understand the past in its own terms or for its own sake but to understand and evaluate the present."[12] Although Gutting is not directly referring to the five daily prayers, "the act of orienting one's body toward a 'source' conjures within the self a transcendental anchor, connecting one to a narrative of faith and existence."[13]

The practice of orienting one's body along the *qibla* as indicated by the *mihrab*'s placement may be expressed in two principal architectural modes: as a simple, demarcated niche on the ground, indicating the sacred direction, or as an embellished or unassuming vertical element in the arterial wall of the *masjid* facing Makkah. Constituting an ontological axis, both the *qibla* and the *mihrab* are universally understood.

Because historically there was no singular accepted method of determining the *qibla*'s direction, we find that jurists were free to exercise reasonable partiality. For example, in the medieval Maghrib of North Africa, a debate gave rise to controversy over the correctness of the *qibla*'s orientation and the position of the *mihrab*.[14] However, even in a most rudimentary or remote setting, the place of prostration (*sujud*) retains an association with the direction of the *mihrab* and *qibla*.[15]

The *qibla* and the *mihrab* evoke a range of meanings and a direct relationship to the spatial practice of Islam (*sunnah*) and the Masjid al-Nabawī al-Sharīf—the Mosque of the Prophet—the seminal *masjid* built in the city of

Madinah around the year 622 CE. At the same time, the term *sunnah* (practice, custom, personal mannerism, model, convention, law, habit, and so on) can be substituted for "tradition," and thus the term *spatial sunnah* conveys explicit spatial features of the seminal *masjid* as a place for education, for the destitute, for communal worship, and for the daily and Friday prayer admitting men, women, and children.

Later generations of builders and patrons considered the seminal *masjid* to be the archetype, excepting a very few art historians who continue to describe the mosque as a house because at one point there were nine private apartments attached. But in so doing, they ignore the edifice's primary function and what remains of it today; this is in keeping with the notion that "there is no place without memory; no memory without place; and since there is no architecture that is not engaged with place, neither is there architecture that is not engaged with memory."[16] The historian's conception could not be further apart and in greater opposition to the etymology of the word *masjid* (mosque), which is related to a place of prostration and the act of prostration (*sa-ja-da* is the Arabic verb meaning "to prostrate").[17]

Ontologically, these convergences and enduring universal traditions have psychological benefits for the believer: they allow the devotee to orient the bodily posture toward the direction of the *Ka'ba*—the universal omphalos, or hub, of Islam. It is the same for every devotee paying heed to the inner experience: they will be inclined to the practice of approaching the sacred orientation. This practice admits the term *ahl al-qibla* (literally, "people/community of the *qibla*"), which suggests a sense of human engagement with the *Ka'ba* and the city of Makkah.

Further, the subtle implications of the potency of facing Makkah create a reassuring component of belief, as the practice conforms perfectly to and is consonant with the Qur'anic injunctions. Finally, this reflection is taken from the perspective that, in the temporal context, the well-known *hadith* (tradition) declares, "The earth has been made a mosque . . . therefore when prayer overtakes a person, they should prostrate wherever they may be."[18]

That said, the mechanisms of the *qibla*, the *mihrab*, and the alignment of the *masjid* operate within the framework of *zaman wa makan* with psychological causes. To state it somewhat differently, the *qibla*, the *mihrab*, and the alignment of the *masjid* "testify to the richness and diversity of the Islamic religious and cultural heritage and provide a unique example of the interplay between science [urbanism, art, architecture, sacred geography] and religion."[19] Accordingly, in every condition of the devotee's *location*, humanity, faith, and practice mean "that the inherent symbolism of the *Ka'ba*, in its shape and the [pilgrimage] rites associated with it, contains in embryo everything expressed by the sacred art of Islam."[20]

Figure 3.2 The Little White Mosque, Abiquiú, New Mexico. The *mihrab* protrudes beyond the *qibla* wall. Photograph. Source: William R. Baker.

Art historian and scholar of Islam Titus Burckhardt provides a convenient synopsis of the philosophical reflection on the symbolic meaning of the *Ka'ba*: "The Ka'ba's role as the liturgical center of the Muslim world," he writes, "is bound up with the fact that it demonstrates Islam's link with the Abrahamic tradition and thereby with the origin of all the monotheist religions."[21]

As the preceding range of hermeneutical reflections demonstrates a multitude of strategies for serious consideration, likewise, we cannot overemphasize the importance of the *Kitab Akhbar Makkah* (Book of Reports about Makkah)—the contribution of ninth-century historian al-Azraqi. The focus that al-Azraqi places on the *Ka'ba* and on Makkah's history connects memory with the meanings residing in the city, emphasizing knowledge, landscape, and eschatology.[22]

Consider, for example, al-Azraqi's assertion that the angels first built the *Ka'ba* and placed it directly below the celestial *Ka'ba*. Then, two thousand years later, it was rebuilt by Adam. After being destroyed by the great deluge (the flood at the time of Noah), Abraham and Ismail rebuilt it on the same foundation. It was once more returned to its inviolable status during the time of prophet Muhammad, when the idols were destroyed.[23] This destruction of the idols suggests that the monotheistic beliefs and practices of earlier prophets (Adam and Abraham) were at this time restored.

Al-Azraqi also provides a detailed description of Adam's house on earth, the *Ka'ba*, and the city of Makkah, all of which he copiously chronicles to ensure that the knowledge is retained in our collective memory. In this way, the palimpsests of sacred geography set the context "through both a perceptual recognition and a theoretical-historical understanding" of the sacredness of the *Ka'ba* and the city of Makkah.[24] As part of our understanding of Makkah's topography, its inviolable sites, sacred places, and spaces shape the devotee's knowledge and discerning sense of being.

Along with the injunction to circumambulate the *Ka'ba*, the Qur'an also specifies the hajj rites, which include being present—on the 9th day of the hajj—on the Mount of Arafat (*Jabal ar-Rahmah*, or the mountain of mercy) and the valley of Mina, where it is believed that Abraham was commanded to sacrifice his son Isma'il. As such, there is something quite specific in the Qur'anic mention of these inviolable sites and in al-Azraqi's copious historical accounts that are inherently symbolic, in that they are indebted to history, "experience, knowledge, and religious belief."[25]

In his many volumes of *Kitab Akhbar Makkah*, al-Azraqi emphasizes the events of history that are most importantly linked to sacred Islamic traditions: the *Ka'ba* (the sacred cube and black stone), the sacred well (*zam zam*), the two hills Safa and Marwa, and, on the outskirts of Makkah, the valley of Mina, all offer hermeneutical meaning to the devotee. It is between Safa and Marwa that the Virtuous Lady Hajar, wife of Abraham, trod back and forth, seven times, in a desperate search for water to save her son, Isma'il, who was dying of thirst. Reenacting that journey has become an essential requirement for all pilgrims.[26] She finally found water at the sacred well—the *zam zam*—after being directed to the spot by the Angel Gabriel (in another narration, the water sprang from the earth where Isma'il dug with his heel). As the lifesaving well miraculously bubbled forth, in her efforts to contain it with sand and stones, Hajar exclaimed, *"Zum zum!"* (Cease flowing!). Muslims consider the *zam zam* water sacred, in that it still flows and is consumed by pilgrims even today.

Several of Makkah's inviolable sites and most sacred religious practices are attached to "divinely inspired" events referenced in the Qur'an, the hadith, and historical narratives—including the Hira cave on the Jabal an-Nur (mountain of light). It is here that Muslims believe the first verses of the Qur'an were revealed to the Prophet Muhammad, with the Angel Gabriel's command, "Iqra!" (meaning *read, proclaim,* or *recite*; Q. 96:1–5).

Similarly, an entire discourse on the hermeneutics of knowledge and light has been undertaken by eleventh-century philosopher Al-Ghazali in *The Niche of Lights* (*Mishkat al-Anwar*), which takes its inspiration from the Qur'anic chapter "The Light"—or *al-Nur*—and the verse of light (Q. 24:35):

God is the Light of the heavens and the earth.
His light is like a niche in which there is a lamp,
the lamp is in a crystal,
the crystal is like a shining star,
lit from [the oil of] a blessed olive tree,
[located] neither to the east nor the west,
whose oil would almost glow,
even without being touched by fire.
Light upon light!
God guides whoever He wills to His light.
And God sets forth parables for humanity.
For God has [perfect] knowledge of all things.[27]

The Niche of Lights opens the ontological question for the possibility of light to be understood as a projection into and onto darkness (ignorance), where darkness is a human and diabolic quality.[28] In other words, the power and the symbolic meaning of "light" takes on ontological meaning through the prism of knowledge. In this way, the metaphorical aspects of *The Niche of Lights* broaden our understanding of the mountain and the cave, and these are among the facets of Makkah's location, power, and spiritual agency, confirmed by the custom of climbing 642 meters to visit the cave. What then emerges from this assertion is a balance of meanings and the premise that *knowledge is a landscape*.

While this kind of labeling is a common academic practice, ontology and architecture extend the assertion beyond the label to include Makkah and the *Ka'ba* as part of the devotee's lifeworld in devotion, spatial orientation, and the annual hajj. The premise that *knowledge is a landscape* includes Islam's cosmological order—lived time and perceived space, which are connected to the concept of being. As such, knowledge transfers to and from the aesthetics of architecture and visual history and the character and roles of representation.

Because knowledge concerns human existence and spatial and visual relationships, we may begin by asking how architecture and ontology and the experiential effect of devotional practices might lead to a mental space. The question is important because mental spaces provide a medium for reasoning and a structuring of experience on two levels. First, on the subjective side, the importance accounts for the Qur'anic injunction to face Makkah. In this case, "structures therefore provide a means [for the devotee] through experience. The structure is an experience effect . . . a set of effects which go beyond the building to the world and the Creator."[29]

This is to say, in the practice of facing Makkah, we are dealing with a "transformatory device" and the relationship of the *Ka'ba* to the external reality that is defined by human cognition.[30] This means it would be wise for us to probe the theophanic experience Ibn al-Arabi had while circling the *Ka'ba* during his hajj to Makkah. In other words, the body (mind and soul) in devotion is part of an order of practices that work from subjectivity and from the worldly perspective—that is, human cognition observes and describes the world through language and meaning. So, if we consider the evocative cadence of the *adhan* (the call to prayer)—by locating the quotidian practice with the reliance on time—we may come to understand *zaman wa makan*, time and place.

In this sense, the cadence of the *adhan* points to Henri Lefebvre's *Rhythmanalysis*, with very different qualifications: it provides an account of the *doxa* and the framework of practices coupled with spatial moments.[31] First, the *adhan* is invested with meaning: explicitly it is made intelligible through its daily iteration; it is a persuasive tradition that operates throughout the world. Second, for the devotee, the performance of the five daily prayers—one of the essential pillars of the faith—are marked by the familiar cadence of the *adhan*'s intonation, which summons the faithful at the instant the prayer is to be performed. Finally, the idea of phonocentrism draws our attention to Philip Glass's 1988 film score No. 16, "From Egypt," a beautiful recording of the *adhan*, composed for the documentary *Powaqqatsi*: *Life in Transformation*.[32] Above all, the privilege is accorded to the voice in the recitation and reading (*qira'at*); the pronunciation, intonation, and caesuras of the Qur'an (*tajweed*); and the common practice of Qur'anic memorization and the recitation of the entire 114 chapters (6,236 verses) during the entire month of Ramadan comprises another corpus of devotional rhythms that serve to enhance human belief and practice.

Beyond the confinement of time and location, the mosque (*masjid*) being a work of art and architecture simultaneously has the potential to evoke meaning and a sense of place when coupled with five cognitive themes: belief, order, space, materials, and symbols. These five ontological themes have their origin in the multilayered exegesis of the Qur'an, which "emerge in short passages, creating an inimitable interplay."[33] While Islam's dogma may reflect a core epistemological emphasis on monotheism, at the same time the correlation of belief, order, space, materials, and symbols informs the spatial language and aesthetic vocabulary. More importantly, the architectural spatial language and aesthetic relate to the *masjid*, but since the meaning in art and architecture are not fixed, they have a part to play, by putting in place a sense of how ontology, aesthetics, and the idea of beauty operate.

To close this discussion, as we have noted, the history and sacred nature of the city of Makkah make for a quite distinctive understanding of geography and even the *qibla* axis; both must be reconsidered with the *stabilitas loci* of an edifice, its location, and its inherent ontological meaning. The point here is to underscore that the understanding of ontology can broaden the architect's volition. Finally, with all the implications that the encounter with place admits, what can an architect learn from the spatial traditions of the mosque? Importantly, the objective interpretation of beauty, architectural manifestations and expressions of the sacred art of Islam, along with the orientation of the *masjid* move within the universal category of the ontological axis—that is, the relationship to Makkah and the *Ka'ba*. In other words, architecture and ontology are part of a particularly poignant hermeneutic discourse, because they must also consider the *stabiltas loci* and the relations among sites.

The Burden of the Architect

In an attempt to address the questions we've raised thus far in this chapter, in this next section we turn our discussion to the Qaytbay funerary mosque complex (Cairo, 1474). Specifically, we will consider how the complex finds its place in the Mamluk era (1251–1517) and also, fast-forwarding more than four hundred years and crossing the globe to Chicago, Illinois, in 1893, looking at the complex's re-creation as an exhibit at the World's Columbian Exposition can help us discuss and better understand *place*.[34]

Critical to our examination of the re-creation on the Chicago fairgrounds is the role played by project architect Max Herz (1856–1919). The complex's Chicago location differs in existential relationship to the lifeworld of fifteenth-century Mamluk Cairo. The problem of time and space "is the practical problem of what it takes to make space . . . to make places from sites where the active place making infrastructure . . . [can support the analysis]."[35] Further, "the architect, like other professions in the modern world distinguished by specialist training (doctors, engineers, etc.), cannot be conceived easily without some notion of 'expertise.' [Additionally], the architect's authority derives from their mastery of certain skills, their fluency in technical vocabularies, and importantly the accumulation of *experience*—'expert' from the Latin *expertus*, the past participle of *experiri*, 'to try.'"[36]

And so, given Herz's decision to restage the Qaytbay complex—to elaborate the play of historical forces—we may begin our discourse by asking, of all the possible examples of architecture that exist in Cairo fin de siècle, why the Qaytbay complex was the best replica for the exposition in Chicago (figure 3.3).

In addition, how are we to evaluate the Qaytbay complex—a thing built in the distant past for a specific purpose and aesthetic that can now only be imitated and can be expected to have neither meaningful status nor creative value in the United States? Because we are no longer dealing with the original but a simulation, the edifice's "'stylistic' component must be complemented by a creative deviation from [its original place]."[37] It is against the paradox of representation and simulation that Baudrillard expands the Foucauldian

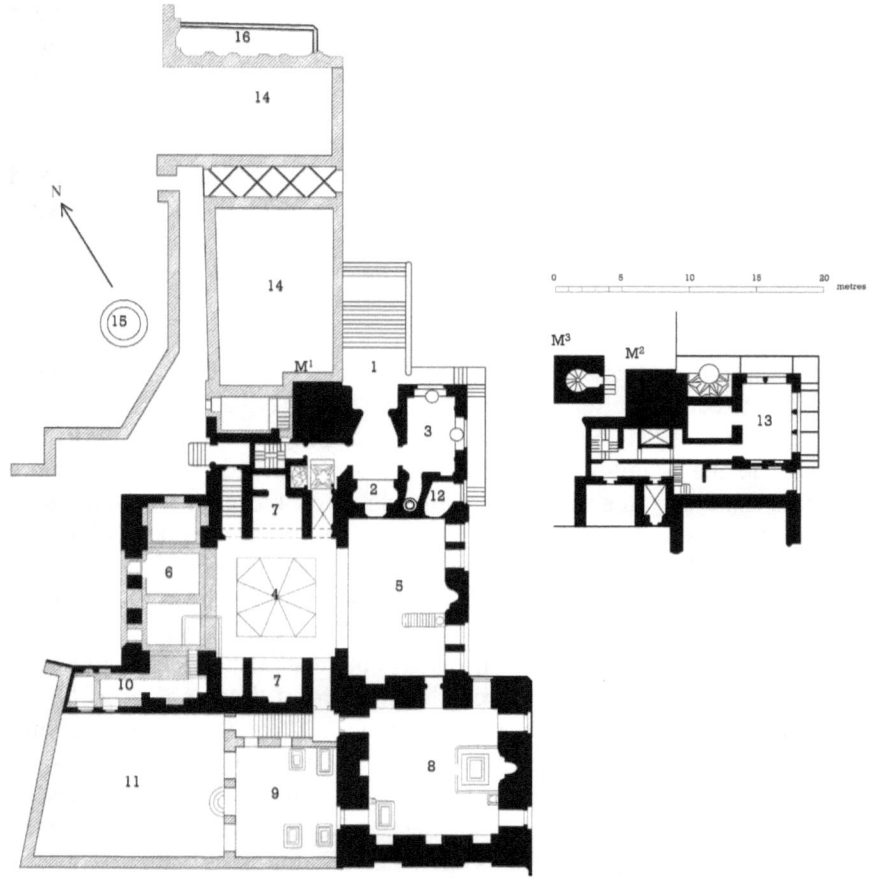

TOMB MOSQUE OF KAIT BEY - 1. Principal Entrance. 2. Vestibule with throne. 3. Sebil. 4. Sahn el-Gamia. 5. Sanctuary with prayer-recess and pulpit. 6. Liwan. 7. Side-liwans. 8. Domed room with cenotaph of Kait Bey. 9. Hall with tombs of Kait Bey's four wives. 10. Library. 11. Uncovered court. 12. Hilweh (chamber) for the Imam. 13. (first floor). Kuttab (elementary school). 14. Administrative offices. 15. Well with water-wheel. 16. Water-trough. 17. Staircase to the minaret. M^1, M^2, M^3. Minaret in the three stories.

Figure 3.3 Qaytbay complex, Cairo, Egypt. Drawing. Source: Muhammed Madandola.

definitions of *resemblances* and *similitudes*—the object of our discussion in previous chapters. Baudrillard argues that simulation is opposed to representation and that "representation stems from the principle of the equivalence... Whereas representation attempts to absorb simulation by interpreting it as false representation, simulation envelops the whole edifice of representation itself as a simulacrum."[38]

This is particularly true in instances like the Chicago Exposition, where buildings built on the fairgrounds were elaborately choreographed and restaged for the public exhibition and where simulation envelops the Qaytbay complex by imitating the original but only providing a false representation—a simulacrum. In this case, what happens when the flow of visual and aesthetic expression between two locations—Cairo, and Chicago—results in a faulty replica of the "real thing"? Moreover, we must ask, did Herz specifically opt to re-create the Qaytbay complex simply to appeal to the psychology of the American spectator?

These questions reflect truth and secrecy and the architect's "quest for experiential and expressive frontiers—a mission of discovery that leads beyond referentiality, beyond imitation, beyond 'reason,' beyond the established generic bounds of [the architect's] disciplined invention, to the edges of coherence and interpretability."[39] Finally, it would take us far beyond the scope of this chapter to discuss all the complex responses to these questions. Nevertheless, our aim is to thrash out an analysis of the structure, "to identify the accidents, the minute deviations—or conversely, the complete reversals—the errors, the false appraisals, and the faulty calculations."[40]

The Qaytbay complex was restaged in the "Street in Cairo" at the Exposition's Midway Plaisance, "a mile-long carnival area adjacent to the main fairgrounds, featuring carnival rides, performances, food stalls, and inhabited 'villages' purporting to display architecture and customs from around the world" (figures 3.4).[41] The replica's *place* holds the potential to affect a *modus vivendi*—that is, a workaround—despite Herz's intention to reproduce the appearance of urban life in Cairo. As the *Chicago Tribune* reported on April 30, 1893, "The Midway Plaisance . . . bears the same relation to the Exposition that the sideshows have to the circus. [Here are] German, Irish, Austrian, Turkish, Javanese, and Egyptian villages, mosques, kiosks, and pagodas, menageries, panoramas, casinos, cliff-dwellers, snake-charmers, Esquimaux. . . . It is . . . a vivacious, cosmopolitan medley."[42]

But Herz's intention, it seems, imparts a fictive web of meanings that are far apart from the innate relationship of the edifice, insofar as it remains bound to time and space. The original Qaytbay complex had been built in 1474 CE by Sultan Qaytbay, and it is in Cairo's Northern Cemetery: "the architecture of this period was not gigantic but tended rather toward refinement of proportions, and it was a golden age for stone carving. Marble work, especially on facades, also played a prominent role in architectural decoration."[43] Thus, even though Herz actually had some familiarity with the Mamluk world, "the mode of being of things that appear [at the Midway Plaisance] defines [a deceptive] simultaneity as well as the series of mutations."[44] In other words, a replica could not help but distort certain critical elements of the complex. In fact, Herz—chief architect of Egypt's Comité de

Figure 3.4 Street in Cairo Exhibition, World's Columbian Exposition, Chicago, Illinois, 1893. Photograph. Source: Library of Congress.

Conservation des Monuments de l'Art Arabe—clearly understood the power, value, and significance of the Qaytbay complex, once even saying of it that "Arab Art in Egypt has never produced a more harmonious ensemble."[45]

Herz's appreciation of the Qaytbay complex may explain why it was chosen to be restaged at the Chicago Exposition; the architect allowed the "original" edifice's continued claims to authority.[46] In other words, he believed the original to be a superlative example of architectural beauty that, therefore, would have public appeal. This judgment and impulse to copy led Herz to succumb to the persuasive power of illusion, mimesis, and enchantment.

In Chicago, the site of the Street in Cairo exhibition and the Qaytbay complex were managed by Herz, with the help of Chicago-based architect Henry Ives Cobb (close associate of Daniel H. Burnham,), with designs supplied by George Pangalo (an Egyptian subject active in the banking sector).[47] In restaging the Qaytbay complex, Herz, Cobb, and Pangalo certainly granted the Mamluk edifice a prominent position on the Midway Plaisance, but one without the promise of aesthetic truth. It is against this distinction that Baudrillard would interpret the edifice's *place* as a simulacrum, insofar as "it is the reflection of a profound reality; it masks and denatures a profound reality; it masks the absence of a profound reality; it has no relation to any reality whatsoever: it is its own pure simulacrum."[48] The simulacrum masks the fragile and the imaginary, knowing that, even when the edifice is skillfully and artistically reproduced, the ethos is to make the real possible. That is, "every aesthetic manifestation implies a showing of itself a reflection . . . in the chain of relations."[49]

It is against this paradox—a reproduction inherently losing something critical in translation—that the public fairgoers were entranced by the Street in Cairo—by the camel rides, the Qur'anic school and public fountain (*sabil-kuttab*), and the salacious belly dancing. But the Qaytbay replica, with its towering minaret, embodied the core of the street exhibit. But again, Baudrillard explains that "when the real is no longer what it is . . . there is a plethora of myths of origin . . . a plethora of truth, of secondary objectivity and authenticity."[50] The exhibition by definition could not convey to the viewer the essential truths that only the original could.

Here the aesthetic manifestation of Mamluk architecture benefits from the analysis of Howaydya al-Harithy, professor of architecture: the Mamluk architecture, she writes, is "governed by urban, social, and political factors, and, as a result, Mamluk monuments cannot simply be read as containers of spaces or objects in space, but rather as complex mediators between interior architectural spaces and exterior urban spaces."[51] As a part of Mamluk urban complexes—the mausoleums, mosques, madrassas, Qur'anic school and *sabil-kuttab*—Lefebvre holds, "it is reasonable to assume that spatial practice, representations of space, and representational spaces contribute in different ways to the production of space according to their qualities and attributes, according to the society or mode of production in question, and according to the historical period."[52] Accordingly, given the web of relations that govern the urban, social and political factors of Mamluk Cairo, it is difficult to understand if it is at all possible for the American public to see the Qaytbay complex as an edifice that reveals the modality of public life and its urban setting.

In this way, amid the Street in Cairo exhibit in its enigmatic location at the Midway Plaisance, the Qaytbay complex is far removed from the poise of meanings, beliefs, and function that al-Harithy describes. That is, the "simulacrum" reveals the deviations and the complete reversals of a spatial order (figure 3.5). And if we accept Lefebvre's proposition, then *there is no aesthetic connection* between the original edifice and the replica, and therefore

Figure 3.5 The entrance to the Street in Cairo Exhibition at the Chicago World's Fair, 1893. Photograph. Source: Library of Congress.

the replica simultaneously blunts and dims aesthetic meaning. In other words, Herz's "mastery of illusion" and mimetic representation "cannot succeed."[53] But we must also remember that this is exactly the sense in which all paradoxes work: "they pale as copies, clichés, and empty appropriations."[54]

To cite Foucault's own prime example, "the new knowledge that emerged in the nineteenth century gave rise to a profound preoccupation with historicity and to the forms of order implied by the continuity of time."[55]

In the context of his discussion, our analysis deconstructs the real origin, the official meaning, and the location of the Street in Cairo exhibit and the Qaytbay replica as a way "to remove the concepts of statement and discourses from the ghetto of ideas, to demonstrate that discursive formations may be regarded as complex."[56] In fact, to describe the urban setting of the Street in Cairo exhibit—using the discursive formula derived from Foucault—we may also conceive of the Midway Plaisance as a "self-regulating conception" that reposits meaning in the action undertaken by the exhibit's team—Herz, Cobb, and Pangalo.

To wrap our heads around the "self-regulating" concept, we consider Foucault, who claims that "knowledge can have a positive voice not only constraining it or eliminating [it] . . . but also producing it."[57] This explains why historians have made the claim that America's first urban mosque was the Qaytbay complex, which "was meant to be a close replica of the Mosque of Sultan Qaytbay in Cairo, to display Islam for American audiences."[58] Any attempt at confirming this claim falls short, because the Qaytbay complex *does not* carry over to the history of the present, and so the assertion fares badly, given what we know of the history of Islam in the United States and the likelihood of the existence of mosques before 1893. In fact, no one really knows for sure how many Muslims were among the contingent of slaves brought to North America, between 1619 and 1808, when the US Constitution officially barred the import of slaves.

The trans-Atlantic slave trade brought upward of 12 million enslaved Africans to the Americas including Muslim Africans from the Ivory Coast, Ghana and the Senegambia (Bilad al-Takrur).[59] Likewise, in the early 1940s, during a survey of Blacks living along coastal Georgia, historian Malcolm Bell Jr. interviewed several subjects who were descendants of former West African slaves and who identified as Muslim. They told Bell that they still performed their daily ritual prayers. One descendant spoke of a building that a slave master had ordered torn down, which, from the description, could have been an "informal Muslim prayer space" (*musalla*) rather than a domicile. From Bell's interviews, we learn that Ben Sullivan, grandson of Salih Bilali—a man abducted into slavery from present-day Mali and known devotee of Islam—was at the time of the interviews eighty-eight years old and living on St. Simons Island off the coast of Georgia.⁶⁰

That Islam had seemingly not survived in the antebellum era in an *organized* practice among Muslim captives does not mean that it did not survive in some defiant, underground form during the era of chattel slavery in the United States. Indeed, the enslaved African Muslim community succeeded in following the precepts of their faith even in captivity. Several stood out as personages of education and knowledge—for example, Omar ibn Said (1770–1863/64)—after whom a mosque at Fayetteville, North Carolina, is now named. And the 2008 documentary *Prince Among Slaves* recounts the true story of Abdul-Rahman ibn Ibrahim Sori, an African prince and Muslim devotee who was abducted and enslaved in the American South for almost forty years (figure 3.6).⁶¹

But even were it true that the Qaytbay mosque replica at the 1893 World's Fair was indeed the first urban mosque in America, two important questions

Figure 3.6 Abdul-Rahman ibn Ibrahim Sori, Muslim ruler and Fula prince. Engraving, c. 1834, originally published in *The Colonizationist and Journal of Freedom*, Boston. Source: Library of Congress.

are in order: Did the edifice set the aesthetic rules for the future of the American mosque? And was the Qaytbay mosque built facing Makkah? As we have discussed earlier, the sacred orientation of a mosque is a core aspect of the *stabilitas loci* and the continuation of religious life; the traditional places time and space in a relationship where the *qibla* axis is visualized and which gives the edifice power over the location through the determination of space and architecture. Simply put, if the replica was not built as a true mosque, we cannot claim it was a true mosque.

Further, in asking whether or not the exhibit reconstruction was a true mosque in America, we must consider the relationship between discourse and buildings; this allows us to overcome the limits of interpretation. Since no drawings exist of the Street in Cairo exhibit and of Herz's mimetic reproduction of the Qaytbay complex, it is fair to assume that subsequent American mosques were not based on its typology. And since plans *do* exist of the original edifice in Cairo—consisting of a mosque, madrassa, mausoleum, and public fountain—we can get some sense of what was restaged on the Chicago fairgrounds. Further, the exhibition's organizers invited cultural displays and buildings from the Muslim world, which were then situated as "anthropological subjects." This all sounds more like a museum exhibit than place of worship.

Against this segregated place along the Midway Plaisance, reserved for *other* non-American spaces and societies, architect Daniel H. Burnham created the "White City," greater than the portion of the fairgrounds, designated for exhibition of beaux arts buildings, industry, technology, agriculture, trade relations, and economics—in short, demonstrations of the endless progress that Europe and America had made since the onset of the Industrial Revolution. Precisely because of Burnham's political and economic beliefs and veneration of progress, we need to keep in mind the idea behind the World's Columbian Exposition: it was to commemorate the four-hundredth anniversary of Columbus's "discovery" (*Sic transit gloria mundi*) of the New World.

To close the discussion, the Qaytbay complex is another indication that "the quasi-continuity on the level of ideas and themes is only a surface appearance" and a disguised form of resemblance. At the same time, we must remember that "the deeper archeological investigation into the modalities of thinking—that is, into governing episteme—reveals a different logic."[62] In fact, the idea of aesthetic distance, as developed by Gilles Deleuze, offers an interesting counterpart to discussions of a deeper discursive investigation of the disguised form of resemblance. Deleuze emphasizes the point that "there is no 'blank canvas,' only visual 'clichés' which are utilized to be deformed such that invisible forces and rhythms can be diagrammed or composed."[63]

From this angle, the deformed perceptions embodied in the replica of the Qaytbay complex may be understood as a discontinuity that reveals the making and remaking of traditional forms of knowledge. In keeping with the Deleuzian observation, the public experience of the Street in Cairo exhibition "leaps from perception to fantasy . . . because the human perception has no choice but to look at individual things, and their presence."[64] At the same time, by marking its position, the possibility of visual proximity and resemblance must come to grips with the basic fact about meaning, which "involves different kinds of correlations, positions, functioning and transformations that go beyond the usual expected understanding of identity and proximity."[65]

As Deleuze insists, the "resemblance and symbolism cannot be done away with but can in fact be the more profound, displaced and disguised form of non-representative."[66] In other words, Herz's mimetic representation of the Qaytbay complex and the "actual" setting of the Street in Cairo were intended to entertain the public as they walked to and fro and to produce a sense of medieval Cairo's "relation to [urban] chaos without becoming chaotic."[67] In the context of this discussion, the Street in Cairo exhibition opens up a dialogue between space, time, and location in consideration of the 1867 Exposition Universelle in Paris and the 1873 Vienna World's Fair, where urban mosques from Cairo had also been staged, displayed, and eventually dismantled.[68]

Having laid out the problem of interpretation we faced with the Qaytbay reconstruction, a discursive analysis of the Islamic Center of Washington, a permanent counterpart, allows for further consideration of the birth of an urban mosque.

The Birth of an Urban Mosque

The Islamic Center of Washington (ICW; Washington, DC, 1957; figure 3.7) was developed by Mario Rossi, Egyptian architect of Italian origin, "with an ensemble of relations that makes them appear as juxtaposed, set off against one another, implicated by each other—that makes them appear, in short, as a sort of configuration."[69] The relationship between the Qaytbay complex and the ICW is immediately clear. First, Rossi's design would suggest that his mosque, when juxtaposed against the original Qaytbay edifice, is a faithful exemplar, making it a meaningful space and experience, allowing "the experience in turn [to produce] knowledge."[70] Second, although it has been asserted that the Qaytbay complex replica was the first urban mosque in America, the ICW, being that it is a "functional" mosque, with a valued origin, challenges this notion. We can trace the ICW's origin to a particular place and time and to a neo-Mamluk "typology."

Architecture and Ontology 103

Figure 3.7 The Islamic Center of Washington, DC. Photograph. Source: Library of Congress.

Our attempt here is to understand Rossi's intention in designing the ICW and to understand to what extent his production is fundamentally important. Because visual language and meaning are important to the émigré and devotee of Islam, the ICW's epigraphic elements give meaning to the edifice. To be sure, "all these [elements] are still nurtured by the hidden presence of the sacred," which perhaps takes us back to Foucault's assertion that "our epoch is one in which space takes for us the form of relations among sites."[71]

Our starting point for the discussion of ICW is a tragic event—the passing of a distinguished Turkish diplomat, Munir Ertegun, on November 13, 1944. Two of the mourners at the funeral parlor—Ambassador of Egypt Mahmoud Hassan Pasha and local businessman and builder-contractor A. Joseph Howar—were lamenting the fact that Washington, DC had no mosque where the funeral prayer (*janaza*) for the deceased could take place. Within a couple of weeks, the Washington Mosque Foundation had been formed, under the leadership of the Egyptian ambassador, with the support of Howar, who had migrated to the US capital at the turn of the century, along with a few diplomats and local Muslim families—all of whom had been unable to participate in a Muslim congregation or religious event and all yearned to worship in a mosque.[72]

In this regard, another event important to our telling was taking place in England at the same time: plans for the London Central Mosque at Regent's Park were being drawn up. That campaign was being led by "Dr. Hassan Nachat Pasha, the ambassador of His Majesty the King of Egypt at the Court of St. James [who] four years earlier had convened a meeting with Muslim diplomats in London to build the London Central Mosque." The decision to build the London mosque was reported in notes of the meeting: "The Muslim Subjects of His Majesty King George IV exceeded in number his Christian Subjects, and that many Moslems [sic *Muslims*] from the British Empire as well as from friendly countries such as Egypt, Iraq and Arabia were having their children educated in British Universities but were deprived of the means of keeping up their religious duties during their studies in England." Almost two weeks after the deed for the London Central Mosque was signed A. J. Howar and Mahmoud Hassan Pasha were to meet in Washington, DC.[73] And so, parallel with the events unfolding in London, the calculated efforts of the Washington Mosque foundation remained the primary nexus of relations between Washington, DC, and Rossi in Egypt and the many sponsors of the project both in the United States and the Middle East.

Muhammad Abdul-Rauf, imam and scholar of Islam, summarizes Rossi's biography: "Professor Mario Rossi in his early life in Egypt became fascinated by the old mosques in Cairo in which he spent long hours contemplating and reflecting on their beauty, and then he came out with his own beautiful concepts which won him wide recognition. . . . As a result of the knowledge he acquired about Islam . . . Rossi became a Muslim late in his life, adopting the name 'Muhammad Mahdi.' He performed the pilgrimage to Makkah in 1381 A. H. (1961 CE) shortly before his death."[74] From 1929 to 1954 Rossi was chief architect for the Ministry of Awqaf in Egypt, "and his approach to mosque design was an evident typological and stylistic innovation that left its mark on the architectural vocabulary of the time, establishing a new eclectic style that became widely adopted in Egypt, . . . Saudi Arabia, and Iraq."[75]

Our focus now shifts to the production of space—Rossi's process of understanding the site while working remotely in Egypt—and the direct practical application of his knowledge and expertise. The Washington Mosque Foundation was guided by the strategic aim stated in its certificate of incorporation, dated February 2, 1945: to be "a religious organization [that provides] a place of worship for the members of the Islamic faith and in furtherance thereof to acquire land and to erect and permanently maintain a mosque within the District of Columbia for the members of the congregation of said faith."[76]

The idea for the Islamic Center of Washington had been formulated in 1944 and the land purchased in 1946 by the Washington Mosque Foundation, Inc. The project to build this vital communal space for the American Muslim community brought in support from fifteen Muslim countries.[77] Here community is constituted with the shared cultural values of the diplomatic corps and the émigré, the primary sponsors of the project. The cornerstone was laid in 1949, and the mosque was finally dedicated on June 28, 1957, by President Eisenhower. At the dedication, the president vowed, "Indeed, America would fight with her whole strength for your right to have here your own church [sic, *mosque*] and worship according to your own conscience."[78]

This important edifice belongs to the historic taxonomy of American architecture and yet has been glossed over; it is not included in the *Source Book of American Architecture*. It is equally surprising that the Dar al-Islam mosque complex at Abiquiú, New Mexico (1981), by architect Hassan Fathy, and the Islamic Cultural Center of New York (1991), designed by architectural firm Skidmore, Owings and Merrill, were also overlooked by the book's editors.[79] The exclusion makes our analysis here all the more important.

To begin our analysis of the Islamic Center of Washington and to better understand Rossi's architectural point of view, we must first examine the question of other spaces and the relation among sites—as it is well known that Rossi did not travel to Washington, DC for the project. Foucault has classified "other spaces" to encode them in his analysis according to their functions, fragmented arrangements, and the relations among sites. Using this type of discursive analysis allows us to trace the origin of the ICW. Further, the typology and spatial configuration of ICW—the discrete cultural elements—inform the aesthetic norms that reside in a neoteric category: diaspora aesthetics. Consider, for example, the habit popular among immigrants of reanimating the past; Muslim immigrants to the United States are no different in this regard, and the ICW's aesthetic treatment has clear ancestral ties. In this way, the relation among sites and other spaces is integral to an émigré's or devotee's cognition, as is a familiar style of architecture evoked through memory.

In any case, it is this mode of diaspora aesthetic that, at first glance, would seem detached from the urban context of Washington, DC. At the same time, the edifice is clearly nurtured by an inviolable tradition—primarily seen in the orientation of the prayer hall and the *qibla* axis. The mosque's prayer hall is covered with a modest clerestory dome, set out at a tangent to conform to the *qibla* axis, which has been calculated on the great circle (fifty-six degrees, thirty-three minutes, fifteen seconds)—or the shortest distance (on the great circle) when facing Makkah. The *qibla* axis, as we have previously noted, originates in the seminal mosque built at Medina in 622 CE and in Qur'anic injunction: the *qibla* axis and the *mihrab*—its concomitant chamber always oriented toward Makkah—are found in all mosques across historical time and geographic space. In the same manner, understanding this and other

106   Chapter 3

traditions is the primary inspiration for Rossi's production of space and his aesthetic language.

The ICW was Rossi's only project in the United States. Indeed, one of my central concerns is the fact that Rossi was not entirely familiar with the American urban context. And so we must ask what part his knowledge—or lack thereof—played when positioning tradition within an alien environment. Although by this time in his career Rossi was already well known for the many projects he had ably completed, the radical task of designing the Washington mosque remotely nonetheless demonstrates his unfamiliarity with the particular urban context of Washington, DC. In addition, the project's urban space and structure furnish an adequate sense of space, "but its justification does not need to be precise or definitive. It can fall far short of proof."[80] This could explain why Rossi's plan for the Washington site is significantly different from his projects in Cairo and Alexandria.

Because Rossi did not travel to Washington, DC, descriptions of the site were probably couriered to him in Egypt via the Washington diplomatic corps, and his drawings for the project had to be converted from metric measurements to feet and inches. Additionally, to comply with US and District of Columbia building codes, DC-based architectural firm Irwin S. Porter and Sons provided Rossi on-site aid with the project. Understanding the remote nature of Rossi's involvement allows us to develop an interpretive understanding of the ICW and explore the architect's aesthetic language, which

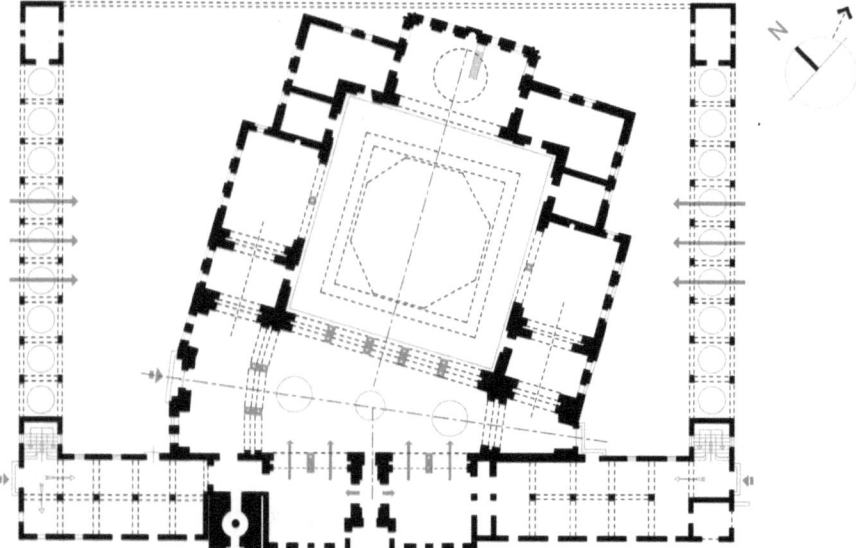

Figure 3.8 Rossi's original drawings for the Islamic Center of Washington, DC. Source: Muhammed Madandola.

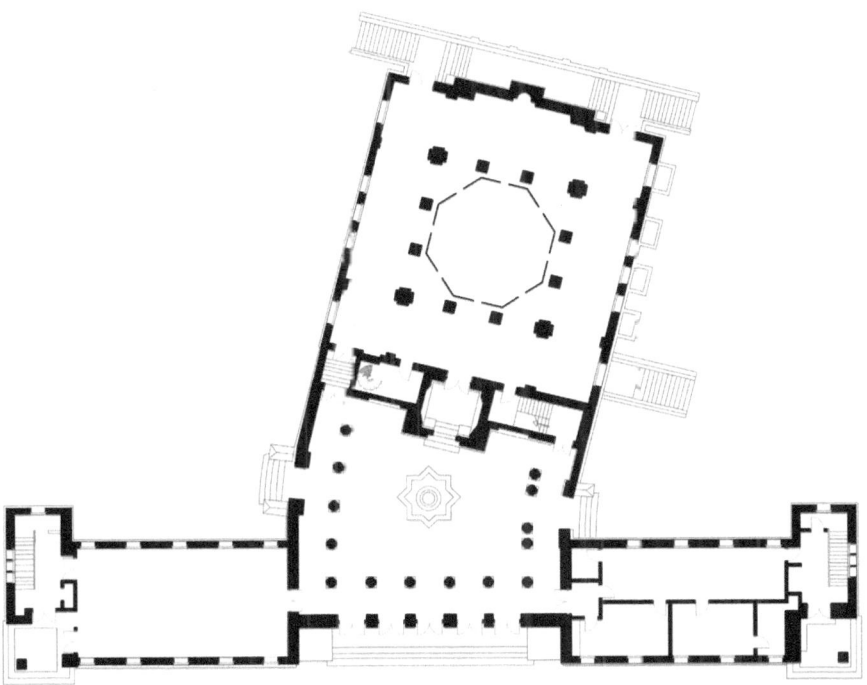

Figure 3.9 Drawing of the modified plan. Source: Muhammed Madandola.

borrows from the immense archive of architectural knowledge that resides in Cairo and Alexandria. Above all, we may discover that Rossi's spatial order for the site expands the characteristics of the typology of the urban mosque (figures 3.8 and 3.9).

Rossi's design occupied a thirty-thousand-square-foot site at the corner of Massachusetts Avenue and Belmont Road—now known as 2551 Massachusetts Avenue, N.W. The land that was purchased in April 1946 for the mosque measured two hundred feet of frontage along Massachusetts Avenue by 150 feet on Waterside Drive and 150 feet on Belmont Avenue. At the time of purchase, it was an empty site, which meant that no need to demolish existing structures saved money.[81] Rossi's plan for the mosque suggests "that spatial practice, representations of space, and representational spaces contribute in different ways to the production of space."[82]

The original plan for the building contained three halls (*iwan*) framed by an exterior double arcade (*riwaq*), which would serve as an *extra muros*—or an internal, enclosed courtyard (*sahn*). However, in the executed plan—a variation on Rossi's original design—the orthogonal arcade of the entry portal runs parallel to the street, serving as the main public entrance to the *sahn* and then to the prayer hall (figures 3.10 and 3.11). The small courtyard is open to the

Figure 3.10 The Islamic Center of Washington, DC. The interior court (*sahn*). Photograph. Source: Mark Susman.

sky and is connected to a *riwaq* consisting of five contiguous "horseshoe" arches demarcating the entry portal—a key part of the facade. Two wings run parallel to Massachusetts Avenue and connect with the courtyard; it is here that the administrative office, the library, and other ancillary functions are

Architecture and Ontology

Figure 3.11 Details of the main prayer hall. Photograph. Source: Mark Susman.

housed. The main body of the building is clad in Alabama limestone, including the 160-foot-high minaret, richly decorated with geometric patterns and epigraphy.

We must remember that the mosque was a cultural undertaking primarily by members of the diplomatic community, with participants from Iran, Egypt,

Turkey, and Saudi Arabia, among other nations. For instance, a magnificent two-ton chandelier made of solid bronze and inlaid with nickel was shipped from Egypt in sections; also sent were the craftsmen and specialists who wrote the Qur'anic verses adorning the mosque's walls and ceiling. Turkey donated the specialized Iznik tiles, along with the craftsmen to install them. Even the rugs were imported from Iran, and they are still in the mosque to this day. But it remains difficult to precisely determine the architectural language used to compose the mosque; the particular vocabulary speaks of an émigré's place of origin (that is, in this particular case, of mosque architecture). This aesthetic expression makes up most stylistic variations in the mosque.

In the essay "The Works of Mario Rossi at Alessandria," Historian James Dickie notes that Rossi's eclecticism "exemplifies the opposite tendency in which Europeans set out consciously to imitate Islamic models. He employs a visual vocabulary lifted entirely from late Mamluk architecture . . . Rossi, therefore, represents the principle of relativism, which holds that architecture must relate to the cultural climate."[83] Rossi's eclecticism underscores a community of meanings that retain traditional links and an interplay of aesthetic resemblances that would otherwise be difficult to understand without careful examination. Attempting to develop a global frame of reference, the "eclecticism" and "relativism" that Dickie references reside in close proximity with the elements that constitute the vocabulary of the Washington mosque and at the same time Rossi's work in Egypt, where he is believed to have completed some 260 buildings (figure 3.12).

The description that we provided of the mosques in Alexandria and Washington DC have precise and determined importance to Rossi's aesthetic volition. In other words, it is in the production of space that Rossi demonstrates his knowledge, being that it is rooted in the Mamluk architectural tradition. This played an important role in planning the mosque in Washington, DC. The plans could also be understood as the architect's statement (in the absence of an avowal): the object of the space is "to [enable] us to repose the rules of ideas and to examine in a new way the relationship between discourse and buildings."[84]

Analogous to the relationship between discourse and buildings is the meta-level question of Rossi's consideration for the urban plan, the compositional elements, the order of epigraphic statements, and the mosque's discursive condition. The epigraphy and geometry were clearly intended to be operative emotive devices and familiar leitmotifs—that is, they were employed to depict both meaning and style. In the same way, the epigraphic treatment includes a host of familiar elements while at the same time the mode of production provides a structure that largely functions as both subject and object, the aim being to summon hermeneutical reflection.

Architecture and Ontology 111

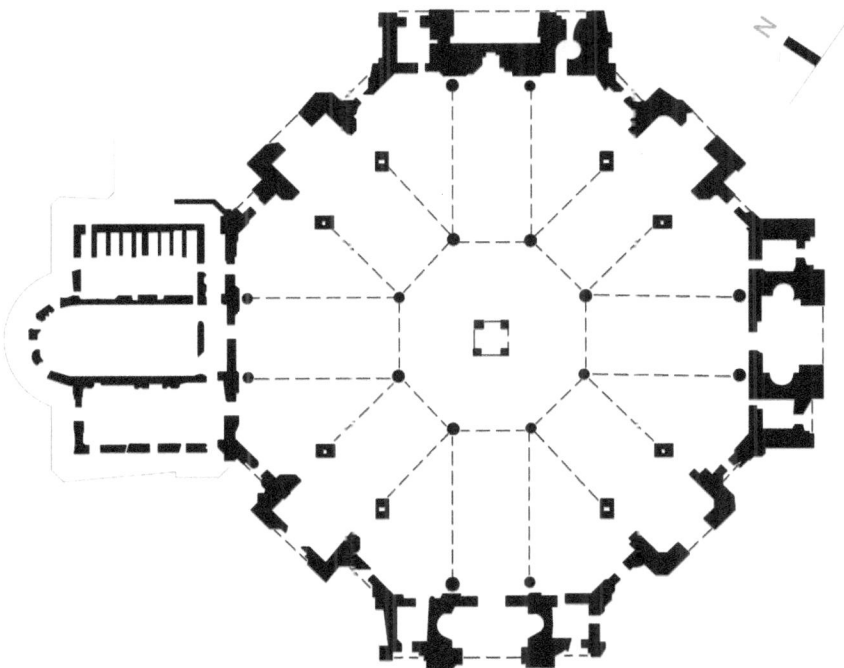

Figure 3.12 The plan for the mosque of Abu al-Abbas al-Mursi (d. 1286, whose tomb it contains), Alexandria, Egypt. Architects Eugenio Valzania and Mario Rossi built it between 1929 and 1945. Drawing. Source: Muhammed Madandola.

In *The Hermeneutics of the Subject*, Foucault addresses the opposition that exists in the Kantian "subject and object" dichotomy: "We will call, if you like, 'philosophy' the form of thought that asks, not of course what is true and what is false, but what determines that there is and can be truth and falsehood and whether or not we can separate the true and the false."[85] As part of the analysis of subject and object, the ethos that constitutes *belief*, *space*, *order*, *materials*, and *symbols* points to three traditional aesthetic themes: (1) Designs derive from plant life—often called arabesque in the West. (2) Epigraphy (emotive visual language) is the most revered art form in Islam because it conveys the word of God. (3) Geometric patterns or tessellations.[86] We could argue that the significance of these three themes summons "hermeneutical reflection" and that undertaking is "acknowledged as a universal process of understanding."[87] In combination and through their repetition, they reinforce the idea "that there is and can be truth and falsehood" that is universally understood by devotees in one part of the world or another—that is, in Egypt or in Washington, DC.

We will most effectively interpret this building's aesthetic through the frame of Islamic epistemology and the role of traditions in Islamic architecture. It is the same with the notion of ontological experience: that is, the devotee's understanding of existence and the world. In their own form of self-reflection and the practice of daily remembrance, ontology passes through, and they reflect upon meanings. Likewise, the discourse on aesthetics is connected to the power of language and ways of knowing, while art remains a distinguishing feature; it is not created ex nihilo.

Rossi's widespread use of epigraphy in the Washington mosque evokes "the philosophical and practical significance of an architecture which links [devotion with the inner and outer experience] art and spiritual concerns."[88] For instance, epigraphy and language play an important role in the devotee's knowledge and understanding, in that they emphasize the meaning of existence, which dogma is derived from the Qur'an and its exegesis. By focusing on the meaning of the inscription, the devotee's faith is amplified.

Notable in the ICW are the verses of the Qur'an that have been arranged in an orderly configuration and in various patterns on the interior walls and ceilings and in the *mihrab* of the prayer hall. They include the Divine Names of Allah (*Asma Allah Al-Husna*) and several familiar and often-quoted verses from the Qur'an, such as *Al-Alaq*, 96:1–5. These are inscribed in large, framed borders of Arabic script (*thuluth*) with smaller framed panels of ornamental Kufic script.

The *mihrab* was built by specialist craftsmen and is located in the prayer space. Ipso facto, it indicates the *qibla*, the devotee's orientation with the *Ka'ba*. The *mihrab*'s decorative treatment follows the Iznik and Bursa tradition of using glazed tiles—blue, red and green, which are commonly found in Ottoman architecture. Two inscription bands run horizontally across the face of the prayer niche (*mihrab*): the upper band reads, "Verily we have seen the turning of your face to the heaven" and the lower band, "surely we shall turn you to a *qibla* that shall please you" (*Al-Baqara*, 2:144).

As in religious buildings elsewhere, difficulties remain regarding the stylistic qualities of this mosque that have mainly been derived from the conventions of Muslim Art. For instance, religious buildings in Cairo and throughout the Islamic world have emblems at their entry portals, but these are mostly to reinforce the image of the patron, to promote religious ideology (the Fatimids, for example) or to celebrate and enhance the aura of the edifice. In the Washington mosque, however, each inscription is primarily intended to further the knowledge of the devotee, and as such they are significant for two reasons: first as a devotional theme and second as an emotive device, with meanings to satisfy remembrance and one's devotional disposition.

However, reading the inscriptions is an overwhelming task for anyone not adept at reading Arabic. As regards the devotee's enthusiasm for knowledge, inscriptions fulfill another expectation by orienting the attention of the faithful from mundane concerns to the wisdom and counsel of the Qur'an. For added emphasis, the main entry to the mosque is designed as a colonnaded cloister surrounding a small court with a decorated fountain. It has an inscription band of Kufic script at the upper part of the facade of the colonnade, which reads, "In houses of worship which Allah has permitted to be raised so that His name be remembered, in them, there [are such as] extol His limitless glory at morning and evening" (Q. *Al-Nur*, 24:36). Thus the colonnade signals an absolute moment in which the devotee moves from the secular domain of the street into the realm of reverential awareness. The entry colonnade with the compelling invitation functions as a threshold.

Architects, critics, and historians have long debated the problem of time and space, while some have sought to preserve the notion that "when a civilization is centered on the sacred . . . the practical is always inextricably linked to the spiritual."[89] Not surprisingly, Henri Lefebvre has noted that "these protracted debates marked the shift from the philosophy to the science of space. It would be mistaken to pronounce them outdated, however, for they have an import beyond that of moments or stages in the evolution of the Western Logos."[90] This point is worth noting because it shows how such "motifs" travel and how the experiential effects are self-evident to the devotee and the temporal world.

To conclude this discussion, a few final remarks are in order. Although Rossi was a non-Muslim in the early part of his life, as Abdul-Rauf has reported he embraced the faith some time before his death in 1961. Nevertheless, he was widely respected in Egypt and was commissioned by the government there to design several mosques.[91] The case of the ICW is different: One of its defining elements may well be the simulation of two modes of reasoning—one that follows *tradition* and the other that accommodates *place*. First, "tradition" embraces convention and origin; it expresses its own mimetic essence by asserting meaning and truth. Second, the "local" seeks identity; in the face of obvious social and cultural realities, it must respond to *place*. Above all, it is due to Rossi's efforts that the ICW reveals the promise of architectural truth that resides side by side with religion and philosophy and as such informs the struggle to come to terms with the location of culture.[92]

The Hermeneutics of the Subject

While in the foregoing discussion we have attempted to study space and time, we have also explored hermeneutic conceptions of the Muslim body/space experience and the sites that are regarded as "sacred spaces" through some sort of divine action or intervention.[93] Consider the Mountain of Mercy (*Jabal ar-Rahmah*), the *Ka'ba*, the Dome of the Rock, and the sacred topographies of Makkah, Madinah, and Jerusalem. However, the closest we can come to achieving a genuine sense of "temporal realism" is in the *Ka'ba* and the tradition of "facing" Makkah along the *qibla* axis.

While this quotidian observance gives meaning to acts of devotion, it also creates "a path for the connection between . . . [body, space, place,] intellect and experience."[94] This understanding exhorts the *Ka'ba*'s position and the fact that it is the universal *omphalos*—the hub. With circumambulation (*tawaf*), the *Ka'ba* maintains a tradition established by the prophets Adam, Abraham, and Muhammad. For the devotee, this knowledge provides a sense of symbolic realism to the acts of devotion that memory holds and the potential to restore the spiritual and monotheistic bond between the individual and the Creator. So, while the *Ka'ba* maintains the perceptual and temporal orientation, the spiritual bond expands the idea of the *qibla* and the *mihrab*, owing to the cosmological understanding of the celestial *Ka'ba*. The spatial identity of the *Ka'ba* and the city of Makkah are significant even from the distant location of a mosque in the United States: the *Ka'ba* remains a devotional "force field of everyday life."[95]

Understanding this confers a new centrality to the architect's volition, since it is an intrinsic factor in the design and production of mosques and devotional spaces. In fact, there is no liturgy in Islam per se (aside from the orientation of the body facing Makkah, the recital of verses of the Qur'an, and the various postures of the prayer); the quotidian forms of worship can be performed in a mosque or in an open field. The commonly held belief is that the whole world is a mosque—except for forbidden spaces or polluted sites.[96] Furthermore, sociologist Hanisah Binte Abdullah Sani explains "that orientation metaphors organize a whole system of concepts with respect to another" and "are rooted in physical and cultural experience, which can serve as a vehicle of understanding a concept only by virtue of its experiential basis."[97]

Justifications for this ontological notion are related to the "concept of public space both in the purpose it serves, and the way users experience it."[98] The case of the basilica is quite different from the mosque. In *The Burden of the Ceremony Master*, scholar of religious iconography Staale Sinding-Larsen goes to great lengths to compare the liturgical regalia of the basilica with the mosque.[99] Sinding-Larsen concludes, "In the Christian service the congregation participates actively, and so do the Muslims in their prayer ritual, but they are not defined as a sacramental community. In the Roman Church a sacramental transformation of a sum of individuals into a supernatural entity is supposed to take place. In the mosque, the community is made up of a summation of all the right-believing, intentionally sincere and correctly performing individuals."[100]

The Burden of the Ceremony Master highlights the practice of observing and the distinct domain of ritual exegesis, liturgy, iconography, and bodily experience, among others. However, Sinding-Larsen defines the clear separation between the basilica and Roman rite and the mosque and acts of veneration: "Clergy and congregation, facing the image of the Virgin Mary during Mass or during the Salve Regina as described by our Ceremony Master, would work their way through texts referring to her and her role."[101] It is important to remember that the Qur'an includes an entire chapter dedicated to the Virgin Mary (Q. 19) and the birth of the Prophet Jesus. However, it is striking that there is no equivalent form of worship of the Virgin Mary or the prophet Jesus or regalia to be found in a mosque or in Islamic worship. In this sense, we may make the claim that, unlike Catholicism, Islam rejects the veneration of icons, relics, idols, and intercession.

It seems that the ceremonial acts and objects of veneration residing in the basilica, when contrasted with the spatial attributes of a mosque, make several key omissions. First, Islam's aniconism is situated within an understanding of the discursive conditions that make up the Muslim body/space experience and the spatial attributes of the mosque as evincing a religious and ontological disposition. Second, for the Muslim, truth, beauty, and belief are connected to the performance of prayer, which has a direct correlation to the ethos of faith and praxis and to the Creator of the universe and the lifeworlds. Third, the annual pilgrimage (hajj), the communal devotion (Friday prayer or *Jumm'a*, the month of Ramadan, and so on) are moments (time and space) that offer serious reflection that may also include the devotee's remaining in the mosque or in a place of quiet repose for a length of time (*I'tikāf*, or seclusion/withdrawal). With this, we can no longer ignore the architect's intention when attempting to decipher the aniconic episteme of Muslim art. In the Islamic Center of Washington, the epigraphy allows for further interpretation of the composition that epitomizes an array of ontological meanings.

While the replica of the Qaytbay funerary mosque complex can be regarded as an anomaly whose short existence in Chicago only serves to disrupt the architectural exchanges, the same is not true for the ICW, where it is evident that Rossi meant to design an operative mosque (*masjid*). At the same time, the *masjid* "in the normative sense [and] as we understand it . . . has the status and resources that go with it, and some of them, as Islamic institutions, function as symbolic markers in urban areas, as illustrated in the case . . . of its official character and often the desire to display its ethno-religious specificity through physicospatial elements (such as architectural elements) and the need for a vast space, or a simple prayer room."[102]

The notion of "perfect imperfection" helps us frame a critical rereading of the Qaytbay edifice: it is an anomaly given the transitory nature of the exposition and Herz's struggle to reconcile the antinomies of time and space. It is Lefebvre who introduced the term *perfect incompletion* and speculates on the architect's volition: "the architect will value the multifunctional and the trans-functional rather than the merely functional. He will cease to fetishize (separately) form and function, and a structure as the signifiers of space." Furthermore, Lefebvre has noted that, "in the place of the formal, or rather formalist idea of perfection, the architect will substitute that of incomplete perfection (which is pursued, which is sought in practice) or, preferably, that of perfect incompletion, which discovers a moment in life (expectations, presentiment, nostalgia) and provides it with an expression."[103]

At the same time, the American Muslim community is a multiethnic, transglobal, and multicultural community; its members are not a monolith. In *Culture and Value*, philosopher Ludwig Wittgenstein makes a point about the cultural undertakings that are commonly pursued by the American Muslim community: "A culture is like a big organization which assigns each of its members a place where [they] can work in the spirit of the whole; and it is perfectly fair for [their] power to be measured by the contribution [they] succeed in making to the whole enterprise."[104] What has not changed, however, is the nature of the challenge that Mario Rossi confronted when designing the mosque in Washington, DC: the possibility of maintaining architecture in a context increasingly dominated by diaspora and the search for identity. In fact, the word "community," from the Latin *communitas* or *communis*, refers to the sense of belonging and attachment to other people or a group for geographical, political, and religious reasons; the inquiry, therefore, shifts our attention to the communal values, implicit in the word *communitas*.

Our critique in chapter 4 considers the question of community, the sense of belonging, and the planning of mosques. This discussion is best suited to address the contentious nature of the legal disputes over *place*. The core of this argument is the claim that "the [place] of mosques reflects a certain dispersion of sites and public space. These [places] also presuppose spatial mobility of the faithful, who can travel there (unlike the Jews, who, for example, cannot use their car on the Sabbath)."[105] The place of the mosque reflects a certain dispersion of sites, and public spaces are inherently shaped by human beings, also serving to suggest that human friendships (and rivalries) are key agents in the production and reception of architectural production. Chapter 4 questions the hidden assumptions and the intentions of competing forces and forms of practice, particularly in situations where distinctions between public religion and political discourses become blurred and where micro-power and local autonomy take control.

NOTES

1. Foucault, *This Is Not a Pipe*, 9–10.
2. Malpas, "Building Memory," 11.

3. William C. Chittick, "Time, Space, and the Objectivity of Ethical Norms: The Teachings of Ibn Al-'Arabī," *Islamic Studies* 39, no. 4 (Winter 2000): 585, emphasis original, reprinted in http://www.iqbalcyberlibrary.net/files/009/IRE-OCT-2004.pdf.

4. Malpas, "Building Memory," 12.

5. Christian Norberg-Schulz, *Intentions in Architecture* (Cambridge MA: MIT Press, 1968), 16, emphasis original.

6. Fontana-Giusti, *Foucault for Architects*, 39.

7. It was at this time that Ibn al-Arabi began writing *Al-Futūḥāt al-Makkiyya* (*The Meccan Illuminations*), a thirty-seven volume opus that was as many years in the writing, recounting his spiritual journey and theology. Here two verses from chapter 72 are quoted in Denis Gril, "Love Letters to the Ka'ba: A Presentation of Ibn 'Arabi's *Tāj al-Rasā'il*," *Journal of the Muhyiddin Ibn Arabi Society* 17 (1995): 52, https://ibnarabisociety.org/love-letters-to-the-kaaba-denis-gril/.

8. Gril, "Love Letters to the Ka'ba," 52.

9. For an extensive discussion of the *mihrab*, see Nuha N. N. Khoury, "The Mihrab: From Text to Form," *International Journal of Middle East Studies* 30, no. 1 (1998): 1–27; and Nuha N. N. Khoury, "The Mihrab Image: Commemorative Themes in Medieval Islamic Architecture," in *Muqarnas: An Annual on Islamic Art and Architecture*, vol. 9, ed. Oleg Grabar, [11]–29 (Leiden: E. J. Brill, 1992). Also see Estelle Whelan, "The Origins of the *Miḥrāb Mujawwaf*: An Interpretation," *International Journal of Middle East Studies* 18, no. 2 (May 1986): 205–23.

10. David A. King, "The Sacred Direction in Islam: A Study of the Interaction of Religion and Science in the Middle Ages," *Interdisciplinary Science Reviews* 10, no. 4 (1985): 327, emphasis mine.

11. Jaan Holt, "Architecture and the Wall Facing Mecca," *Via: The Journal of the Graduate School of Fine Arts—University of Pennsylvania*, 5, *Determinants of Form* 5 (1982): 25, emphasis original.

12. Gutting, *Foucault*, 50.

13. Hanisah Binte Abdullah Sani, "Corporeal Poetics of Sacred Space: An Ethnography of *Jum'ah* in a Chapel," *Space and Culture* 18, no. 3 (2015): 302.

14. Akel Ismail Kahera, "The Accuracy of the Qibla Axis (*Inhiraf al-Qibla*): A Legal Debate," *Al-Shajarah: Journal of the International Institute of Islamic Thought and Civilization* 8, no. 2 (2003): 191.

15. Kahera, *Deconstructing the American Mosque*, 38.

16. Malpas, "Building Memory," 13.

17. See Akel Ismail Kahera, "Image, Text, and Form: Complexities of Aesthetics in an American *Masjid*," *Studies in Contemporary Islam* 1, no. 2 (Fall 1999): 73, text available at https://www.academia.edu/37564285/Image_Text_and_Form _Complexities_of_Aesthetics_in_an_American_Masjid.

18. *Sahih Muslim*, Book 004, number 1056, 1057 with other narrations 1058 and 1060, available at https://d1.islamhouse.com/data/en/ih_books/single/en_Sahih _Muslim.pdf

19. David A. King, "The Sacred Direction in Islam: A Study of the Interaction of Religion and Science in the Middle Ages," *Interdisciplinary Science Reviews* 10, no. 4 (1985): 327.

20. Titus Burckhardt, *The Art of Islam: Language and Meaning*, fore. Seyyed Hossein Nasr, intro Jean-Louis Michon (Bloomington, IN: World Wisdom, 2009), 1.

21. Titus Burckhardt, *The Art of Islam*, 1, emphasis original.

22. See Muhammad ibn 'Abd Allah al-Azraqi, *Kitab Akbar Makkah*, (ed) Dr. Abdul Malik Dahesh, (Maktabat al-Asadi, n.p. 2003). Also see Oleg Grabar, "Upon Reading Al-Azraqi," *Muqarnas* 3 (1985): 1–7.

23. Al-Azraqi, *Kitab Akbar Makkah*, 74.

24. D'Ascoli, *Public Space*, 112.

25. Hirst, *Space and Power*, 165.

26. Al-Azraqi, *Kitab Akbar Makkah*, 100; It is during the hajj and *umrah* pilgrimages that the faithful reenact Hajar's desperate search for water, walking seven times between Safa and Marwa. In honoring the memory of Hajar, pilgrims also acknowledge the hardships she faced and contemplate the ultimate reward she received of water from the *zam zam* well.

27. Surah *al-Nur,* The verse of light (Q. 24:35)

28. Abū-Ḥāmid Muḥammad Ibn-Muḥammad Al-Ġazzālī, *The Niche of Lights: A Parallel English-Arabic Text*, trans., intro., and annot. David Buchman (Provo, UT: Brigham Young University Press, 1998), xxxii-xxxiii.

29. Hirst, *Space and Power*, 165.

30. Hirst, *Space and Power*, 165.

31. D'Ascoli, *Public Space*, 62. And see Henri Lefebvre, *Éléments de rythmanalyse (Rhythmanalysis)* (Paris: Éditions Syllepse, 1992).

32. Philip Glass, "From Egypt." No. 16, a recording of the Azan (*adhan*), in the soundtrack for *Powaqqatsi: Life in Transformation*, a 1988 documentary film., directed by Godfrey Reggio (dist. United States: The Cannon Group, available online at https://www.youtube.com/watch?v=ZVE-a-24prE.) The film is the sequel to Reggio's experimental 1982 film, *Koyaanisqatsi: Life Out of Balance* (dist. United States, Island Alive, New Cinema). It is the second film in Reggio's *Qatsi* trilogy.

33. Saidah Saad, Naomi Salim, Hakim Zainal, and Shahrul Azman Mohd Noah, "A Framework for Islamic Knowledge via Ontology Representation," paper presented at the International Conference on Information Retrieval and Knowledge Management (CAMP), Shah Alam, Selangor, Malaysia, March 16–18, 2010, 312, available at https://www.researchgate.net/publication/224138969_A_framework_for_Islamic_knowledge_via_ontology_representation.

34. Fontana-Giusti, *Foucault for Architects*, 45.

35. Ian Buchanan and Gregg Lambert, eds., *Deleuze and Space* (Edinburgh: Edinburgh University Press, 2005), 2.

36. Chris Moffat, review of *Expertise and Architecture in the Modern Islamic World*, ed. Peter Christensen, *Reviews in History* (February 2019): 1, https://reviews.history.ac.uk/review/2306, emphasis original.

37. Lindsay Jones, "The Hermeneutics of Sacred Architecture: A Reassessment of the Similitude between Tula, Hidalgo and Chichen Itza, Yucatan, Part I," *History of Religions* 32, no. 3 (1993): 219.

38. Baudrillard, *Simulacra and Simulation*, 6.

39. Faubion, *Essential Works*, xx.

40. Foucault, "Nietzsche, Genealogy, History," 81.

41. Kimberley Kutz Elliott, "The World's Columbian Exposition: The Midway," *Smarthistory*, July 29, 2021, https://smarthistory.org/worlds-columbian-exposition-midway/.

42. As quoted in Zeynep Çelik, *Displaying the Orient: Architecture of Islam at Nineteenth-Century World's Fairs*, Comparative Studies on Muslim Societies 12 (Berkeley and Los Angeles: University of California Press, 1992), 50.

43. Behrens-Abouseif, *Islamic Architecture in Cairo: An Introduction* (Cairo: American University in Cairo Press, 1989), 43.

44. Fontana-Giusti, *Foucault for Architects*, 30.

45. Herz quoted in István Ormos, "Between Stage Décor and Reality: The Cairo Street at the World's Columbian Exposition of 1893 Chicago," in *Studies in Memory of Alexander Fodor*, Arabist series 37, ed. Kinga Dévényi (Budapest: Csoma de Kőrös Society, 2016),??, text available at https://www.academia.edu/36405172/Between_Stage_Décor_and_Reality_The_Cairo_Street_at_the_Worlds_Columbian_Exposition_of_1893_at_Chicago_Studies_in_Memory_of_Alexander_Fodor_The_Arabist_Budapest_Studies_in_Arabic_37_Budapest_2016_pp_115_134_2016_.

46. Buchanan and Lambert, *Deleuze and Space*, 6.

47. The *New Yorker* recently referred to Burnham as "the most successful power broker the American architectural profession has ever produced"; Herz's exhibit, in other words, would have had important boosters. See Paul Goldberger, "Toddlin' Town: Daniel Burnham's Great Chicago Plan Turns 100," March 1, 2009, *New Yorker*, "https://www.newyorker.com/magazine/2009/03/09/toddlin-town. And see Ormos, "Between Stage Decor and Reality," 47.

48. Baudrillard, *Simulacra and Simulation*, 6.

49. Mersch, *Epistemologies of Aesthetics*, 150.

50. Baudrillard, *Simulacra and Simulation*, 6.

51. Howayda al-Harithy, "The Concept of Space in Mamluk Architecture," *Muqarnas* 18 (2001): 73.

52. Lefebvre, *Production of Space*, 46.

53. Mugerauer, *Interpreting Environments*, 31.

54. Mersch, *Epistemologies of Aesthetics*, 143.

55. Foucault as analyzed by Fontana-Giusti, *Foucault for Architects*, 31.

56. Hirst, *Space and Power*, 156.

57. Foucault as analyzed by Gutting, *Foucault*, 51.

58. Sally Howell, "Laying Groundwork for American Muslim Histories: 1865–1965," in *The Cambridge Companion to American Islam*, ed. Juliane Hammer and Omid Safi (New York: Cambridge University Press, 2013), 45.

59. Thomas Lewis, "transatlantic slave trade." *Encyclopedia Britannica*, 22 Sep. 2021, available at https://www.britannica.com/topic/transatlantic-slave-trade.

60. After Bell (1913–2001) photographed and interviewed many coastal Georgia Blacks as part of the Works Progress Administration Program in the early 1940s, the findings were published in the monograph *Drums and Shadows: Survival Studies among the Coastal Georgia Negroes* (Savannah Unit, Georgia Writers' Project [U.S.], Works Progress Administration, fore. Guy B. Johnson, photos. Muriel Bell

and Malcolm Bell Jr. [Athens: University of Georgia Press, 1940]). See specifically, pp. 179. In 1984, historian Allan D. Austin brought to our attention the importance of the history of Islam in the United States with the publication of *African Muslims in Antebellum America: Transatlantic Stories and Spiritual Struggles* (the 1997 edition is published in New York by Routledge).

61. Dir. Andrea Kalin and Bill Duke (Unity Productions Foundation, 2008), watch at https://www.upf.tv/films/prince-among-slaves/watch/). In truth, no one really knows how these early Muslims worshipped or if they were allowed to worship at all; and much more problematic is the dating of the first mosques on American soil.

62. Both quotations drawn from Fontana-Giusti, *Foucault for Architects*, 30.

63. As analyzed in Eugene B. Young, "'Francis Bacon: The Logic of Sensation,'" in *The Deleuze and Guattari Dictionary*, Bloomsbury Philosophical Dictionaries series, Eugene B. Young, with Gary Genosko and Janell Watson (New York, Bloomsbury, 2013), 145.

64. Mersch, *Epistemologies of Aesthetics*, 78–79.

65. Fontana-Giusti, *Foucault for Architects*, 39.

66. Deleuze as quoted in Young, "'Francis Bacon: The Logic of Sensation,'" 145.

67. István Ormos, "Cairo Street at the World's Columbian Exposition of 1893 in Chicago: A New, Fresh Reading," in *Dialogues artistiques avec les passés de l'Égypte: Une perspective transnationale et transmédiale*, ed. Mercedes Volait and Emmanuelle Perrin (Paris: Publications de l'Institut national d'histoire de l'art, 2017), 9, text available at https://books.openedition.org/inha/7201.

68. Ormos, "Cairo Street," 9.

69. Foucault, "Des espaces autres," 22.

70. Hirst, *Space and Power*, 161.

71. Foucault, "Des espaces autres," 23.

72. Muhammad Abdul-Rauf, *History of the Islamic Center: From Dream to Reality* (Washington, DC: Colortone Press, 1978), 12.

73. All quotations in this paragraph drawn from Abdul-Rauf, *History of the Islamic Center*, 13.

74. Abdul-Rauf, *History of the Islamic Center*, 13.

75. Mariangela Turchiarulo, "The Construction of Al-Mursi Abou al-'Abbas Mosque, Alexandria," paper presented at the 2nd International Balkans Conference on Challenges of Civil Engineering, BCCCE, Epoka University, Tirana, Albania, May 23–25, 2013, p. 1084, text available at https://core.ac.uk/download/pdf/152489497.pdf.

76. Abdul-Rauf, *History of the Islamic Center*, 13.

77. In *The History of the Islamic Center*, Muhammad Abdul-Rauf lists the countries as Afghanistan, Saudi Arabia, Iran, Egypt, Pakistan, Syria, Qatar, Turkey, Morocco, Yemen, Iraq, Tunisia, Sudan, Indonesia, and Libya, 95.

78. Abdul-Rauf, *History of the Islamic Center*, 74–75; and Eisenhower as quoted in Andrew Glass, "Eisenhower Dedicates DC Islamic Center, June 28, 1957," *Politico*, June 28, 2018, https://www.politico.com/story/2018/06/28/eisenhower-dedicates-dc-islamic-center-june-28-1957-667325.

79. The omissions are poignant, given that the *Source Book* bills itself as a "comprehensive . . . survey of 500 of America's most distinguished buildings." G. E. Kidder Smith, *Source Book of American Architecture: 500 Notable Buildings from the 10th Century to the Present* (New York: Princeton Architectural Press, 1996), back jacket.

80. Faubion, *Essential Works*, xxix.

81. Abdul-Rauf, *History of the Islamic Center*, 16.

82. Lefebvre, *Production of Space*, 46.

83. James Dickie, "The Works of Mario Rossi at Alessandria," Amate Sponde . . . Presence of Italy in the Architecture of the Islamic Mediterranean, *Environmental Design: Journal of the Islamic Environmental Design Research Centre*, nos. 9–10 (1990): 94, https://s3.us-east-1.amazonaws.com/media.archnet.org/system/publications/contents/3237/original/DPC0789.pdf.

84. Hirst, *Space and Power*, 157.

85. Michel Foucault, *The Hermeneutics of the Subject: Lectures at the Collège de France, 1981–1982*, vol. 3, ed. Frédéric Gros, trans. Graham Burchell, English series ed. Arnold I. Davidson (New York and Basingstoke: Palgrave-Macmillan, 2005), 15.

86. For further discussion of these three themes see W. K. Chorbachi, "In the Tower of Babel: Beyond Symmetry in Islamic Design, *Computers & Mathematics with Applications*, vol. 17, 4:6 (1989): 751–89; Carol Bier, "Geometry in Islamic Art," *Encyclopaedia of the History of Science, Technology, and Medicine in Non-Western Cultures* (2015): 1–21

87. Jones, "Hermeneutics of Sacred Architecture," 225.

88. Hirst, "Space and Power," 161.

89. Emma Clark, *The Art of the Islamic Garden* (Ramsbury, Marlborough, and Wiltshire, UK: The Crowood Press, 2010), 27.

90. Lefebvre, *Production of Space*, 2.

91. Abdul-Rauf, *History of the Islamic Center*, 25.

92. Take, for example, the following: Barbara Daly Metcalf, ed., *Making Muslim Space in North America and Europe*, Comparative Studies on Muslim Societies series 22 (Berkeley: University of California Press, 1996); Kahera, *Deconstructing the American Mosque*; Gulzar Haider, "'Brother in Islam, Please Draw Us a Mosque': Muslims in the West; A Personal Account," in *Expressions of Islam in Buildings*, ed. Hayat Salam, 155–66 (Singapore: Concept Media/The Aga Khan Award for Architecture, 1990); and Omar Khalidi, "Approaches to Mosque Design in North America," in *Muslims on the Americanization Path*, ed. Yvonne Yazbeck Haddad and John L. Esposito, 399–424 (New York: Oxford University Press, 1998). Most of the mosque-building of the last fifty years corresponds to migration trends from the regions of the Muslim world. No known Muslim religious buildings survive in the United States from the antebellum period; recall that the first African Muslims from West Africa were abducted to the United States in 1619. These demographic fluctuations in turn shaped art criticism, which developed in many directions through new challenges and crises.

93. See David S. Gutterman and Andrew R. Murphy, "The 'Ground Zero Mosque': Sacred Space and the Boundaries of American Identity," *Politics, Groups, and Identities* 2, no. 3 (2014): 368–85.

94. Hirst, *Space and Power*, 161.

95. D'Ascoli, *Public Space*, 134.

96. *Sahih Muslim*, Book 004, number 1056, 1057 with other narrations 1058 and 1060; Places you should not perform the prayer . . . in a bathroom, camel pen in a graveyard, available at https://d1.islamhouse.com/data/en/ih_books/single/en_Sahih_Muslim.pdf

97. Sani, "Corporeal Poetics," 302.

98. D'Ascoli, *Public Space*, 134.

99. Likewise, the Great Mosque of Damascus emerges most prominently as a concept of spatial transformation, given that the edifice has experienced three or more iterations in its history: first as the Temple of Jupiter, second as the Church of John the Baptist (a cenotaph honoring the head of John the Baptist still resides there), and finally as the Umayyad Mosque, circa 715 CE.

100. Staale Sinding-Larsen, *The Burden of the Ceremony Master: Image and Action in San Marco, Venice, and in an Islamic Mosque; The Rituum Cerimoniale of 1564* (Rome: G. Bretschneider, 2000), 144, text available at https://folk.ntnu.no/staalesl/BurdenNet.pdf.

101. Sinding-Larsen, *Burden of the Ceremony Master*, 85.

102. Julie Elizabeth Gagnon and Annick Germain, "Espace urbain et religion: Esquisse d'une géographie des lieux de culte minoritaires de la région de Montréal," *Cahiers de géographie de Québec* 46, no. 128 (January 2002): 149, https://www.erudit.org/fr/revues/cgq/2002-v46-n128-cgq2700/023038ar/.

103. Both Lefebvre quotations pulled from D'Ascoli, *Public Space*, 34.

104. Ludwig Wittgenstein, *Culture and Value*, ed. G. H. von Wright, with Heikki Nyman, trans. Peter Winch (Chicago: University of Chicago Press, 1980), 4.

105. Gagnon and Germain, "Espace urbain et religion," 148.

Chapter 4

Place, Biopolitics, and Legal Discourses

This struggle may be a moral one, or it may be a physical one, and it may be both moral and physical, but it must be a struggle. Power concedes nothing without a demand. It never did and it never will.

—Frederick Douglass, 1857[1]

The instruments of control that Foucault describes in regard to the power/knowledge nexus can be applied to another of his statements—"that certain ideological conflicts which underlie the controversies of our day take place between pious descendants of time and tenacious inhabitants of space."[2] At the same time, it is "another medium through which power is communicated and exerted, as well as something that comes to be and comes to be understood as a result of the power relations surrounding it."[3] On the one hand, the claim makes it possible to identify the power/knowledge nexus, and the discursive method provides explanatory power that comes forth in the litigation of *place*, police power, and other means of control. On the other hand, society is vastly dominated by the power of the public discourse and social media, which is an instrument of influence that is "always a certain way of acting upon another person or persons. . . . All of these constitute a block of capacity-communication-power."[4]

In this chapter, we discuss a sampling of cases describing how the place of the mosque is tied to micro-powers and biopolitics. Take, for example, the 2010 controversy over the construction of Cordoba House/Park51—also known as the "Ground Zero mosque—in Lower Manhattan. The building plans included a *musalla* (a simple *intra muros* prayer space) and accommodation for a host of community functions. Inclusion of the *musalla* raised doubts among critics of the site plans, which only goes to illustrate the many complexities of place.

The year 2010 marked a decided increase in litigation throughout the United States concerning the Religious Land Use and Institutionalized Persons Act (RLUIPA), often involving disputes over the placement of mosques—right around the time that the "Ground Zero mosque" controversy boiled over in New York City.[5] Three additional court cases—*The Islamic Center of Mississippi. v. City of Starkville*, *The Islamic Center of Murfreesboro v. Rutherford County*, and *The Islamic Society of Basking Ridge v. Bernards Township*—amplify the language of the power/knowledge nexus by analyzing the litigants' claims, the wording of various zoning ordinances, and the implications of the site-planning decisions, which were all considered paramount to regulating land use in the United States.[6]

"Land use controls," argues Michael Allan Wolf, scholar of environmental law, "are caught in a swirling snowstorm of ideological, political, legal and popular controversy." Above all, "it is no exaggeration to say that the judicial acceptance of modern environmental law is an important legacy of *Euclid v. Ambler*"—a landmark 1926 Supreme Court case ruling in favor of zoning for the public welfare.[7] Wolf helps us distinguish between competing biopolitical regimes informing land use—or, specifically in our case, the place of the mosque: the power of the zoning board ("police power") and the local autonomy of the courts. These regimes converge with influence to impact local communities—and specifically for our discussion, the Muslim community. And in its localized form, "Foucault insisted that micro-power, in particular power located in sites away from the central locations of macro-power, had become a defining characteristic of power."[8]

Over the four years in which *The Islamic Center of Murfreesboro v. Rutherford County* was contested—between 2010 and 2014—antimosque opponents, riled by "fears about Islam, sharia law and terrorism," attempted to block the construction of an Islamic center in the town of Murfreesboro, Tennessee.[9] In the absence of compromise between the two camps, the two opposing sides staked their claims in two camps: there were the proponents of self-determination—that is, of authority over the body, space, and place—and defendants of nativist ideology, which they used to identify "enemy," "friend," and "patriot."

Land disputes over plans to build mosques and Islamic centers around the United States are stoked by publications such as *Mosques in America: A Guide to Accountable Permit Hearings and Continuing Citizen Oversight*, which markets itself to the "many communities . . . stymied by Islamist cultural schemes in concert with the political Left's attacks on citizens who defend American traditions and constitutional principles."[10] In truth, the purpose of books like *Mosques in America* is to empower the antimosque litigant to "compete for dominance by criticizing, mis-describing, undermining, or disregarding" the First Amendment clause.[11]

Between 2000 when the RLUIPA was passed and 2015, of the forty total cases opened by the US Department of Justice's Civil Rights Division that involve the contested building and use of mosques or Islamic schools, twenty-nine were initiated between 2010 and 2015 alone.[12] By 2020, which marked the twentieth anniversary of RLUIPA passage, "the largest number of filings involved Islamic mosques and schools and Christian churches, schools, and other institutions, with each representing approximately 35 percent. Jewish synagogues, schools, and institutions were the next group, representing 20 percent. Other filings have involved Hindu and Buddhist groups, each representing 4 percent, and one filing each on behalf of Sikh and Native American groups."[13]

The centrality of RLUIPA disputes has caught the attention of the Pew Research Center, whose findings reveal a seismic shift in US public attitudes over the first decades of the twenty-first century concerning land use by Muslim groups. One 2012 Pew report lists at least fifty-three RLUIPA cases in which "the opposition [to the location of a mosque] has centered on neighbors' concerns about traffic, noise, parking, and property values—the same objections that often greet churches, [temples, synagogues,] and other houses of worship."[14]

Starkville, Mississippi: A Place in the Bible Belt

Let us open our discussion of contested Muslim spaces in the United States by reviewing the case of *The Islamic Center of Mississippi v. City of Starkville*, litigated in the late 1980s. The dispute concerns police power and controlling influence wielded by Starkville, Mississippi's, Board of Aldermen and the lawful notice provided by the Islamic Center of Mississippi to establish a *musalla*—a simple *intra muros* prayer space—adjacent to the Mississippi State University campus. In the court filings, the *musalla* is referred to as "the mosque."

This particular legal dispute preceded the RLUIPA legislation introduced in 2000, which protected religious land use and institutionalized persons. To summarize the argument the Islamic Center brought against the city, Starkville's Board of Aldermen was giving preference to Starkville's churches, which bias was in violation of the Constitutional rights of Muslim citizens. In this discussion, we are *not* suggesting that a church or site planned for explicitly Christian use isn't an important edifice but, rather, that the city of Starkville's ordinance maps plotting church approvals corroborate the plaintiff's struggle to be granted equal treatment under the law where the controlling influence of the board "might wish to pursue one or two interpretations over others."[15] In other words, the board was permitting the building of churches but was blocking the building of a single mosque.

The plaintiff's complaint shows us what coexistence between affective groups really looks like within the dominant "White/Christian" territory, the South, and the Bible Belt—as the strip of Southern states was first described by celebrated American essayist and satirist H. L. Mencken in 1924. "The old game, I suspect, is beginning to play out in the Bible Belt," Mencken had written. Indeed, the "Bible Belt" appellation is important to our discussion here: it aptly names the type of provoked resistance to the Muslim community "where the old game" was playing out in Starkville.[16]

To distinguish which types of localized power were at play in the dispute between proponents of the Islamic center and its opponents, we must consider first the fact that religious identities are not shaped by ideologies alone. That is, it is not the mere fact that the Islamic center's opposition came from avowed, outspoken *Christians* per se, but by people raised in a particular cultural context. Ideologies are also determined over time by *discourses* that explore the virtues of democracy and inequality, their public affect, and, in this case, the irruptions of segregated venues for Blacks—as had been codified in the South's Jim Crow laws.[17]

Let us contextualize the micro-powers at play in terms of "the old game" being played in the South: Foucault tells us that "we are always subject to power" but also "are always exercising power," which can be exercised to the disadvantage of many citizens.[18] The long-term behavior of others—in this case, the entrenched culture of white Southerners in the late 1980s—requires a specific context in order to play out—in this case, the subjugation of Black Americans and other ethnic groups. Hence our analysis of the Starkville case must consider other, similar cases.

Recall our exploration of the Mosque Theater in chapter 2, where we learned that in Richmond, Virginia, Blacks were being excluded from entering the Mosque unless they agreed to be seated in the segregated "negro section," in compliance with the Virginia statute. A suit was brought by "plaintiff negro citizens" seeking full access to public facilities in *Brown v. City of Richmond*. At issue was that the City of Richmond, which owned and operated the Mosque and had frequently leased it for performances and events for the public, and, at the same time, "had always required said lessees to segregate all patrons . . . [for all events] given at the Mosque." The Court reversed and voided the statute.[19]

The gradual and steady eradication in the courts of Jim Crow laws by a series of carefully crafted lawsuits had emboldened Black Americans in their push for civil rights. But when Muslim groups in Mississippi and Tennessee had no recourse but to sue for fair treatment in the 1980s and even in 2012, much of their battle was against entrenched Jim Crow thinking. *The Islamic Center of Mississippi v. Starkville* shows the dynamic interplay of competing power holders: the court of law and the city's board. The Islamic Center had been told by the board that it ought to erect its mosque outside of the city limits, which would have created a mobility and access burden for devotees. The center challenged the board's biased understanding of location and boundary, which had privileged the establishment of religious facilities for only a segment of the Starkville population—white Christians.

Political theorist Stuart Elden argues that territory and boundary are "more than merely land, and go beyond terrain, but [are] a rendering of the emergent concept of 'space' as a political category: owned, distributed, mapped, calculated, bordered and controlled."[20] We can apply this to our consideration of the case—and specifically the effects of the Starkville board's micro-power. In "Where to Pray: Religious Zoning and the First Amendment," scholar of constitutional law Mark W. Cordes offers important insight into micro-power and the Pareto criterion—where the conditions for one group cannot be improved without worsening the conditions of another. A state is empowered to take into account the circumstances where inequality is omnipresent. "Although in theory minimal scrutiny is applied to zoning controls," Cordes writes, "the amount of scrutiny actually applied varies widely among the states, with a few states closely scrutinizing zoning decisions in a manner reminiscent of Lochner-era substantive due process."[21] Thus the unpredictability and instability of the Starkville board's "police power," so to speak, could be envisioned as scrutiny and control but also as the disruption of social norms, and "many legal scholars are properly skeptical of the distinction between *de jure* and *de facto* segregation. Where private discrimination is pervasive, they argue, discrimination by public policy is indistinguishable from *societal discrimination*."[22]

Considering the Pareto criterion—where it is a zero-sum game, and no group can benefit without disadvantaging another group—the issue of micro-power and control becomes critical "with regard to time, place and manner of restrictions on expressive activity and . . . precision of regulation, and available alternatives for the exercise of the restricted right."[23] In the Starkville case, the court considered whether the plaintiff's complaint about building a mosque was covered by the "church" zoning ordinance of Starkville and whether the city's board had acted in a manner consistent with the First Amendment's Establishment Clause.

The plaintiff's complaint had been clearly defined in the case file, highlighting the forms of control and police power used to prevent their building a mosque within Starkville city limits: "The zoning ordinance of the City of Starkville, Mississippi, prohibits the use of buildings as churches in all of the areas within the city limits near the campus of Mississippi State University unless an exception is granted by the City Board of Aldermen."[24] The problem, the Islamic Center would find, would be getting the board to grant an exception.

We might say that in denying the request to build the mosque within city limits the board was wielding their power within "their spatial reach."[25] But under what circumstances is their use of power justified? The question might seem simple, but the issue grew complicated when specifically considering Starkville's Muslim community. In other words, is the board's judgment to deny an exception invested in the First Amendment, *or* is the First Amendment being used as a means to exclude a non-Christian community?

The case file tells us that "while the city ordinance restricts the use of any property in this type of residential area or in the City's commercial district as a church, 25 churches, all Christian, are located in similarly regulated areas. Sixteen of these churches occupied their present sites before the ordinance became effective, and nine moved in thereafter with the benefit of an exception." The board's interest in supporting the constituents of the twenty-five churches is obvious, having granted them exceptions, but they withheld the same consideration from the Muslim community seeking to build a single mosque: "only the Islamic Center has ever been denied an exception. Because the City has failed to establish that the Board based its denial of an exception to the Islamic Center on a sufficient reason or that it has not favored Christian churches over Muslim mosques," the court held that "the Board's action violates the free exercise of religion clause."[26]

The dispute's origins can be traced in part back to 1977, when the Muslim community had decided it needed a mosque to serve both the students at the Mississippi State University and the greater Starkville Muslim community—especially during the month of Ramadan and for Friday prayers. So the community began negotiations with the city of Starkville to identify a suitable location. "In 1982, still lacking an established place for worship, members of the Islamic Center appointed a search committee to locate a building that they could use as a mosque. Because [only a] few . . . Muslim students had cars, the committee sought a site within walking distance of the campus."[27] As a pure zoning issue, the Starkville board would have been operating well within its powers to grant an exception for the mosque to be built within city limits. They had done so multiple times when petitioned by Christian communities.

The first location the Islamic Center's search committee had identified was a building at 212 South Nash Street—about a ten-minute walk from Mississippi State University's campus. As a precaution, and so as to fully comply with the city's zoning ordinance, the committee chair "wrote to the City's building codes official and its liaison representative with the Planning Commission, about the site." The official responded, informing the committee "that the location would not be approved because of inadequate parking." The search committee then proposed another location—this time at 525 University Drive, which had adequate parking and "was located across the street from a church. The Planning Commission rejected the committee's request for permission to use this site because of the heavy traffic on University Drive."²⁸

These early rejections, although not yet generating any serious pushback from the Muslim community, do "suggest the need for a clear understanding of a municipality's ability to regulate religious activities."²⁹ But what produced confusion was the persistent and inevitable response that the search committee received on numerous occasions from city officials, saying that any given proposed location for the mosque would not be approved by the city's planning commission.

In April 1983—six years after the Muslim community of Starkville had first identified the need for a mosque—the search committee made a third written request to the city "for permission to use property at the corner of Jarnigan Street and Lumas Drive, across the street from a church." Again they were told that the location "would not be approved because it created too much traffic congestion," and likewise a proposed "site at 523 University Drive met the same reception."³⁰ After considering the search committee's proposal for yet another property, this one situated at 204 Herbert Street, only one block from the university, the same city official told them their choice was an "excellent location. If you can buy it."³¹

The official's odd response might merely have meant that the committee's long search was finally over. But it is also characteristic of the individual exercise of power: Foucault reminds us, "we must indeed presuppose the free act in the analysis of power relations." And he also famously notes, "where there is power, there is resistance."³²

Nevertheless, the "commissioners agreed that if the Islamic Center could purchase the Herbert Street property and supply the parking the city ordinance required, they would recommend that the Board of Aldermen approve the site." Agreeing with the city official's tentative terms for approval, the search committee then bought the property in September 1983, "prepared a schematic drawing showing the location of the existing structure . . . and the proposed parking area, 18 spaces . . . [and] submitted this to the Planning Commission, which recommended approval."³³

But things did not go smoothly: The committee's representative "then went to the City Office to obtain a building permit to make the necessary improvements," and initially the city employee tasked with issuing permits refused to act, "because the building was not approved for congregational worship."³⁴ The confusion continued.

First, "the city electrical inspector intervened, and the permit was issued with designated use as 'commercial.'" Then, the following day, a representative from the Islamic Center was asked to return the permit, which was then changed to "residential." Keep in mind that "the City's zoning ordinance requires final approval by the Board for the use of property for a church when that use requires an exception to the provisions of the ordinance. Consequently, the Planning Commission submitted its recommendation to the Board for approval."[35]

The other focal point is that the Board of Aldermen always had the power to grant the Islamic Center permission to establish a mosque. But their "method of power lies in its prohibition, its 'rejection, exclusion, refusal, blockage, concealment, or mask.'"[36] On November 22, 1983, a reporter informed the representative of the Islamic Center that "the Board . . . would consider the request that evening and that, because of neighborhood opposition, the Board would likely reject the recommendation." At the meeting, the city official "recommended that the Board grant the exception, but a neighborhood resident, representing property owners in the area, spoke in opposition . . . the resident based his opposition on 'congestion, parking, and traffic problems' in the neighborhood. The Board then voted unanimously to deny the exception without . . . giving any reasons."[37]

In their complaint to the court, the Islamic Center contended that there is *prima facie* evidence that the city's zoning ordinance was invalid for at least three reasons: First it would force members of the Muslim community to worship in an *extra muros* location—"the least acceptable part of the City . . . in a county outside the City's boundaries." Second, in denying the Islamic Center an exception, the board violated the free exercise of religion. Third, "the Board's action was arbitrary," thus denying the Islamic Center and its members due process.[38]

Starkville officials offered a spurious rebuttal: "The City maintained that the ordinance did not inhibit the free exercise of religion because churches may be built either in the R-E districts or outside the city limits and it maintained that the Board's refusal to grant an exception for the Herbert Street location is based on a secular purpose, visiting only an incidental burden on religion."[39] The city's evaluation of the dilemma adds to the confusion, suggesting a lack of empathy or discretion and sounding more like an attempt to escape accountability than sound grounds for refusing an exemption.

We must highlight a point that is almost as critical: the lower court concluded that "standing alone, the denial of the Herbert Street zoning application is not enough upon which to base an inference of discrimination. . . . The actions of the Board were supported by valid traffic considerations, and there is no evidence to suggest that it improperly considered plaintiffs' religion in reaching its decision." In the end, the court found that "the ordinance did not infringe upon the Islamic students' right to free exercise of religion."[40]

There is, however, another reason for being "loath to allow the inevitable . . . to count as being ethically neutral." According to jurisprudential scholar Karl Llewellyn, "that reason goes back to our test for Truth."[41] With this in mind, let's consider the next statement from the court documents: "The district court then held the zoning ordinance had not violated substantive due process because it was a legitimate exercise of the City's police power, not clearly arbitrary or unreasonable and having a substantial relation to the public safety or general welfare."[42] So, the question remains. "who has the power to make other people act in a certain way?"[43]

Scholar of political philosophy Mathias Klitgård Sørensen argues that "Foucault insists that disciplinary power cannot be possessed, acquired, seized or shared, but has purely *structural* origins. However, power can factually speaking only be said to exist when materially manifested. . . . Power relations have multiple origins and can only be found at its point of application: the (possible) actions of subjects as described above."[44] In this regard, and concerns for the rule of law, in the *Starkville* decision the court cites the Supreme Court's decision in *Schad v. Borough of Mount Ephraim*: "The power of local governments to zone and control land use is undoubtedly broad and its proper exercise is an essential aspect of achieving a satisfactory quality of life in both urban and rural communities. But the zoning power is not infinite and unchallengeable; it must be exercised within constitutional limits."[45]

Here the dominant interest is again a caveat: "The burden placed on relatively impecunious Muslim students by the Starkville ordinance is more than incidental, and the ordinance leaves no practical alternatives for establishing a mosque in the city limits. There is no other place in the City within reasonable distance from the campus where the students may establish a place of worship, and the ordinance forbids the use of property they already own for worship services."[46] And still in regard to "the rule of law itself . . . right law must be intelligible, intellectually accessible, to the people whom that law is to serve, whose law it is."[47] That is, the rules must serve not only a few, the immediate, but also the needs of the larger population. In the meantime, a paradox arises, informing the board's judgment: "as disciplinary force, power relations decide upon possible actions of subjects."[48]

And so, the Islamic Center appealed the decision, upon which the Fifth Circuit Court concluded that "the City's approval of applications for zoning exceptions by other churches suggests that it did not treat all applicants alike. This undermines the City's contention that the Board denied a zoning exception to the Muslims solely for the purposes of traffic control and public safety." The appellate court declared the city ordinance unconstitutional as applied to the Islamic center and enjoined "the City of Starkville from enforcing the ordinance against the use of the property at 204 Herbert Street for public worship."[49]

But let's not leave it at that without stating that when the law comes to a closer good in light of reason, reshaping and redirecting, the law is "at its high best."[50] In its reversal of the lower court's decision, the district court reached the "conclusion that the Board of Aldermen denied an exception to the Islamic Center for reasons other than considerations of traffic control and public safety and that it applied different standards to approving a Muslim mosque than it had adopted for worship facilities of other faiths. Moreover, the City has failed to show the importance of its purpose or that it could not have been accomplished by means less burdensome to the Muslim faithful."[51]

I opened this chapter with Frederick Douglass's contention that "power concedes nothing without a demand." With this in mind, we must also remember that Starkville's board was populated by folk who'd grown up under Jim Crow and whose near ancestors had participated in the slave trade, had fought a war to maintain it, and had believed that a slave was only three-fifths the value of a white person.[52] The three-fifths math squares nicely with official policies of racial segregation. We keep this in mind when considering whether or not the Starkville Board of Aldermen was *upholding* the First Amendment by withholding permission to found a mosque or *hiding behind* it.

So it isn't difficult for us to imagine the American legacy of unequal justice, stretching on a time line back into history, and the corresponding fight for fair and dignified treatment under the law: In 1619, the first ship carrying enslaved peoples arrived on America's shores. In 1870, Jim Crow laws were codified, curtailing the rights of recently freed Black Americans. In 1954, the civil rights movement gained momentum, finally ending legal enforcement of Jim Crow in 1965. In 2013, the Black Lives Matter movement coalesced around police brutality against Black Americans. Through all of this, the struggle for social justice has been threatened by religious fundamentalism and its cohort, white supremacy.

As we recall, it took passage of the 1964 Civil Rights Act to remedy the three-fifths formula—to outlaw discrimination in the United States based on race, color, religion, gender, and national origin. But in 1988 Mississippi, what sort of sway did the twenty-four-year-old legislation hold in Starkville, Mississippi? Would it be enough to validate the equal rights of the local Muslim community? Were there enough "good" Christians in the heart of the Bible Belt who would support the promises of the First Amendment and support the local Muslim community's right to worship and have unfettered access to a mosque? Further, while by 1988 legislation already existed making it unlawful to discriminate against any person, the Starkville ordinance was at that same time granting the free exercise of religion to local churches while also imposing burdensome restrictions on the Muslim community.

The Starkville board's powers and responsibilities are defined thorough general state statutes, and, hence, the board is strongly sustained by the state.[53] But "despite various constitutional issues that arise in this setting, until recently, church zoning decisions have been the exclusive realm of the state courts. Most states, although recognizing the legitimacy of some zoning controls on churches, have traditionally restricted a municipality's ability to regulate church location. Surprisingly, these restrictions usually have been based on substantive due process and not First Amendment grounds." Above all, "the general thesis . . . is that, although churches can be made subject to zoning ordinances and other forms of land use controls, Supreme Court precedent indicates that the Constitution requires application of the intermediate level of review to ordinances regulating churches, rather than the mere rationality standard normally applied to zoning ordinances."[54]

As we will see in the subsequent sections of this chapter, our examination of place, discursive relations, and micro-power is further enhanced by two additional examples of juridico-discursive power—that is, repressive, punishing power. The unifying feature of the power struggle Frederick Douglass spoke about resides in the battle against white supremacy—waged in Starkville, Mississippi, and New York City. In Manhattan, yet another Muslim community had to wrestle for equal treatment under the law and demand their constitutional right of free practice of religion.

PARK51: THERE IS NO GROUND ZERO MOSQUE

The beginning of wisdom is to call things by their right names.

—Attributed to Confucius, *Analects*

In 2010, a contentious debate dominated American discourse. In Manhattan, a former Burlington Coat Factory, located at 45–51 Park Place, was under consideration to be retrofitted into a community-oriented facility. The project was "itself inspired by the Manhattan Jewish Community Center (JCC) which offers a wide range of programs and activities, including but not limited to Jewish culture."[55] The adaptive reuse program for the old department store building was called Cordoba House, which was to be fitted with a five hundred–seat auditorium, a performing arts center, a culinary school, a theater, a fitness center, a swimming pool, a basketball court, child-care facilities, a bookstore, an art studio, a food court, a memorial to the victims of the September 11 terrorist attacks, and an open-air *musalla* in which one to two thousand people would be able to gather for informal prayer. While Cordoba House's plans had been drawn up to function like the Manhattan JCC, it is important to note that the JCC, though explicitly Jewish in identity, was not publicly referred to as a "'synagogue' or 'temple' although Shabbat dinners are held there on Friday nights, Sukkah host rooftop dinners during Sukkot and menorah-lighting ceremonies occur during Hanukah."[56]

And yet, when plans for Cordoba House were announced, a sizable and public pushback stopped the project's forward momentum. The lack of empathy for the project was mainly driven by negative public reaction to plans for the *musalla* and the building's location—a mere two blocks from "Ground Zero," where thousands of people had died after terrorists had piloted two commercial airplanes into the World Trade Center's Twin Towers, which had collapsed. In the years since the 2001 tragedy, the country had begun to think of the site as sacred ground; in 2006, heavy construction had begun for a memorial, intended to commemorate the 2,977 killed there.[57] But in the intervening years, many had also begun to blame Islam for the deranged attack of an isolated group of extremists who identified as Muslim.

A Muslim community center in Lower Manhattan was called thoughtless, insensitive—even dangerous. In their panic, media pundits, congressional legislators, and public antagonists failed to consider the similarity between the Manhattan JCC and the Cordoba House plans, which failure resulted in widespread opposition to the project. In the face of public vitriol, the Cordoba House appellation was changed to Park51—a nod to the address—in hopes of quelling the uproar. But it also allowed for naive acquiescence to another popular label being put on the project: "the Ground Zero mosque."

With popular conflation of Islam with terrorism and the ensuing public hysteria, it is no wonder that Cordoba House—Park51, the Ground Zero mosque—would escape "the dilemmas of truth and falsehood and of being and nonbeing."[58] Additionally, in all the chaos and hand-wringing, the public did not understand the difference between a *musalla* and a mosque—or *masjid*. This confusion passed from subject to object, departing from the Confucian admonition to *call things by their right names*. I believe that the cultural dislocations of the old Burlington Coat Factory—Cordoba House, Park51, Ground Zero mosque—enable us to re-pose the conditions wherein public perception has the power to alter the identity of place.

On the one hand, *place* is bound by biopolitics—and, in the United States, the precarious ideological claim that "America is a Christian country." This assertion seemed a sufficient basis on which to question the propriety of a Cordoba House and became part of the larger debate over whether or not Ground Zero ought to be considered *sacred ground*. This terminology raises a few questions: What makes ground sacred? Is the abandoned department store building—which had suffered collateral damage as the Twin Towers fell that day in 2001—sacred ground or a profane space?

On the other hand, as the debate raged, and because use of the label "Ground Zero mosque" had become so widespread, public understanding of the Cordoba House project was distorted, and the specious ties that the project had to the September 11 tragedy were reinforced. Before long, the public had adopted the *Ground Zero mosque* label, overriding the *right name*, Cordoba House. But was the proposed structure even a *mosque*? In this way, *calling things by their right names* allows us to think about time, space, and place as "one of the pre-occupations of power."[59]

The first point to be made in our exploration of time, space, and place requires a bit of history. The Cordoba House was publicly associated with the Spanish city of Córdoba's long history of Muslim rule, which had spanned from the eighth to the thirteenth centuries CE. This link was underscored by right-wing pundit Newt Gingrich and others.[60] As we discussed in the introduction, the Córdoba Mosque was around this same time at the center of public debate after a local bishop had enjoined the public to cease acknowledging its history as a mosque and instead refer to it solely as a Christian space of worship. Above all, I want to suggest that the false appraisal of the Cordoba House in Manhattan resides in the "far reaches of [history] which hold the greatest potential to illuminate the nature of thought, because the [Córdoba Mosque dispute] express[es] nothing but thought."[61]

In their opposition to the plans for Cordoba House, detractors disregarded the fact that the facility was intended to serve real people. Between the "stubborn visual associations linking Muslims [to the fall of Córdoba with] . . . the practice of Islam . . . with perceptions of Muslims and Islam [that] are often shaped by the media," the community needs that the center would have fulfilled were ignored.[62] Obviously the callbacks to Muslim rule in Europe did "not serve as a norm . . . in trying to uncover . . . discursive practices insofar as they give rise to a corpus of knowledge."[63] Rather, they were used disingenuously to stoke xenophobic resentments and fears. The negative commentary about Cordoba House stubbornly failed to account for time, space, and place—the history of Córdoba, Spain—and was instead largely prejudiced by the language of "difference." The language of difference is often used to manufacture public consent and public doubt.

The second point to be made in our exploration of time, space, and place is that in their desire to foster public doubt in the project, opponents failed to shift the discourse away from blatant Orientalist tropes. The public perception of Cordoba House was fabricated knowledge, woven of rhetoric, stereotypes, and bias. In other words, they failed to raise legitimate grounds for concern. As early as 1981, Edward Said was drawing our attention to the fact that the "negative images of Islam continue to be very much more prevalent than any others, reducing Islam to not what it is . . . but to what prominent sectors of a particular society take it to be."[64] As the battle over the "project moved to center stage, it occupied the headlines of major newspapers and becoming the buzz on talk shows, news reports and websites around the nation and the world."[65] The media frenzy over the plans to build Cordoba House correspond to another setback to the freedoms of Muslim Americans and to calm, rational discourse: It seems almost certain that, since its passage in 2001—a mere forty-five days after the towers fell, while the rubble of the World Trade Center still burned—the Patriot Act has been instrumental in marginalizing Muslims in America. In the tumultuous post–9/11 era, the US Muslim community was targeted, as anti-Islamic sentiment grew and the Muslim community was forced to grow wary and vigilant. One bombastic Christian preacher even threatened to stage a massive "global" Qur'an burning—which would have proven a horrifying insult to Muslim sensibilities.

The third point to be made in our exploration of time, space, and place is that, in the competing arguments for and against the building of Cordoba House, the opponents weaponize the language of denunciation and the project's "relationship to the city.... This relationship bears upon questions of architecture's disciplinary autonomy, its agency in the change and transformation of the city, and the possibility of its politics."[66] In this case, we can see the importance of other types of urban spaces and places. However, the planned facility's proximity to Ground Zero made the project's detractors even more suspicious of the true nature of Cordoba House, and this facade of suspicion undercut and hindered the likelihood that it could ever be viewed as valuable to the entire lower Manhattan community.

Underscoring the above points, we also know that one mosque—Masjid Farah—was founded in 1985 in the vicinity, on West Broadway, about twelve blocks from Ground Zero. In fact, the vacant Burlington Coat Factory space was being used by the Masjid Farah community as a spillover prayer space long before opposition to Cordoba House erupted.[67] The erasure of this knowledge and the inclusion of the *musalla* in the Cordoba House proposal promoted the public perception of resemblances to something exotic, suspicious, dangerous.

But additional questions remain: How are mosques and prayer spaces publicly received, and how do they give rise to biopolitical preoccupation with place? In the wake of the controversy, the perception that emerged about Cordoba House demonstrates that "when modes come into existence, they acquire extensive parts. They acquire a size and duration: each mode endures as long as its parts remain in the relation that characterizes it."[68] In other words, the production of space/place has biopolitical significance, as does the public meaning that was attached to Cordoba House—and, more precisely, to "the part that characterizes it," the *intra muros* musalla.

Political scientists David S. Gutterman and Andrew R. Murphy argue that to call the Cordoba House "a mosque seems to inappropriately substitute a part [the *musalla*] for the whole in a manner that obscures rather than illuminates the proposed . . . many purposes. After all, "in conventional usage *mosque* tends to be used analogously to other houses of worship (e.g., *churches, synagogues, temples, and mosques*) where the performance of rituals and the conduct of worship represents the primary activity taking place onsite."[69]

In an attempt to quiet the hysteria, liberal pundit Keith Olbermann expressed his thoughts on the narrative of the Ground Zero mosque thus:

> There is no training ground for terrorists. There is no insult to the victims of 9/11. There is no tribute to medieval Muslim subjugation of The West. There is, in fact, no "Ground Zero mosque." It isn't a mosque.
>
> A mosque is a Muslim holy place in which only worship can be conducted. What is planned for . . . Park Place, New York City, is a Community Center. It's supposed to include a basketball court. And a [culinary] school. It's to be thirteen stories tall and the top two stories will be a Muslim prayer space.[70]

Olbermann's commentary calls out the rhetorical weaponization of the appellation "Ground Zero mosque" meant to otherize Cordoba House and to awaken bigotry and fear. Additionally, the controversy shows how prejudices and biopolitics are omnipresent and enable the public discourse; it highlights the biopolitics while recalling the forms of power relationships and the ideological conflicts underlying the question of *place*.[71] This would mean that the freedom to build must be bargained for.

It is perhaps in this manner that Cordoba House paved the way for a discursive interpretation of place. It must not be forgotten that even while the parts of the Cordoba House were to be largely used for public and nonreligious activities, it was the *musalla* that had provoked use of the term "Ground Zero mosque." This observation takes us to remarks made by Supreme Court Justice John Paul Stevens—which would appear to take a rational view of the controversy:

> I suspect that many New Yorkers who lost friends or relatives as a result of the terrorist attack on the World Trade Center on 9/11 may have reacted to the news that Muslims are planning to erect a mosque or a religious center in the neighborhood much as I reacted to the sight of the Japanese tourists on the *Arizona*. Perhaps some of them may have thought: "This is no place for a mosque; Muslims killed innocent Americans here; they should build their places of worship in Afghanistan or Iraq or anywhere else, but not here."
>
> But then, after a period of reflection, some of those New Yorkers may have had second thoughts . . . the Muslims planning to build the mosque are not responsible for what an entirely different group of Muslims did on 9/11.[72]

I end this discussion of place where we started: with the Confucian admonition to *call things by their right names*. At Ground Zero, a new battle has since emerged, about whether or not to call the site a "sacred" place, when we know that the active place-making infrastructure remains governed by zoning laws, micro-powers, and governmentality and that infrastructure can be readily disenfranchised by the rhetorical power of the public discourse.[73] In other words, who has the prerogative to determine the "sacred" from the "profane"?

As on September 13, 2001, crews worked to clear the mounds of rubble that had once been the Twin Towers, they discovered a section of steel beam enjoined with a column, which "became known as the Ground Zero Cross[;] it inspired people around the world as it was moved from site to site in Lower Manhattan . . . to the National September 11 Memorial and Museum."[74] The cross-shaped piece of wreckage was an important part of what led many to designate the ruins "sacred ground"—which would eventually give rise to questions of inclusion and exclusion when the Cordoba House project was announced. "The broader concern [was] that the project would somehow violate the Ground Zero site, and, thus, as a sign of 'respect' should be moved to a different location, an argument that was invariably articulated in 'spatial language' as groups debated the physical and spatial presence of the buildings in question, their relative proximity, and even the shadows they cast."[75]

Religious studies scholar Jeanne Halgren Kilde notes that "almost immediately after the attacks, then-mayor of New York City Rudolph Giuliani publicly termed the site 'sacred ground,' and the phrase was repeated over and over in the press. But what did the term 'sacred' mean with respect to this site? What is 'sacred ground'—or, in the more common parlance, 'sacred space'?"[76] This attraction to "sacred ground" may be attributed to an enduring and unrequited longing to attach transcendent meaning to a place of horror and tragedy. But "instead, it is a single-minded condition, a state of fixation or obsession [with the cross and with Christianity], the inextricable companion . . . to maintain either appearances or its own boundaries . . . (and so, distracted) . . . exceeds itself and the boundaries of the ordinary world—its meanings."[77]

Lee Leviter's essay "The Myth of Christian Innocence Reinforces Anti-Semitism" painfully illustrates the ways in which rhetoric has led to the erasure of the Jewish identity, but his observations can be easily applied to Islam and other faiths. Citing Paul Kivel's *Living in the Shadow of the Cross*, Leviter explains "that this erasure is part of 'Christian hegemony,' and the notion that Christian values and ideas dominate every aspect of American life . . . that this domination operates through common ideas rooted in Christian thought, through the personal power of individual members of the clergy, and through networks of churches and church affiliates."[78] Kivel's account would suggest that a society's ability to understand themselves and the history of the present is necessarily biased or fabricated and unlikely to provide the "will to truth," meaning it is even less likely to serve as a repository of knowledge.

In the same manner, scholars of rhetoric Ekaterina V. Haskins and Justin P. DeRose write that "given the iconic status of the Twin Towers, it is not surprising that the bulk of popular and critical discourses over the future of Ground Zero has dwelt on how best to restore the wounded skyline and to fill the gaping hole in lower Manhattan. Although the issues of urban development and economic revival are bound to influence the destiny of Ground Zero, the symbolic and political value of commemoration after 9/11 is also likely to impact the design of the memorial on the site of the tragedy."[79]

Admittedly, the cultural and religious values between the East and West—between Christianity and Islam—fundamentally differ in the public perception. But what concerns me most is the rhetoric coming from the demagogues of power and the characterizations that underline the everyday practice of Muslims in America, their *doxa*, and their established norms, that the rhetoric must deride so that the so-called American values can be implicitly extolled and ultimately reinforced. It is clear, for instance, that the prime test of place resides in biopolitical shifts.

It is for this reason that I have undertaken this critique of Cordoba House as an urban site that can be interpreted as evincing a political disposition. Furthermore, the project's opponents believed that the "spaces of experience" has been intimately linked to diaspora, to the multicultural, transhistorical, and transglobal flow of Islam's cultural and religious practices in the United States. These commonly held views are often merged with prejudice about racial and religious identity when the demagogues see it fit to exploit the sensibilities attached to diaspora and identity politics. For instance, consider the political propositions drawn in Amy Waldman's American Book Award–winning novel, *The Submission*: "When word leaks that the winning choice [for the Ground Zero memorial] was designed by a Muslim [architect], a nationwide uproar follows, reminiscent of the real-life one . . . over plans to build a mosque near ground zero. The jury is dismissed as a bunch of elitist Manhattan artists, oblivious to the nation's feelings."[80]

Space/place is never neutral, and thus it reiterates the battle for self-representation. The opponents of self-determination no longer recognize Cordoba House and certainly its place in Lower Manhattan. The vitriolic language of antimosque sycophants used against Cordoba House was again to reemerge, this time in Rutherford County, Tennessee, where a dispute over land use pitted the local Muslim community against vocal opposition.

Murfreesboro, Tennessee: Opprobrious Language

In *The Zoning of America*, environmental law scholar Michael Allen Wolf writes that a particular 1926 Supreme Court case—*Euclid v. Ambler*—elucidates the validity of place "as a central component of our land use regulatory regime [that] has continued to evolve since its origins during the opening decades of the twentieth century." *Euclid*'s critics, Wolf is quick to note—planners and architects, the proponents of "smart growth" and "new urbanism"—consider the Court's decision for the plaintiff "primitive" and a great contributor to urban sprawl.[81]

Sixty-one years after the *Euclid* decision, scholar of constitutional law Mark W. Cordes wrote of the case's reverberations: it "involved a challenge to a comprehensive zoning ordinance in its totality, alleging that the restrictions imposed on the claimant's land violated substantive due process. The court viewed zoning as a form of economic and social legislation and stated that a zoning ordinance would be unconstitutional only if it was 'clearly arbitrary and unreasonable, having no substantial relation to the public health, safety, morals, or general welfare.'"[82]

For later writers, such as political scientist Kathleen Moore, the problem of place provides an opportunity for a sociopolitical critique of zoning and the adverse conditions of distance and proximity. Moore's 1995 study *Al-Mughtaribūn: American Law and the Transformation of Muslim Life in the United States* underscores the fact that the micropolitical discourse did not begin with the tragic events of September 11, 2001. In "There Goes the Neighborhood: Mosques in American Suburbs," chapter 6 of her volume, Moore explores multiple instances of zoning irregularities, drawing particular attention to two cases, originating in Rochester, New York, and Freemont, California, before the 2000 passage of the Religious Land Use and Institutionalized Persons Act.[83]

What we learn from Moore is that all politics is local, and so is all land-use planning. But in early 2010, after a sign was planted in a vacant lot announcing plans for the "Future Site of Islamic Center of Murfreesboro," a firestorm erupted that consumed not only the city of Murfreesboro, Tennessee, but the national media as well, going on to became even more contentious than the Ground Zero mosque controversy, which was unfolding concurrently, about nine hundred miles northeast.[84]

This is broadly how the Ground Zero mosque controversy traveled across the Hudson River into Basking Ridge, New Jersey, and stretched its tentacles across the United States, all the way down to Murfreesboro, seat of Rutherford County, Tennessee. The vicious rhetoric that halted the Cordoba House project in Manhattan became part of a national conversation infected with Islamophobia, nativism, and xenophobia. These fights over land use and location force us to recognize the very real obstacles facing practicing Muslims in America and, more generally, the fragility of freedom of religion.

Perhaps the most provocative challenge the Islamic Center of Murfreesboro faced in this whole ordeal would be posed by four residents of Rutherford County in a brazen attempt to not only obstruct free practice of religion but deny the existence of the religion altogether. The court case that grew from the controversy remains "one of the most striking examples of anti-Muslim sentiment in land use matters," writes civil rights attorney Eric Treene. "*U.S. v. Rutherford County* [is] a RLUIPA case that the United States brought in the U.S. District Court for the Middle District of Tennessee to protect the right of the Islamic Center of Murfreesboro . . . to move into a new mosque."[85]

More precisely, antimosque proponents sought the court's consideration to stop the project after the Islamic Center of Murfreesboro received unanimous approval in May 2010 from the Rutherford County Planning Commission to build a 4,500-square-foot mosque as part of the fifty thousand-square-foot plan on Veals Road in Rutherford County, Tennessee (figure 4.1). While the site was purchased in 2009, the Muslim community had been established in Rutherford County since 1960; ICM was incorporated in 1997, and the planned facility would serve the needs of the approximately three hundred Muslim families and a cohort of Muslim students from the nearby Middle Tennessee State University.[86]

In fact, the antimosque argument is a tacit implication that the Rutherford County Planning Commission "had no discretion of initiative powers other than those expressly authorized by state statutes."[87] In this argument, the matter of the power/knowledge nexus is left open for better or for worse, and opponents of the mosque presented their case as an emotive obsession

Figure 4.1 The Islamic Center of Murfreesboro, Tennessee. Photograph. Source: Christopher McCoy.

with control and jurisdiction. In an effort to garner support, they made wide-ranging innuendoes and ad hominem references to the *shari'ah*, amplifying and animating the public debate, particularly on social media and in the press. But above all, the provocation also suggested that ownership of the land must remain alien to any rational or objective discourse or meaning that one could attach to ICM's proprietary status.

The desire for control wherein knowledge is generated through ad hominem claim making and subjugated knowledge—dominant forms of knowledge that emerge within a social order—exhorts us to take notice. In "Of Other Spaces," Foucault makes the argument that in order to understand how heterotopias acquire meaning, we need to consider how "today's anxiety concerns space in a fundamental way, no doubt much more than time. Time probably only appears as one of the possible games of distribution between the elements that are spread out in space."[88] In fact, this is exactly what Foucault means when he argues that different types of cultural, public, institutional, and discursive spaces—bath houses, cemeteries, prisons (and mosques)—push the boundaries of the power/knowledge nexus and create or juxtapose spatial relationships that are contradictory or transforming. Furthermore, within the ambit of an effective power/knowledge critique, even with the provocation of the publication *Mosques in America*, do the litigants really grasp the form of relations at stake?

Certainly "the enormous work of [twentieth-century French philosopher] Gaston Bachelard and the descriptions of the phenomenologists have taught us that we are living not in a homogeneous and empty space but, on the contrary, in a space that is laden with [*heterotopic*] qualities, a space that may also be haunted by [the power demons]."[89] Drawing upon the power/knowledge nexus, the framework of distance and location becomes the subject of the Murfreesboro dispute and also brings into play a host of power relations.

To approach the theme of power/knowledge and the intersection of law, according to Foucault, "power exists only when it is put into action, even if, of course, it is integrated into a disparate field of possibilities brought to bear upon a permanent structure."[90] This also means that the Islamic Center of Murfreesboro was a "permanent structure" that had been functioning in Rutherford County since 1982. The controversy began after ICM "purchased land for [a community center] and applied for site-plan approval. After considering the proposal at a regularly scheduled, advertised meeting, the county approved the site plan."[91]

While it is true that "the Rutherford County Planning Commission followed the law and treated the mosque the same way it would have treated any other religious assembly," the case probes the interstices of biopolitics and power/knowledge relationships, and the legal challenges that ICM was involuntarily forced to confront. Though the Rutherford County Planning

Commission approved the site use plan at the end of May 2010, "in July, a rally by several hundred mosque opponents in the Murfreesboro square called for the construction of the mosque to be stopped."[92] Furthermore, the Rutherford County Planning Commission, the US Department of Justice, the Chancery Court, and the state's courts were drawn into a legal dispute to deal with the range of egregious acts primarily sustained by anti-Muslim sentiment. "The site was subject to vandalism, arson, and a bomb threat between 2010 and 2012."[93]

The local matters regarding the ICM case were multifaceted, since "zoning laws are sometimes used to discriminate against religious groups." It is for this reason that "RLUIPA was passed . . . to protect religious assemblies and institutions from discrimination in the land use regulation process—defined as landmarking and zoning. The law also protects against unjustifiably burdensome land use regulation . . . including those in the Muslim community."[94]

In addition, Michael Allan Wolf has noted, "hindsight makes it appear that many of the eventual abuses of zoning were not only inevitable but intentional. The historical record, however, instructs us that this appearance is deceiving."[95] Relying on the state court to settle the case would mean that the court would need facts and the defendant's lawyers' arguments would rely on such facts to make their points. The court battle was first fought under the terms of the county's site-plan approval, given the power that local zoning boards hold, and to understand the facts and conditions of the case.

The most pivotal conclusion was that when "some residents held protests and eventually filed two lawsuits against the county in September 2010 and in September 2011, seeking to halt construction of the mosque, they alleged in part that Islam is not a religion and that Muslims posed a threat to the neighborhood."[96] Emboldened by their campaign to stop the project and to challenge the county's power/knowledge, "in September 2010, four county residents sued in state's chancery court to try to stop construction of the mosque. Among the allegations were claims that there had been inadequate notice to the public under the Tennessee Open Meetings Act for the meeting that approved the mosque, that the mosque would promote terrorism and seek to overthrow the U.S. government, and that the mosque thereby posed a risk to the safety of the community."[97] So, the question remains: Can the residents' lawsuits against Rutherford County refute ICM's ownership rights over their own land?

The project's opponents made two assertions in their legal argument: first, "alleging a violation of their Due Process rights in approval of the mosque," and, second, "that the county should not have treated the mosque as it would have a church, because Islam is an ideology, rather than a religion, and thus a mosque is not a place of worship but a nonreligious assembly."[98] The residents' claim that Islam is not a religion but an ideology was an idiopathic avowal that ignored otherwise universal recognition of 1.9 billion adherents. Their assertion, in fact, would also suggest that, in relation to Islam, ICM is pars pro toto—a part taken from the whole, or that represents the whole. The opponents' claim that Islam is not a religion defines a wholly disparate mode of power, control, and biopolitics, which prompted the United States to submit an amicus brief, detailing what should have been the uncontroversial position that the federal courts, Congress, and the executive branch had consistently "recognized" that Islam is, indeed, "a religion."[99]

The stage was then set for a showdown between the litigants and the Department of Justice. On October 18, 2010, the DOJ filed an amicus brief—*Estes v. Rutherford County Regional Planning Commission*—with the Chancery Court for Rutherford County, Tennessee; the brief forcefully argued that Islam is a legitimate religion. Indeed, any reasonable legal strategy concerning the extensive scope of the First Amendment would be grounded in the understanding that the court's judgment cannot be based on the spurious claim that Islam is not a religion.

In any case, at first, the state judge "dismissed most of the opponents' claims but in May 2012 ruled that the county did not provide adequate notice of the approval meeting for the mosque and thus prevented the mosque from opening. In June 2012 the mosque filed suit against the county in federal court alleging religious discrimination," and the DOJ filed an objection in support of the mosque opening, "questioning the state court ruling."[100]

The county treated the chancery court decision as a restraint on ICM's rightful exercise of occupancy while ignoring the underlying legislative predicament: "the Islamic Center's goal had been to complete construction in time to hold Ramadan services in the new mosque by the start of Ramadan on July 20, 2012. The mosque was completed on July 13, but the county informed the mosque that it was bound by the chancery court order not to issue a certificate of occupancy."[101] The Department of Justice undertook an inquiry as a potential violation of the Religious Land Use and Institutionalized Persons Act and in response to the opponents' use of rhetorical language to target and undermine the self-interest of the ICM.

Soon after, "On July 18, 2012,"

> the U.S. Attorney for the Middle District of Tennessee . . . sued Rutherford County asking [the] U.S. District Court Judge . . . for an emergency order to allow worshippers into the building in time for the holy month of Ramadan, which began on July 19, 2012. This lawsuit marked the beginning of the federal court involvement in the case of the Murfreesboro Mosque. At this time, opponents of the mosque filed a motion in U.S. District Court stating that they should have been, but were not, included in the federal lawsuit filed . . . against Rutherford County.[102]

This case raises specific questions about the appropriation of land and public encounters with place making from social, religious, and cultural perspectives, "because religious traditions persist, space matters, and in thinking about sub-urban and urban space, American Muslims have been constructing mosques and Islamic centers for several decades now in towns, cities and neighborhoods where they reside."[103] The Islamic Center of Murfreesboro ultimately won their suit, despite further appeals and new lawsuits put forth by their opponents, which prolonged the litigation through June 2014, at which point the last lawsuits were finally dismissed by the federal courts.

No obvious attempt was made by the opponents to remedy their own understanding of Islam in terms of accepting the legitimate presence of the ICM's location and the communal need for religious accommodation. But above all, the claim of four litigants that Islam is not a religion attempts to erase Islam's 1.9 billion adherents and to test the modes of domination and subjectivation. The issue as interpreted by the chancery courts was whether or not Rutherford County's approval was still valid despite the litigants' assertion that Islam is not a religion. However, "after final inspection, Rutherford County issued a certificate of occupancy, and on Aug. 10, 2012, the Muslim community in Murfreesboro entered their new mosque for the first time for prayer."[104]

Consistent with Foucault's methodological orientation, the ideological and biopolitical frameworks for thinking about ICM, and the "forms of community control, surveillance, administration and formation of populations of human individuals . . . these apparatuses of power are linked in a constitutive interdependence."[105] This understanding has exhorted geographer and environmental scholar Gordon L. Clark to argue "that the doctrine of local matters is incredibly fragile." In his treatise *Judges and Cities*, Clark appeals to the idea that "in general, local matters [are] best understood as a rhetorical device used to justify juridical discretion."[106]

While Clark's interpretations may be valid, they also show that "land use controls are caught in a swirling snowstorm of ideological, political, legal and popular controversy."[107] By focusing on biopolitics and the power/knowledge nexus—and especially the RLUIPA—we offer another caveat to Clark's interpretation: the impact of uneven spatial mobility. More precisely, uneven mobility can be understood as a contingent form of relations among sites (and often a contested form of control) and a contributor to the vicissitudes of biopolitics.

Thus, one of the main purposes of the RLUIPA is to go beyond a limited history of religious land uses that affect synagogues, temples, and mosques and that has traditionally narrowed down to a static understanding of the First Amendment Establishment Clause. RLUIPA offers insights as to how the courts and litigants might grasp "other spaces" used for communal or religious interaction even if it means examining the limits of police power and the failures of zoning ordinances. Above all, in reviewing the "police" power of the planning board or a litigant's complaint, the initiation of a lawsuit points to the different moments of the legal process that are the basis of RLUIPA.

These reservations aside, with the 2000 passage of the RLUIPA, groups like the ICM were given a chance to remedy the adverse claims made by their opponents; "the land use section codifies the constitutional protections for religious freedom and against religious discrimination provided under the free exercise clause, the Free Speech Clause, and the Equal Protection Clause and provides [the] mechanism for the protection of these rights."[108]

Despite the urge to ignore the ugly bias and egregious acts that can so often offend the religious devout, the Murfreesboro decision shows how US law can be wielded for the "protection for religious freedom and against religious discrimination." RLUIPA "Section 2(a) prohibits land use regulations that impose a 'substantial burden' on the religious exercise of a person or institution, unless the government can show that it has a 'compelling interest' for imposing the burden and that the regulations further that interest in the least restrictive way."[109] This designation seems to be important to showing why antidiscrimination policies are adopted and recognizes that the legal frameworks for thinking about religious land use that have governed criticism since 2000 are inseparable from the context of racial and social justice and civil rights—and, more recently, the burgeoning xenophobic propaganda, political rhetoric, and nativist ideology pervasive in the United States.

Furthermore, in their 2012 report, "Controversies Over Mosques and Islamic Centers Across the U.S," the Pew Research Center confirms that the greatest obstacles faced by communities seeking to build a mosque—"the same objections that often greet churches and other houses of worship"—or acquire land are micropolitics, communal attitudes, and egregious forms of discrimination, coupled with a lack of trust in the planning process.[110]

In our discussion of the Murfreesboro case, we have attempted to challenge asymmetrical notions of place and the imposition of a *mute* contestation. And yet the question remains: What conclusions can be drawn from the use of such opprobrious language and from these egregious forms of contestation? What does it say about those who opposed the placement of the Islamic center? There is certainly more to explore here, so our concluding remarks provide a final reflection by focusing on mobility justice.

What might a further critique into mobility justice look like? Sociologist Mimi Sheller explains that "uneven [spatial] mobility . . . refers to a terrain, the built environment, and the ways in which [public] space . . . may be splintered in ways that connect some places while disconnecting others."[111] That is, the codification of the law may be touched by the better angels of our nature, but it's humans who will apply the law, and often imperfectly. One way of understanding *uneven spatial mobility* is to look at how government power is wielded in a given community: do the community's police power and its micro-power regimes make it difficult if not virtually impossible to extend the concept of empathy to out-groups? ICM had to take legal action to protect itself from Murfreesboro's biased protection of—and the ensuing disconnecting effects of—their entire community's First Amendment rights. Oftentimes, "othered" groups in the United States—especially non-Christian faith communities—are forced to resort to lawsuits as their only remedy against a lack of empathy toward them and against constraints made on their spatial mobility; the courts are regularly applied to for the preservation of a biopolitical climate free of fear, dissonance, and bias. Sheller's essay offers an antidote to the fundamental divergences that have emerged in the Murfreesboro case over distance, proximity, and location.

The adversaries who want to control access or restrict spatial mobility will no doubt continue their efforts, but the intervention of the Department of Justice provided the necessary "juridical power" to combat their aims. Furthermore, because the Murfreesboro case also speaks to acts of oppression and xenophobia, "the term juridical [power] describes an arrangement and a representation of power rather than the law. . . . Modern law operates between Foucault's concepts of government and discipline. It provides a key way in which government decisions can adjust the relationships between disciplinary institutions."[112]

In summary, in the foregoing discussion we saw how various attempts have been made to come to grips with the benefits and challenges of location, which are perhaps most acute in rural America, where for the most part immigrant adherents make up the majority of the mosque population. Put simply, while a mosque's place raises questions of xenophobic attitudes, the resulting bigoted behavior is perhaps an indication of what Tocqueville had already described in 1835: He concluded his magnum opus, *Democracy in America*, "by observing that God favored democracy because it was more just; this stood as Tocqueville's ultimate endorsement of the democratic revolution. So even the broad shape of his argument reveals how closely religion fits into his thinking."[113]

Such thinking prevails today among right-wing factions, evangelicals, and nativists, and it is most present in churches for a single purpose: coupling patriotic hysteria with religious fervor. Yet it is also worth noting that, despite Tocqueville's admiration for the power that religion can extend over a society, "*Democracy in America* cites and criticizes two different examples of the religious power moving beyond its sphere and intruding in the political and social realm: Puritanism and Islam." Tocqueville "found many of the

[Puritan] efforts to legislate behavior offensive; such things, he wrote, 'shame the human spirit.'"[114]

But what about the inclusion of non-Christian faiths that upon moving into places like Murfreesboro are taken to be hostile? Or, to put it another way, are the dominant white Christian folks likely to coinhabit spaces with those who do not look like them religiously, socially, or culturally? This characteristic of suburban life is in fact "*simulacral* space that is doubtless the still-hidden contemporary locus . . . [of contestation] but this space of the double, this hollow of the *simulacrum* is where Christianity became enchanted with its Demon, and where the Greeks feared the glittering presence of the gods with their arrows. Distance and proximity of the same, where we others now find our only language."[115]

Tocqueville tells us that in their minds they completely confuse Christianity and freedom, a conclusion enabling him to avoid judging how sincerely Christian Americans are. "Americans believe religion to be useful, but it will appear to be useful only if they believe in it because it is true, rather than as a political institution. Religion cannot be 'well understood' in the manner of self-interest." Tocqueville "was even more severe, condemning Islam for setting forth not only religious doctrine but also specific social and political arrangements and even scientific theories. That intrusive nature, he stated bluntly, disqualified Islam for any role in modern democratic society."[116] In his avowal, Tocqueville sets his critique on religion, philosophy, and politics but discounts Islam's scientific contribution to the development of the Western world.[117]

Mathematician Nikos A. Salingaros reminds us that "stubborn and non-correcting behaviors have of course been documented throughout history, though this has not made the slightest difference to their continued misapplication. Philosophers have known for a long time that human beings are not rational, confusing as we do abstraction with reality. Friedrich Nietzsche cynically and perceptively observed, 'Men believe in the truth of anything so long as they see that others strongly believe it is true.'"[118] So, the main point to be gleaned from these events is that the opponent's opprobrium is clearly reflected in the avowal that *Islam is not a religion*.

At the outset I pointed out how Foucault's power/knowledge nexus and the particularities of juridical power interrogate these complex exchanges and divergences—that is, power/knowledge offers a discursive strategy. It is quite "possibly the most often quoted part of the Foucauldian legacy . . . the analysis of power relations as fundamental to social relations and our knowledge of the world and ourselves. It informs an array of [discursive] techniques, and these [components] converge in what Foucault . . . emphasizes as his main interest: *subjectivity*, i.e., the way we relate to ourselves: 'I am such and such a person who acts in such and such ways.'"[119]

As we have imagined, in the manner of "subjectivity" the sub-rosa argument is implicitly about racial profiling with the ultimate aim of stymying any form of consent that may be perceived to be a legitimization of the adherents of Islam. Likewise, the opprobrium is inseparable from the racialization and burgeoning xenophobic attitudes that have become widespread in the aftermath of the terrorist attacks of September 11. Together, these forms of subjectivity are a common accumulation of the epistemic effects of the power/knowledge nexus, and, as we will discover in the Basking Ridge case, the will to truth "does not prevent the possibility that consent may be a condition for the existence or the maintenance of power."[120]

Basking Ridge, New Jersey: The Battle for Place

The community of Liberty Corner in Bernards Township, New Jersey, "traced its name back to the American Revolution, and the whole town took great patriotic pride in the role it had played in the independence struggle, as a stronghold for George Washington's army" (figure 4.2).[121] In 2011, in search of a prayer space for their expanding community, the Islamic Society of nearby Basking Ridge, New Jersey, purchased a property in Liberty Corner. "Not too far from the proposed location for the mosque, in the yard of its Presbyterian church, founded in 1717, stood an ancient tree known as the 'Holy Oak,' where Washington is said to have picnicked with the Marquis de Lafayette."[122] The National Register of Historic Places says that "Liberty Corner is in many ways a typical crossroads hamlet, centered among gently

Figure 4.2 Washington Tavern, Basking Ridge, New Jersey. Photograph. Source: Library of Congress.

rolling agricultural lands with a strong rural character. The town's center is formed by a tiny triangular green at the intersection of the . . . roads marked by a flagpole, the successor to the 'liberty pole' erected by patriotic colonists in the eighteenth century which eventually gave the village its name. The Liberty Pole site is marked by a large boulder upon which is placed a commemorative bronze tablet."[123]

At this point in our exploration of place, it will not surprise you to learn that the Islamic Society of Basking Ridge began to experience immediate pushback to their plans to found a mosque in the storied neighborhood. While I explore the oppositional discourse across the battle for Liberty Corner, the "techniques of subjugation" are weighted toward the power/knowledge nexus, "irrational groupthink," and contradictions. But the problem does not stop there. In the struggle that unfolded between the local Muslim group and their opponents, a key question remains: How did a small-town land use dispute turn into a biopolitical and ideological war with such divisive implications? Nikos A. Salingaros, architectural theorist, has attributed such behaviors to "'cognitive dissonance' . . . a state of physical anxiety to which we instinctively react in a defensive manner. We are programmed to counteract its occurrence. Studies in political science and psychology reveal strong innate mechanisms for preserving misinformation so as to avoid cognitive dissonance."[124] In other words, once we believe a thing to be true, we emotionally invest in it and are then less likely to be swayed by evidence to the contrary.

First, my goal in exploring the fight for Liberty Corner is to understand the competing interests for exclusive control underlying "one of the prime effects of power."[125] "We can understand this resistance to change within the framework of social learning and evolutionary adaptation."[126] And as Foucault has noted, "one of the prime effects of power [is] that certain bodies, certain gestures, certain discourses, certain desires, come to be identified and constituted as individuals."[127]

My second goal in this exploration is to show how the Foucauldian emphasis on discourse is important and thereby renders the differences and contradictions in the power/knowledge nexus. So we may ask to what extent the Foucauldian power/knowledge nexus helps us understand the instances of police power and Nietzsche's "the will to truth"—both of which are evident in the court case arising from the Liberty Corner dispute: *The Islamic Society of Basking Ridge v. Bernards Township*.[128]

My third goal in this discussion is best stated by Foucault: "Through the effects and the domain of the law and the oppositional discourse, power is employed and exercised by individual agents." In exploring this court case, we discover the fragility of police power—that is, "those aspects of it that are most familiar, most solid, and most intimately related to our bodies and to our everyday behavior."[129]

How to best adjudicate competing claims is not always obvious. On one level, the law is a useful tool for evaluating unequal claims and voices in the land use dispute that has claimed our attention; the law provides judicial discretion to substantive meaning, given the circumstances in a dispute. But the dispute also draws our attention to "the system of right, [and] the domain of the law, [that] are permanent agents of these relations of domination, these polymorphous techniques of subjugation."[130] Finally, in speaking about the power/knowledge nexus, it will be helpful for us to explore a few examples of intense opposition faced by religious communities—in *The Islamic Society of Boston v. Boston Herald, Inc.* and *North Jersey Vineyard Church v. Township of South Hackensack et al.*[131]

In a heightened atmosphere of Islamophobia following the September 11 terrorist attacks, in 2011 the Islamic Society of Basking Ridge (ISBR) "purchased a four-acre property in a zone where a house of worship was a 'permitted use' under the Township's zoning ordinance."[132] At another level, the power/knowledge nexus features prominently in the Liberty Corner dispute. If there is a linkage between Liberty Corner and the ISBR's decision to build the mosque, "there is in fact a built-in resistance to new ideas that do not conform to accepted practices, even when such practices are demonstrated to be failures."[133]

We can piece together the egregious conflict that emerged between the Islamic society and anti-Islamist neighbors in the court documents and in journalist Andrew Rice's piece for *The Guardian*, "The Fight for the Right to Be a Muslim in America"[134]: Court documents reveal that "in April 2012, the ISBR applied to the Bernards Township Planning Board . . . for approval of its site plan to build a modest 4,252-square-foot mosque containing a 1,594-square-foot prayer hall. That application fully complied with all zoning requirements."[135] Yet the ISBR's plan to build the mosque at Liberty Corner set off a storm of controversy and opposition from the neighbors and townsfolk. "'The neighbors near this proposed mosque did not sign up to live next to this house of worship,' said one resident, who broke down sobbing as she spoke. 'They have been members of a quiet residential neighborhood for decades, and do not look forward to having their routines and lives disrupted.'" These remarks provide valuable insight into what is considered to be forms of knowledge, that emerge as a set of distinctive temporalities or representations of location, and in so doing, "Liberty Corner considered itself separate from the older and wealthier village of Basking Ridge, though they were both part of the same larger township, and few outsiders recognized the geographical distinction."[136]

In December 2015, the town's planning board voted to reject the proposed mosque, citing inadequate parking in the area. "The township's parking ordinance specifies that one parking spot must be available for every three seats in a church. The term *church* in the municipal ordinance is defined to encompass all houses of worship, including mosques. The ISBR's original application had accommodated a maximum of 150 worshippers in its prayer hall and, accordingly, provided 50 parking spaces applying the three-to-one ratio."[137] That the township had still rejected the proposal despite the Islamic society's compliance exemplifies the police power of the township. But the battle did not end there.

In an apparent move to stymie the future construction of the mosque at Liberty Corner, the township also adopted a new ordinance that would effectively prevent the Islamic Society from building on its own site: "The proposed amendment doubled the required minimum lot size [for a house of worship] from three acres to six acres and significantly increased the standards for lot coverage, floor area ratio, and building and parking setbacks."[138] The rigid enforcement of parking restrictions has a long history of being used to exclude out-groups and constrain their mobility; thus, given its intersections with land use, parking allowance has become a longstanding controversial topic among architects and planners. "After much trial and error, the Board adopted a proposal from an objector that required a massive parking lot with 107 parking spaces. This for a congregation that, at the time of application, peaked at 65 worshippers for one weekly afternoon service."[139] The antimosque residents "confined their criticisms to the nimby issues: drainage, parking, landscaping, and the like. They convinced the board that a mosque would need more parking spaces than a church, because midday worshippers would come alone. When the Islamic Society submitted a new plan, with a larger parking lot, the mosque's opponents protested that, too. It quickly became clear that the opposition was not solely concerned with parking."[140]

Zoning ordinance as a discursive system can change and are fundamental in evaluating the architecture of an edifice and its location. Evaluating the ordinances makes up the structure of the episteme and the source of rejection and it is perhaps for this reason that the township ignored all of ISBR's proposals designed to address parking concerns, "including a proposal to split the largest weekly service into two services, similar to the practice of area churches," should parking ever become a constraint due to future growth.[141] Thus ordinances, we come to understand, exist to exclude certain buildings—therefore making them *heterotopic*, or out of place, within the conventions of acceptance. In an effort to make the proposed mosque "fit into its suburban surroundings, it had been designed to resemble a mini-mansion, with gray clapboard siding, a pitched roof with asphalt shingles, dormer windows and minarets disguised as chimneys. But the architecture did little to defuse tensions with the surrounding neighborhood."[142]

Feeling they had no other recourse, the ISBR filed a lawsuit against the township, complaining that opposition to the project "was a 'well-funded machine that was substantially grounded in anti-Muslim animus.'"[143] One of the ISBR's key grievances was that "this community opposition evolved into a well-funded machine that recruited objectors and coached them to channel their opposition through the permissible language of land use: parking, buffer and screening requirements, [storm water] management, and so on. A community group—the Bernards Township Citizens for Responsible Development—was formed specifically to oppose the mosque."[144]

Here we note how the grievance is part of the assumption the ISBR made about religion and identity in America: they had assumed free religious practice was accorded to them as to any other. Thus, while the language of the ISBR complaint is powerful, I also want to suggest opposition groups—proponents of protonational and nativist identity—within the United States nowadays use the power of social media to drive a considerable amount of exclusionary rhetoric, which alone makes us question whom the Constitution truly protects. Although social media is often called an indispensable tool, it is also a political instrument. Antimosque opposition "tactics [were] once unwritten, spread through websites and word of mouth, but more recently they were set down in a book titled *Mosques in America: A Guide to Accountable Permit Hearings and Continuing Citizen Oversight.*"[145]

Over the last three decades, the "methods of handling contradictory information within settings requiring urgent action"—like in the spur of the moment reacting to a distraught and distressingly worded message shared through social media, warning of imminent danger—"while obviously appropriate at the evolutionary level of early humans, wreak havoc with our present-day rationality."[146] The social media discourse can count as legitimate knowledge, though we cannot forget that the words and images constructed there are communicated within a very specific social frame of reference.

The social media opposition to the ISBR's proposed mosque was less concerned with empathy or reason than it was motivated by Islamophobia, which, "like all prejudices, is rooted in ignorance." Emails that opponents of the mosque sent one another "contained jokes about Muslims, pigs and Barack Obama," whom one resident called "'the product of fools, raised by idiots and coddled by affirmative action. Behold the beast.'" Another resident suggested that the ISBR member who had undertaken the mosque planning couldn't possibly be "'a real moderate Muslim.'"[147] The ISBR's opposition cannot be characterized as a niche group of hysterics: "a Cato Institute survey found that 47% of all Republicans—and a quarter of Americans overall—would support a ban on building new mosques in their communities."[148]

Once a falsehood or misrepresentation of the truth has been shared, its capacity to affect, distort, or even completely shut down the discourse remains dependent on a multitude of deceptive details that can contribute to its power. With the hateful language swirling among the ISBR mosque's opponents, "something else deeper and darker seemed to be at work. Some residents openly discussed Islamophobic conspiracy theories, such as the idea that the mosque was meant to send a message of conquest, due to its proximity to the town's September 11 memorial. Such crackpot notions promoted by far-right ideologues . . . used to be confined to the margins of the internet." But, as we recall from the Murfreesboro discussion, "there is, literally, an anti-mosque playbook" backing "the theory that Muslims are engaged in a secret plot to impose sharia law on the US." The book *Mosques in America* calls itself "a 'how-to manual for patriotic Americans who are ready to counter the leading edge of Islamic supremacism.'"[149]

The ISBR realized that their opposition wasn't truly worried about inadequate parking. In their complaint, they wrote how "Congress noted that zoning laws often place the ability of religious groups to assemble for worship 'within the complete discretion of land use regulators,' who often have 'virtually unlimited discretion in granting or denying permits for land use and in other aspects of implementing zoning laws.' RLUIPA's Senate sponsors also observed that 'churches and synagogues cannot function without a physical space adequate to their needs and consistent with their theological requirements.'"[150] Again, this was not a case of citizens impassioned about law enforcement and rigid adherence to local statutes. This was a case of bigotry wielding capricious interpretation of the law for its own ends.

Part of the reason that otherwise neutral or even well-intended regulations can be so misused "has to do with the country's labyrinthine land-use laws, which leave most control to state and local governments, which are in turn vulnerable to the furies of angry mobs. Part of it has to do with America's love of litigation. The inherently confrontational and intrusive legal process had a radicalising effect on [Liberty Corner], driving some opponents of the development to extremes."[151] The resulting firestorm of Islamophobia, which in an earlier age of less virtual connectivity might have petered out over time, was fanned by newer technologies enabling the instantaneous transfer of information. The antimosque opponents' hateful language and misinformation could be immediately and thoughtlessly shared, creating a self-reinforcing atmosphere of aggression and fear.

In their "zeal to prevent ISBR from establishing [the mosque]," the defendants also realized "that a simple denial of Plaintiffs' application would have allowed for a renewed application. Accordingly, defendants also changed the rules wholesale."[152] They introduced zoning ordinances that—as is often the case with many such rules in the United States—were primarily biopolitical in intent. "By its very nature, therefore, zoning tolerates imprecision. That is, it does not regulate land based on the actual external effects generated by a particular use, but upon generalizations about the anticipated impact of that type of use. This inevitably results in some imprecision, since a particular use might be more or less compatible with its surroundings than is normal for that category of use."[153]

Drawing upon this history of zoning used for biopolitical exclusion, economist Richard Rothstein notes that "other influential zoning experts made no effort to conceal their expectation that zoning was an effective means of racial exclusion. . . . Ernst Freund, the nation's leading authority on administrative law in the 1920s, observed that preventing 'the coming of colored people into a district' was actually a 'more powerful' reason for the spread of zoning during the previous decade than creation of single-family districts, the stated justification for zoning."[154] Zoning ordinances, in other words, have never been neutral.

The ISBR had originally assumed the township was acting in good faith, however. "When ISBR submitted its original plan to the board,"

> the only rule Bernards Township had to govern how much parking space they needed to provide was a provision in the local zoning ordinance. The rule says that for "churches, auditoriums and theaters . . . 1 space for every 3 seats or 1 space for every 24 linear inches of pew space is sufficient." Because . . . the Society hoped to one day cater to 150 congregants, their plan provided for 50 parking spaces, more than twice as many as would have been necessary at the time. The piece of land they purchased for three-quarters of a million dollars was also located and sized with this in mind.[155]

With the township's strategic change in zoning regulations, the ISBR was beginning to confront the board's will to truth. And "instead of waving ISBR's proposal through, like they'd always done with submissions for Christian churches and the town's two synagogues, [the township] sent the Society back to the drawing board with changes they had to make and then, when they returned, demanded changes to the changes. They kept the scam going for three and a half years and 39 hearings, vastly more than any other applicant had to endure . . . in the form of parking requirements."[156]

Basking Ridge is a wealthy, educated, and gentrified community, attracting the upper class, the nouveau riche, and, it must be said, white Christians. All too often, it has closed ranks to protect the status of the townsfolk by encoding strict enforcement of zoning principles meant to exclude, which "may well have had a racial intent."[157] Zoning restrictions used for gatekeeping is quite common, writes Richard Rothstein, since historically, zoning has had "two faces. One face, developed in part to evade a prohibition on racially explicit zoning, attempted to keep African Americans out of white neighborhoods by making it difficult for lower-income families, large numbers of whom were African Americans, to live in expensive white neighborhoods. The other attempted to protect white neighborhoods from deterioration by ensuring that [unwanted building types—like mosques, synagogues, and temples] could not locate in them."[158]

The ISBR was beginning to understand the game being played. But their opponents and the township would not admit to any ulterior, racial motives and instead persisted in treating the Islamic society as bad actors. "By the perverse logic of the mosque opponents, it was the Islamic Society that had brought discrimination upon itself, by suing over discrimination. There was only one thing the Muslims could do to prove themselves worthy neighbors: go somewhere else."[159]

As in the case of the mosque opposition in Murfreesboro, Tennessee, where the Islamic community was hit with lawsuits, protests, and even an arson attack, the Department of Justice intervened on behalf of the Islamic Society of Basking Ridge, citing noncompliance with the Religious Land Use and Institutionalized Persons Act, which "specifically bans local governments from discriminating against religious organizations when it comes to land use."[160] In 2016, the DOJ filed a lawsuit in which they claimed that in rejecting the mosque plans, the township had violated the ISBR's rights.[161]

"The township," the suit conceded, "has the authority to regulate and restrict the use of land and structures within its borders."[162] But, the DOJ contended—and the court agreed—the township's shifts in strategy, alteration of regulations, and delays in the ISBR mosque approval process had been unprecedented, resulting in the violation of the ISBR's First Amendment rights. "On 31 December 2016, a federal judge issued a preliminary decision in the Basking Ridge case, finding that the planning board had exercised 'unbridled and unconstitutional discretion' in requiring the mosque to have more parking than other houses of worship."[163]

As the court has noted, "this case arises from the purported religious discrimination by Bernards Township against a local Islamic society, ISBR, in connection with a site plan approval application to build a mosque. Defendants allegedly engaged in impermissible discriminatory conduct following receipt of ISBR's application dated April 20, 2012, until they ultimately denied ISBR's application on January 19, 2016."[164] Tocqueville reminds us that democracy "brought its own potential benefits and dangers. The moral responsibility for promoting the first and avoiding the second rested with human beings."[165]

The opposition had "accused Muslims of deception," while "the Islamic Society, in its lawsuit, alleged that many of the neighbors were presenting a false front, using preservationist sentiment to disguise their real, less respectable fears."[166] For example, Nikos A. Salingaros has written of biases and our blindness to them: "Human physiology can lead people who have acquired false beliefs to stubbornly persist in holding them. Intelligent persons conform to irrational groupthink, employing a stock of tools to fight against any idea that conflicts with those already held."[167] And so the power holders, who are just as subject to irrational biases and blindness to them, can wield their authority and call it fairness and upholding the law; it is the less powerful who suffer.

Exploring this growing emphasis on power and domination as it occurs in relation to other minority communities helps us understand institutional authority and power. Enmeshed in these circumstances—the societal contingencies and particularly racial and political currents—authority and power are connected in complex ways. As author Richard Rothstein notes in *The Color of Law*, "Only in 2015, after the murder of nine black church members by a white supremacist youth in Charleston did the trustees of Clemson University adopt a resolution dissociating themselves from [Benjamin] Tillman's 'campaign of terror against African Americans in South Carolina that included intimidation and violence.' But the trustees can't take his name off [campus's Tillman Hall] unless the state legislature authorizes it, and the legislature has not done so."[168] Even as perspective and the historical narrative shifts, once-lionized figures may with the passage of time come to be despised, but it's the power holders who determine who gets enshrined and who gets kicked out of the neighborhood.

In hindsight, we can call Bernards Township's opposition to the Islamic Society of Basking Ridge *religious discrimination*. Perhaps one of the keys necessary to "successfully" discriminating is wielding police power, which is also a form of effective control Foucault addresses: "They are the manifold relations of power which permeate, characterize and constitute the social body, and these relations of power cannot themselves be established, consolidated nor implemented without the production, accumulation, circulation and functioning of a discourse."[169]

This dispute was local, and yet it is a microcosm of the biopolitical struggle for justice and equality being waged throughout the United States—a struggle "to ensure, sustain and multiply life, to put this life in order."[170]

ON THE SUBJECT AND POWER

Writing about "The Subject and Power," Foucault states that, "as far as this power is concerned, it is first necessary to distinguish that which is exerted over things and gives the ability to modify, use, consume, or destroy them—a power which stems from attitudes directly inherent in the body or relayed by external instruments."[171] I believe that we have adequately demonstrated the biopolitical contestations in Starkville, Murfreesboro, and Basking Ridge. It is obvious that biopolitical power permeates "the production of truth" and that, as Foucault has noted, the problem is, rather, "what rules of right are implemented by the relations of power in the productions of discourses of truth?"[172]

On the one hand, place "is no longer merely the economic object of land, nor a static terrain, but . . . a vibrant entity, within its frontiers, with its specific qualities."[173] On the other hand, biopolitics is a critical discussion with a view to changing the way we think about what it takes to ensure the life of a community and to put life in order—that is, what methods are used to control public spaces and places of communal gathering.

Accordingly, Foucault notes that "we are subjected to the production of truth through power, and we cannot exercise power except through the production of truth." Perhaps among the key aspects of place—which is also a form of effective body/space control—are the "manifold relations of power which permeate, characterize and constitute the social body, and these relations of power cannot themselves be established, consolidated nor implemented without the production, accumulation, circulation and functioning of a discourse."[174]

Let us take as our first example the conflict in Starkville, Mississippi, in which the city's Board of Aldermen denied the Islamic Center a waiver to establish a mosque within city limits, instead attempting to banish them to an *extra muros* location. The board's rules seem to have been arbitrarily applied, as, according to court documents, the rules used to exclude the Islamic Center were not enforced against Maranatha House, a student organization where Christian worship takes place, located right next door to the Islamic Center's proposed location within the city, at 204 Herbert Street. In addition, Maranatha House's membership was twice as large as the Islamic Center's, they had half as many parking spaces as the Islamic Center had allotted for their own facility, and Maranatha House's services were quite audible from the street. Furthermore, the city had not prohibited the parking of cars on the street for Maranatha House members, although when explaining its refusal to allow the Islamic Center to occupy a facility within city limits, "it argued that on-street parking is not permitted on Herbert Street."[175]

In aggregate, is this not the city's attempt to rob the Islamic Center of its lawful rights? These facts make it clear that the city's ordinances and bias policies are discriminatory. As sociologist Ali Rattansi notes, "the justification of hostility and discrimination on grounds of culture [and religion] . . . is mostly a rhetorical ploy . . . that has gradually been established in Western liberal democracies."[176] In other words, the high ideals of democracy are skirted with obfuscation and misrepresentation.

The conflation of Islamophobia and biopolitics in the Murfreesboro case shows how "inevitably ... the term 'racism' has also become subject to social forces and political conflict."[177] In their attempt to identify Islam as hostile to their own territory—the South, the Bible Belt—the antimosque opposition took the form of a rhetorical opprobrium: *Islam is not a religion*. Islam, they insisted, in the face of the facts, is an ideology and therefore cannot qualify for the legal rights granted to a church or Christian community. The opprobrium was meant to banish the Muslim community.

We must also remember that "the 'good' life recruited subjects as if for their own benefit inciting them to internalize a discipline [Christianity] that visibly subjected them to its account of what constituted the good."[178] On the other hand, the anecdote of the drunken fellow and the foot-washing Baptist is a good example of the Christian rhetoric: "The drunken fellow put a gun to the head of a foot-washing Baptist in Upland Tennessee. The drunk ordered the Baptist to utter a vile imprecation regarding Jesus Christ. The Baptist was in no mood to be a martyr; in fact, he desperately wished to save his own hide. But he was a true believer, and he could not make the words pass his lips, try as he might, and his brains were blown out."[179]

But above all, this code of behavior and its form of subjectivation (and subjective knowledge) is a signifying spatial practice, and Foucault is most valuable in seeing the parallels in the triad and that "power is not a thing or a quantity we possess or lose but a relation of a struggle."[180] Is this perhaps the struggle of which Frederick Douglass spoke (figure 4.3)? And is this what Omar ibn Said and Abdul-Rahman each wrote of after they had been abducted from their homelands, transported to the United States, and enslaved?

To grasp the biopolitical issues at stake, let us take a moment to recall the history of enslaved African Muslims in the antebellum South, the historical legacy of race relations, and the struggle for equality and justice. Fula Islamic scholar Omar ibn Said (1770–1863/64) wrote that the struggle (*jihad*) resided in his heart, was spoken with his tongue, and was written with his hands, and ultimately he would use the pen (*jihad al-Qalam*) to effectively use the power of the Qur'an to condemn his treatment.[181] Likewise, Abdul-Rahman questioned the "good" men of Mississippi; they had, after all, profited off of his suffering and enslavement. His *jihad* was constituted by speaking about the New Testament, its laws, and the will to truth.

By the year 1831—the year of Nat Turner's Rebellion and the year that Tocqueville landed in New England—African Muslims had been a vivid presence among the enslaved in Mississippi and the South for over two hundred years. It was also in 1831 that Omar ibn Said penned his autobiography during his enslavement on the Owen estate in North Carolina (figure 4.4). *The Life of Omar ibn Said* provides an occasion for rethinking rhetorical strategies of spirituality to challenge the dichotomies of servitude and freedom.[182]

Figure 4.3 Frederick Douglass. Photograph. Source: Library of Congress.

By quoting *al-Mulk* (Q. 67, The Dominion) in the opening of his autobiography—to contrast his servile condition as a slave to all humanity's servile condition to Allah—Omar ibn Said reveals and undermines the mendacity of slavery. It was precisely his recognition of the fact that servitude was an aberrant practice that gave him the opportunity to find an escape from the torture and subjugation of his mental and physical condition. By turning the narrative

Figure 4.4 Omar ibn Said. Photograph. Source: Beinecke Rare Book and Manuscript Library, Yale University.

of his autobiography into an epistemological tool against the unlawfulness of slavery, Omar provided a new framework for understanding the human struggle and experience. While the details of his *jihad* are unclear, it is worth noting here that classical jurists had distinguished four ways by which the believer could fulfill *jihad* obligation against injustice and oppression: by the heart (secretly opposing), the tongue (by speaking), the hands (by writing), and the sword (in combat in a just war).[183]

Similarly, West African Muslim prince Abdul-Rahman ibn Ibrahim Sori had been forced into servitude in Natchez, Mississippi, for forty years before he was able to return to West Africa with the help of abolitionist sympathizers. Like Omar ibn Said, Abdul-Rahman had personally suffered through the egregious conditions of slavery. He had to know the power of the servile estate, and this made him highly skeptical of Christianity—which precepts slaveholders used to justify their actions. A copy of the New Testament translated into Arabic had been given to him (just as an Arabic-translated Bible had been given to Omar), and after reading it, Abdul-Rahman said, "I tell you the Testament very good law; you follow it you no pray often enough; you greedy after money." Was the scripture given to him a byproduct of biopolitical power and subjugated knowledge? Considering the profoundly moral and religious vision of his own faith, at the very least, Abdul-Rahman's statements are evidence of his resistance and conviction: "You good man; you join the religion. . . . See you want more land, more neegurs [sic *niggas*]; you make neegurs work hard make more cotton. . . . Where you find dat in your law?"[184]

With this condemnation, Abdul-Rahman clearly believed that a person should not be called a "good" Christian even if they say they adhere to Christian scripture yet in practice observe laws unsympathetic to freedom, justice, and human decorum.[185] His avowal introduces another view of law and justice that could have been widely held by others who had suffered slavery. Indeed, any reasonable conclusion concerning the statements of Omar ibn Said and Abdul-Rahman—and of Frederick Douglass—is perhaps found in the earliest examples of resistance to slavery and the efficacy of liberation theology. The statements of Omar and Abdul-Rahman are evidence "that any sound socio-jurisprudence turns on the analysis of what institutions of law is for, how it goes around, with one's fighting convictions."[186]

Race is still an issue despite the efforts of those who fought to pass the Civil Rights Act, the Voting Rights Act, the RLUIPA, and any number of other congressional acts introduced to combat racism. In general, one expects intellectual advocacy and action to show a somewhat similar effect in scholarship to advance the struggle that Douglass spoke of. Even the most progressive scholars of race and religion today have overlooked the Muslim presence in antebellum America, choosing instead to focus on their own Christian inklings, notwithstanding the very few publications that have emerged over the last two decades.

The subject of *place*, territory, and boundary is hardly scratched in this summary. Further research and scholarship may approach the writings of Omar ibn Said, Abdul-Rahman ibn Ibrahim Sori, and other Muslims in the United States in an entirely different manner—or at least in tandem with the current intellectual discourse. At least this brief account of Omar ibn Said and Abdul-Rahman ibn Ibrahim Sori shows how racial attitudes and stereotypes that pervaded in the antebellum South and later in the Bible Belt also existed in Starkville and Murfreesboro. These stories represent spatial differentiation, forms of exclusion, the religious status of Christianity, and an unwillingness to promote social integration.

Therefore, the arguments put forward by the antimosque opponents in the Murfreesboro case in some ways recall Foucault's arguments in *Discipline and Punish*: "It considers the ways in which societies have penalized those who reject their norms."[187] And one of the ways this becomes possible is through the police power of the township, in the Basking Ridge case, where the abuse of power was even more egregious. The township held thirty-nine hearings to debate the location of the mosque in efforts to delay granting approval and went even further by changing the zoning laws and adding additional restrictions for parking requirements. In other words, "the categories we all recognize not only make this account possible, but also call us to account, and by so doing bring us into line with the norms and properties that culture itself constructs."[188]

The Basking Ridge case and the other cases we have discussed in this chapter help us understand why certain people want to dominate by "invoking what Foucault calls the 'reverse discourse' as basis of resistance to the norm itself."[189] The court's ruling in the suit brought by the Islamic Society of Basking Ridge agrees that the ISBR's rights had been willfully violated.

Another aspect of our discursive analysis of the three cases would suggest that they are equally biopolitical. In this regard, Nikos A. Salingaros has noted that "the unavoidable tendency to conform easily overrides both rational behavior and moral inhibitions." Evidence in the cases "demonstrates again and again how normal persons ignore their sensory apparatus to trust a false piece of information only because it is the accepted group opinion."[190]

Further, "societies recruit us as subjects, subject us to their values, and incite us to be accountable, responsible citizens eager indeed to give an account of ourselves in terms we have learned from the signifying practices of those societies themselves." Literary critic Catherine Belsey notes that these practices and "these associations depend (of course) on differences—between . . . substantial fragile [subjects]."[191] This would also suggest that in the United States, race, ethnicity, and religion are fragile subjects that are widely contested and that "ethnic identities are constantly subjected to formation and re-formation and to contextual negotiation."[192]

NOTES

1. "West India Emancipation," speech delivered at an event celebrating the twenty-third anniversary of the emancipation of West India, Canandaigua, New York, August 3, 1857, text archived at https://rbscp.lib.rochester.edu/4398.

2. Foucault, "Des espaces autres," 22.

3. Foucault as analyzed in Laurie, "Foucault and the Power of Texts," *The Social Construction of Literature* (blog), October 12, 2014, Rutgers.edu, https://soclit14.blogs.rutgers.edu/2014/10/foucault-and-the-power-of-texts/.

4. Michel Foucault, "The Subject and Power," *Critical Inquiry* 8, no. 4 (Summer 1982): 786 and then 787.

5. *The Religious Land Use and Institutionalized Persons Act of 2000* (RLUIPA), Public Law 106–274, U.S. Statutes at Large 114 (2000): 803–807, https://www.govinfo.gov/content/pkg/STATUTE-114/pdf/STATUTE-114-Pg803.pdf.

6. See *The Islamic Center of Mississippi, Inc., et al., Plaintiffs-appellants, v. City of Starkville, Mississippi, Defendant-appellee*, 876 F.2d 465 (5th Cir. 1989); *The Islamic Center of Murfreesboro and Dr. Ossama Bahloul v. Rutherford County, Tennessee*, "Plaintiffs' Memorandum of Law in Support of Plaintiffs' Application for a Temporary Restraining Order or Preliminary Injunction," United States District Court, Middle District of Tennessee, Nashville Decision, July 18, 2012, available at https://becketpdf.s3.amazonaws.com/Memo-in-Support-of-TRO-07.18.12.pdf.pdf; and *The Islamic Society of Basking Ridge et al. v. Township of Bernards et al.*, No. 3:2016cv01369, Document 81 (D.N.J. 2016), https://becketpdf.s3.amazonaws.com/ISBR-v.-Twp-of-Bernards-et-al_Complaint.pdf, https://law.justia.com/cases/federal/district-courts/new-jersey/njdce/3:2016cv01369/330708/81/.

7. Michael Allan Wolf, *The Zoning of America: 'Euclid v. Ambler'* (Lawrence: University Press of Kansas, 2008), 4 and then 3, emphasis original. And also see *Village of Euclid, Ohio v. Ambler Realty Co.*, 272 U.S. 365 (1926). In this case, the US Supreme Court sided with the Village of Euclid, Ohio, allowing them to establish limits to land development that would impact the town. "In short, the Court ruled that zoning ordinances, regulations, and laws must find their justification in some aspect of police power and [be] asserted for the public welfare. Benefit for the public welfare must be determined in connection with the circumstances, the conditions, and the locality of the case." "*Village of Euclid v. Ambler Realty Co.*," Wikipedia, last modified July 30, 2021, https://en.wikipedia.org/wiki/Village_of_Euclid_v._Ambler_Realty_Co.

8. Nickolas James, "Law and Power: Ten Lessons from Foucault," *Bond Law Review* 30, no. 1 (2018): 35–36, https://pure.bond.edu.au/ws/portalfiles/portal/27624577/Law_and_Power_Ten_Lessons_From_Foucault.pdf, discussing Michel Foucault, *The Will to Knowledge: The History of Sexuality*, trans. Robert Hurley (London: Penguin Books, 1998), 1:26.

9. Pew Research Center, "Controversies Over Mosques and Islamic Centers Across the U.S.," PewForum.org, September 27, 2012, p. 1, https://assets.pewresearch.org/wp-content/uploads/sites/11/2012/09/2012Mosque-Map.pdf.

For more on the protracted legal battle, see Bob Smietana, "Murfreesboro Mosque Fight Laid to Rest after Supreme Court Ruling," *Washington Post*, June 3, 2014, https://www.washingtonpost.com/national/religion/murfreesboro-mosque-fight-laid-to-rest-after-supreme-court-ruling/2014/06/03/0da487c0-eb49-11e3-b10e-5090cf3b5958_story.html.

10. Karen Lugo, *Mosques in America: A Guide to Accountable Permit Hearings and Continuing Citizen Oversight* (N.p.: CreateSpace Independent Publishing Platform, 2016), cover description, available at https://centerforsecuritypolicy.org/wp-content/uploads/2016/12/Mosque_in_America.pdf.

11. James, "Law and Power," 32.

12. Eric [W.] Treene, "Zoning and Mosques: Understanding the Impact of the Religious Land Use and Institutionalized Persons Act," *The Public Lawyer* 23, no. 1 (Winter 2015): 3, archived at https://docplayer.net/46988863-Zoning-and-mosques-the-public-lawyer-winter-2015.html.

13. US Department of Justice, "Report on the Twentieth Anniversary of the Religious Land Use and Institutionalized Persons Act," Justice.gov, September 22, 2020, p. 15, https://www.justice.gov/crt/case-document/file/1319186/download.

14. Pew Research Center, "Controversies Over Mosques," 1.

15. Gordon L. Clark, *Judges and Cities: Interpreting Local Autonomy* (Chicago: University of Chicago Press, 1985), 145.

16. H. L. Mencken had written this in the November 19, 1924, edition of the *Chicago Daily Tribune*, referring to the states in the US South whose popular culture is largely determined by adherence to conservative Christian mores. Here Mencken is believed to have coined the term *Bible Belt*, which usage antedates the previously known date of 1926, found in historical dictionaries. Mencken as quoted in Fred R. Shapiro, ed., *The Yale Book of Quotations*, fore. Joseph Epstein (New Haven, CT: Yale University Press, 2006), 512

17. Racial segregation of American citizens began to be legally enforced throughout the US South from the 1870s through 1965, but the culture and ideologies encoded during that hundred-year span had existed for much longer and did not simply change overnight with passage of civil rights legislation. Progress was incremental, and a series of well-considered lawsuits had been slowly chipping away at the "separate but equal" precedent decided in *Plessy v. Ferguson* (163 U.S. 537 [1896]). White power holders did not cede their advantage quietly. *The Islamic Center of Mississippi v. City of Starkville* was playing out in the courts a mere twenty years after passage of the Voting Rights Act, meaning many of the Islamic center's opponents would have come of age under Jim Crow.

18. As analyzed in James, "Law and Power," 35..

19. *Brown v. City of Richmond*, 204 Va. 471 (1963).

20. Stuart Elden, "Land, Terrain Territory," *Progress in Human Geography* 34, no. 6 (2010): 810.

21. Mark W. Cordes, "Where to Pray? Religious Zoning and the First Amendment," *University of Kansas Law Review* 35, no. 4 (1987): 697n1, https://commons.lib.niu.edu/bitstream/handle/10843/16450/Cordes%2035%20U%20Kan%20L%20Rev%20697%201987-HeinArticle.pdf. And see Lochner v. New York, 198 U.S. 45 (1908). During the Lochner era (1897–1937), the Supreme Court made a practice of "strik[ing] down economic regulations adopted by a State based on the Court's own notions of the most appropriate means for the State to implement its considered policies." *Central Hudson Gas & Electric Corp. v. Public Service Commission*, 447 U.S. 557, 589 (1980) (Justice Rehnquist, dissenting). And see "Lochner era," Wikipedia, last modified July 26, 2021, https://en.wikipedia.org/wiki/Lochner_era.

22. Richard Rothstein, *The Color of Law: A Forgotten History of How Our Government Segregated America* (New York: Liveright Publishing Corporation, 2018), 14, emphasis original.

23. Cordes, "Where to Pray?" 701.

24. *Islamic Center of Mississippi, Inc., et al., Plaintiffs-appellants, v. City of Starkville, Mississippi, Defendant-appellee*, 840 F.2d 293, 294 (5th Cir. 1988).

25. Clark, *Judges and Cities*, 150.

26. *Islamic Center of Mississippi*, 840 F.2d 293.

27. *Islamic Center of Mississippi*, 840 F.2d 293.

28. *Islamic Center of Mississippi*, 840 F.2d 293.

29. Cordes, "Where to Pray?" 701.

30. *Islamic Center of Mississippi*, 840 F.2d 293.

31. *Islamic Center of Mississippi*, 840 F.2d 293.

32. Both Foucault quotations pulled from Mathias Klitgård Sørensen, "Foucault on Power Relations," 2. Irenees.net, September 2014, http://www.irenees.net/bdf_fiche-notions-242_en.html.

33. *Islamic Center of Mississippi*, 840 F.2d 293.

34. *Islamic Center of Mississippi*, 840 F.2d 293.

35. *Islamic Center of Mississippi*, 840 F.2d 293.

36. Sørensen, "Foucault on Power Relations."

37. *Islamic Center of Mississippi*, 840 F.2d 293.

38. *Islamic Center of Mississippi*, 840 F.2d 293.

39. *Islamic Center of Mississippi*, 840 F.2d 293.

40. *Islamic Center of Mississippi*, 840 F.2d 293.

41. Karl N. Llewellyn, "On the Good, the True, the Beautiful, in Law," *The* University of Chicago Law Review 9, no. 2 (1942): 251, https://chicagounbound.uchicago.edu/cgi/viewcontent.cgi?article=1983&context=uclrev.

42. *Islamic Center of Mississippi*, 840 F.2d 293.

43. Sørensen, "Foucault on Power Relations."

44. Sørensen, "Foucault on Power Relations," emphasis and parenthetical original.

45. *Islamic Center of Mississippi*, 840 F.2d 293. And see Schad v. Borough of Mount Ephraim, 452 U.S. 61, 68 (1981).

46. *Islamic Center of Mississippi*, 840 F.2d 293.

47. Llewellyn, "On the Good," 249.

48. Sørensen, "Foucault on Power Relations."

49. *Islamic Center of Mississippi*, 840 F.2d 293.

50. Llewellyn, "On the Good," 264.

51. *Islamic Center of Mississippi*, 840 F.2d 293.

52. For some perspective, consider that records indicate the last survivor of American enslavement was a man named Peter Mills, who had been born on October 26, 1861, and was a year and two months old when the Emancipation Proclamation was issued, legally freeing all enslaved peoples in the United States. Mills died on September 22, 1972, at the age of 110. Records further indicate that Sylvester McGee, the last formerly enslaved American to die in the State of Mississippi, where the *Starkville* case played out, had died at the astonishing age of 130, on October 15, 1971—a mere six years before the Islamic Center had initiated its search for a mosque in the city of Starkville. See "List of the Last Surviving American Enslaved People," Wikipedia, last modified October 21, 2021, https://en.wikipedia.org/wiki/List_of_last_surviving_American_enslaved_people.

53. Clark, *Judges and Cities*, 149.
54. Cordes, "Where to Pray?" 698 and then 701.
55. Gutterman and Murphy, "'Ground Zero Mosque,'" 373.
56. Gutterman and Murphy, "'Ground Zero Mosque,'" 373.
57. "National September 11 Memorial and Museum," Wikipedia, last modified October 12, 2021, https://en.wikipedia.org/wiki/National_September_11_Memorial_%26_Museum.
58. Faubion, *Essential Works*, xxii.
59. Jean-Michel Brabant, "Response," trans. Gerald Moore, in *Space, Knowledge and Power: Foucault and Geography*, ed. Jeremy W. Crampton and Stuart Elden (Aldershot, Eng.: Ashgate, 2007), 25.
60. See, for example, Newt Gingrich, "Newt's Statement on the Proposed 'Cordoba House' Mosque at Ground Zero," *Gingrich 360* (website), July 22, 2010, archived at https://web.archive.org/web/20190930005239/https://www.gingrich360.com/2010/07/mosquestatement/.
61. Faubion, *Essential Works*, xx.
62. Chao, "Oppositional Banality," 28.
63. Faubion, *Essential Works*, xxvii.
64. Edward W. Said, *Covering Islam* (London: Routledge and Kegan Paul, 1981), 144.
65. Robert M. Bosco and Lori Hartmann-Mahmud, "The Securitization of Park51," *Peace Review: A Journal of Social Justice* 23, no. 4 (2011): 531.
66. Katharina Borsi, Tarsha Finney, and Pavlos Philippou, "Architectural Type and the Discourse of Urbanism," *The Journal of Architecture* 23, nos. 7–8 (October 2018): 1093, https://www.tandfonline.com/doi/pdf/10.1080/13602365.2018.1513478.
67. Anne Barnard, "In Lower Manhattan, 2 Mosques Have Firm Roots," *New York Times*, August 13, 2010, https://www.nytimes.com/2010/08/14/nyregion/14mosque.html.
68. Deleuze, as quoted in Eugene B. Young, "Duration," in *The Deleuze and Guattari Dictionary*, Bloomsbury Philosophical Dictionaries series, Eugene B. Young, with Gary Genosko and Janell Watson (New York, Bloomsbury, 2013), 100.
69. Gutterman and Murphy, "'Ground-Zero Mosque,'" 373. In fact, the Qur'an names "monasteries, churches, synagogues, and mosques" as places of worship (Q. 22:40).
70. Keith Olbermann, "Olbermann: 'There Is No Ground Zero Mosque,'" *NBC News*, August 16, 2010, https://www.nbcnews.com/id/wbna38730223.
71. Buchanan and Lambert, *Deleuze and Space*, 2.
72. John Paul Stevens, remarks delivered at the National Japanese American Memorial Foundation 10th Anniversary Gala Celebration, Washington, D.C., November 4, 2010, text archived at https://www.supremecourt.gov/publicinfo/speeches/sp_11-04-10.pdf, emphasis original.
73. Buchanan and Lambert, *Deleuze and Space*, 2.
74. Rick Hampson, "Ground Zero Cross a Powerful Symbol for 9/11 Museum," *USA Today*, last modified May 15, 2014, https://www.usatoday.com/story/news/nation/2014/05/13/911-ground-zero-museum-cross-world-trade-center/8907003/.

75. Jeanne Halgren Kilde, "The Park 51/Ground Zero Controversy and Sacred Sites as Contested Space," *Religions* 2, no. 3 (2011): 297, text available at https://www.mdpi.com/2077-1444/2/3/297/htm.

76. Kilde, "Park 51/Ground Zero Controversy," 299.

77. Faubion, *Essential Works*, xviii, parenthetical original.

78. Lee Leviter, "The Myth of Christian Innocence Reinforces Anti-Semitism," *Sojourners*, April 30, 2020, https://sojo.net/articles/myth-christian-innocence-reinforces-anti-semitism.

79. Ekaterina V. Haskins and Justin P. DeRose, "Memory, Visibility, and Public Space: Reflections on Commemoration(s) of 9/11," *Space and Culture* 6, no. 4 (November 2003): 378.

80. Description of Waldman's book drawn from Michiko Kakutani, "The Right Architect with the Wrong Name," *New York Times*, August 15, 2011, https://www.nytimes.com/2011/08/16/books/the-submission-by-amy-waldman-review.html. And see Amy Waldman, *The Submission: A Novel* (New York: Farrar, Straus and Giroux, 2011).

81. Wolf, *Zoning of America*, 154 and then 3. And see *Village of Euclid, Ohio v. Ambler Realty Co.*, 272 U.S. 365 (1926).

82. Cordes, "Where to Pray?" 702.

83. Kathleen M. Moore, *Al-Mughtaribūn: American Law and the Transformation of Muslim Life in the United States*, SUNY Series in Middle Eastern Studies (Albany: State University of New York, 1995).

84. Wolf, *Zoning of America*, ix; "Islamic Center of Murfreesboro," Wikipedia, last modified October 27, 2021, https://en.wikipedia.org/wiki/Islamic_Center_of_Murfreesboro.

85. *United States v. Rutherford County, Tennessee*, No. 3:12-cv-00737, 2012, WL 2930076 (M.D. Term, filed July 18, 2012, as cited in Treene, "Zoning and Mosques," 3.

86. Laura Blackwell Clark and Barbra Newman Young, "The Murfreesboro Mosque: To Build or Not to Build?" *Forum on Public Policy* 2012, no. 2 (2012), https://4e429266-b6af-4a71-83d3-81ca05731064.filesusr.com/ugd/553e83_91272a6d006444b49636f87f89e9e589.pdf.

87. Clark, *Judges and Cities*, 152.

88. Foucault as analyzed in Faubion, *Essential Works*, 177.

89. Faubion, *Essential Works*, 177.

90. Foucault, "The Subject and Power," 788.

91. US Department of Justice, "Justice Department Files Lawsuit Requiring Rutherford County, Tenn., to Allow Mosque to Open in City of Murfreesboro," press release, Justice.gov, July 18, 2012, https://www.justice.gov/opa/pr/justice-department-files-lawsuit-requiring-rutherford-county-tenn-allow-mosque-open-city.

92. Treene, "Zoning and Mosques," 4.

93. Pew Research Center, "Controversies Over Mosques," 19.

94. Treene, "Zoning and Mosques," 3.

95. Wolf, *Zoning of America*, 154.

96. Pew Research Center, "Controversies Over Mosques," 19.

97. Treene, "Zoning and Mosques," 5.
98. Treene, "RLUIPA and Mosques: Enforcing a Fundamental Right in Challenging Times," *First Amendment Law Review* 10, no. 2 (Winter 2012): 350, https://scholarship.law.unc.edu/cgi/viewcontent.cgi?article=1147&context=falr.
99. Treene, "RLUIPA and Mosques," 350.
100. Pew Research Center, "Controversies Over Mosques," 19.
101. Treene, "Zoning and Mosques," 5.
102. Clark and Young, "Murfreesboro Mosque," 7. And see *United States v. Rutherford County, Tennessee*, No. 3:12-cv-00737, 2012, WL 2930076 (M.D. Term, filed July 18, 2012.
103. Akel Ismail Kahera and Bakama Bakamanume, "Houston Mosques: Space, Place and Religious Meaning," in *The Changing World Religion Map: Sacred Places, Identities, Practices and Politics*, ed. Stanley D. Brunn (Dordrecht: Springer Netherlands, 2015), 2374.
104. Clark and Young, "Murfreesboro Mosque," 7.
105. Foucault, *Power/Knowledge*, 239.
106. Clark, *Judges and Cities*, 159.
107. Wolf, *Zoning of America*, 4.
108. Treene, "RLUIPA and Mosques," 341.
109. Treene, "RLUIPA and Mosques," 341.
110. Pew Research Center. "Controversies Over Mosques," 1.
111. Mimi Sheller, "Theorising Mobility Justice," *Tempo Social* 30, no. 2 (2018): 23, https://www.revistas.usp.br/ts/article/view/142763/142049.
112. Sørensen, "Foucault on Power Relations."
113. James T. Schleifer, "Tocqueville, Religion, and Democracy in America: Some Essential Questions," *American Political Thought* 3, no. 2 (2014): 255.
114. Schleifer, "Tocqueville, Religion, and Democracy," 259.
115. Faubion, *Essential Works*, 154.
116. Schleifer analyzing and quoting Tocqueville in "Tocqueville, Religion, and Democracy," 259.
117. For example, algorithms (al-Khawarizmi), optics (ibn Haitham), philosophy (ibn Rushd), medicine (ibn Sina), sociology and architecture (Sinan), and economics (ibn Khaldun et al.)
118. Nikos A. Salingaros, "Cognitive Dissonance and Non-adaptive Architecture: Seven Tactics for Denying the Truth," *Doxa* 11 (January 2014), text archived at https://applied.math.utsa.edu/~yxk833/CognitiveDissonanceandNonadaptiveArchitecture.html, revised from an earlier version published online by *P2FF Wiki*, last modified February 3, 2011, https://wiki.p2pfoundation.net/Cognitive_Dissonance_and_Non-adaptive_Architecture. Within this extract, Salingaros quotes Kenneth S. Friedman, *Myths of the Free Market* (New York: Algora Publishing, 2003).
119. Sørensen, "Foucault on Power Relations," emphasis and parentheticals original.
120. Foucault, "Subject and Power," 788.

170   *Chapter 4*

121. Andrew Rice, "The Fight for the Right to Be a Muslim in America," *The Guardian*, February 8, 2018, https://www.theguardian.com/news/2018/feb/08/how-to-stop-a-mosque-the-new-playbook-of-the-right.

122. Rice, "Fight for the Right to Be a Muslim."

123. National Park Services, "National Register of Historic Places—Registration Form," listing for Liberty Corner Historic District, Somerset County, New Jersey, August 6, 1991, p. 2 of 4, available online through the NP Gallery: Digital Asset Management System (website), US Department of the Interior, date accessed October 15, 2021, https://npgallery.nps.gov/GetAsset/93096fd2-00f5-42ac-980f-9267ff3ae80d.

124. Salingaros, "Cognitive Dissonance," 1.

125. Foucault, *Power/Knowledge*, 98.

126. Salingaros, "Cognitive Dissonance," 1.

127. Foucault, *Power/Knowledge*, 98.

128. See *The Islamic Society of Basking Ridge et al v. Township of Bernards et al.*, No. 3:2016cv01369, Document 81 (D.N.J. 2016), https://becketpdf.s3 .amazonaws.com/ISBR-v.-Twp-of-Bernards-et-al_Complaint.pdf, https://law.justia.com/cases/federal/district-courts/new-jersey/njdce/3:2016cv01369/330708/81/; *The Islamic Society of Basking Ridge et al. v. Township of Bernards et al.*, civil action no. 16–1369 (MAS) (LHG), case 3:16-cv-01369-MAS-LHG, document 93, opinion, filed in the US District Court, District of New Jersey, December 31, 2016, https://www.govinfo.gov/content/pkg/USCOURTS-njd-3_16-cv-01369/pdf/USCOURTS-njd-3_16-cv-01369-1.pdf; and *United States v. Bernards Township* (D.N.J. 2016) 16-cv-1369, archived at https://becketpdf.s3.amazonaws.com/Bernards-Township-Complaint.pdf.

129. Foucault, *Power/Knowledge*, 96 and then 80.

130. Foucault, *Power/Knowledge*, 96.

131. *The North Jersey Vineyard Church v. South Hackensack, New Jersey*, United States District Court, New Jersey Division, case no. 14–07759 WJM-MF; *The North Jersey Vineyard Church v. Township of South Hackensack et al.*, no. 2:2015cv08369, document 30 (D.N.J. 2016).

132. *The Islamic Society of Basking Ridge et al v. Township of Bernards et al.*, No. 3:2016cv01369 (D.N.J. 2016), at 2, https://becketpdf.s3 .amazonaws.com/ISBR-v.-Twp-of-Bernards-et-al_Complaint.pdf, https://law.justia.com/cases/federal/district-courts/new-jersey/njdce/3:2016cv01369/330708/81/.

133. Foucault, *Power/Knowledge*, 98.

134. Read Rice's piece in full at https://www.theguardian.com/news/2018/feb/08/how-to-stop-a-mosque-the-new-playbook-of-the-right.

135. *The Islamic Society of Basking Ridge et al v. Township of Bernards et al.*, No. 3:2016cv01369 (D.N.J. 2016).

136. Rice, "Fight for the Right to Be a Muslim."

137. *Bernards Township* (D.N.J. 2016) 16-cv-1369, at 4.

138. *Bernards Township* (D.N.J. 2016) 16-cv-1369, at 8.

139. *Bernards Township* (D.N.J. 2016) 16-cv-1369, at 16.

140. *NIMBY* is an acronym for "not in my backyard." Quotation pulled from Rice, "Fight for the Right to Be a Muslim."

141. *Bernards Township* (D.N.J. 2016) 16-cv-1369, at 16.

142. Rice, "Fight for the Right to Be a Muslim."
143. Rice, "Fight for the Right to Be a Muslim."
144. *Islamic Society of Basking Ridge*, civil action no. 16–1369 (MAS) (LHG), case 3:16-cv-01369-MAS-LHG, at 3.
145. Rice, "Fight for the Right to Be a Muslim."
146. Salingaros, "Cognitive Dissonance," 1.
147. Rice, "Fight for the Right to Be a Muslim."
148. Rice, "Fight for the Right to Be a Muslim." Rice's data drawn from Emily Ekins, "The State of Free Speech and Tolerance in America," Cato Institute, October 31, 2017, https://www.cato.org/survey-reports/state-free-speech-tolerance-america.
149. Rice, "Fight for the Right to Be a Muslim."
150. *Islamic Society of Basking Ridge*, civil action no. 16–1369 (MAS) (LHG), case 3:16-cv-01369-MAS-LHG, at 11.
151. Rice, "Fight for the Right to Be a Muslim."
152. *Islamic Society of Basking Ridge*, civil action no. 16–1369 (MAS) (LHG), case 3:16-cv-01369-MAS-LHG, at 6.
153. Cordes, "Where to Pray?" 702.
154. Rothstein, *Color of Law*, 65.
155. David Meyer Lindenberg, "In New Jersey, a Long-Overdue Mosque Will Finally Be Built," *Mimesis Law*, January 9, 2017, http://mimesislaw.com/fault-lines/new-jersey-long-overdue-mosque-will-finally-built/15248.
156. Lindenberg, "In New Jersey."
157. Rothstein, *Color of Law*, 217.
158. Rothstein, *Color of Law*, 69.
159. Rice, "Fight for the Right to Be a Muslim."
160. Rice, "Fight for the Right to Be a Muslim."
161. Rice, "Fight for the Right to Be a Muslim." And see *Bernards Township* (D.N.J. 2016) 16-cv-1369.
162. *Bernards Township* (D.N.J. 2016) 16-cv-1369, at 2.
163. Rice, "Fight for the Right to Be a Muslim," quoting *Bernards Township* (D.N.J. 2016) 16-cv-1369, at 56.
164. *Islamic Society of Basking Ridge*, civil action no. 16–1369 (MAS) (LHG), case 3:16-cv-01369-MAS-LHG, at 5.
165. Tocqueville as quoted in Schleifer, "Tocqueville, Religion, and Democracy," 255.
166. Rice, "Fight for the Right to Be a Muslim."
167. Salingaros, "Cognitive Dissonance," 1.
168. Rothstein, *Color of Law*, 69.
169. Foucault, *Power/Knowledge*, 93.
170. "Foucault's Biopolitics and State Racism," *Law and the Humanities LLM* (blog), Kent Law School, University of Kent, February 15, 2019, https://blogs.kent.ac.uk/lawandthehumanities/2019/02/15/foucaults-biopolitics-and-state-racism/.
171. Foucault, "Subject and Power," 786.
172. Foucault, *Power/Knowledge*, 93.
173. Elden, "Land, Terrain, Territory," 810.

174. Foucault, *Power/Knowledge*, 93.

175. *Islamic Center of Mississippi*, 840 F.2d 293.

176. Ali Rattansi, *Racism: A Very Short Introduction* (Oxford: Oxford University Press, 2007), 8.

177. Rattansi, *Racism*, 8.

178. Catherine Belsey, *Poststructuralism: A Very Short Introduction* (Oxford: Oxford University Press, 2002), 54.

179. Tom Wolfe, *From Bauhaus to Our House* (New York: Bantam Books, 1982), 46.

180. Catherine Belsey, *Poststructuralism*, 55.

181. Akel Ismail Kahera, "'God's Dominion': Omar ibn Said's Use of Arabic Literacy as Opposition to Slavery Disposition," *The South Carolina Review* 46, no. 2 (2014): 128.

182. Kahera, "'God's Dominion,'" 133. The historical narrative represents Omar as both a savant and a slave who used Arabic and Qur'anic rhetorical strategies of protest and concealment to endure his captivity, which reemphasizes the power of writing in precarious, life-threatening circumstances. In his use of rhetorical strategies and tropes, Omar continuously negotiates between his faith and his enslavement.

183. Kahera, "'God's Dominion,'" 128 and then 130.

184. Austin, *African Muslims*, 76.

185. Austin, *African Muslims*, 76.

186. Llewellyn, "On the Good," 224.

187. Foucault as analyzed in Belsey, *Poststructuralism*, 53.

188. Belsey, *Poststructuralism*, 53.

189. Catherine Belsey, *Poststructuralism*, 55

190. Salingaros, "Cognitive Dissonance," 3.

191. Belsey, *Poststructuralism*, 53 and then 16.

192. Rattansi, *Racism*, 89.

Postscript

The foregoing chapters are, broadly speaking, a discursive analysis of the hierarchic ensemble of places, sacred spaces and profane spaces, protected places and open, exposed places, urban places and rural places; all of this concerns the real life of people.[1] I also believe that the real life of people is sufficiently rich to permit an account of the place of the mosque and its temporal history. Therefore, our focus has enabled us to re-pose the question of "other spaces" and the Foucauldian triad—space, knowledge, and power—to cast a critical light on certain ideological conflicts that underlie the biopolitical properties of *space* and *place*.

On the one hand, the chapters have demonstrated that the Muslim body/space has the capacity to assert meaning and truth. In other words, the meanings of *space* and *place* are based on the understanding of the Muslim body/space experience, and truth is based on understanding and meaning; but of course, as I have noted, there are disorders and environments where differences about meaning and truth emerge.[2] On the other hand, the assertion is significant for at least three reasons.

First, while Foucault did aim to elevate the history of the present, his "critique of those margins has the character of an epistemological rehabilitation; even more, it has the character of ontological reconnaissance. 'Hence, for Foucault, the general domain of *savoir* [is the] domain not of things known but of things to be known, one way or another, with less or with greater rigor from one instance to the next.'"[3]

Second, with the domain of things to be known, I have attempted to tease out Gordana Fontana-Giusti's observation that "it is in the nature of human thought to operate through encountering, experiencing and defining problems," whether their conditions and effect are the formal or neoteric properties of *place*.[4] Similar claims have been made by Gilles Deleuze, Pierre-Félix Guattari, Yves Grafmeyer, and others; we will have more to say about this later. It follows that if the mosque occupies a neoteric *place* in society and in the West, then the dispute over what a mosque is and the competing ideologies of place were clearly omnipresent in the battle over Cordoba House/Park51 (aka the Ground Zero mosque). To reconcile the battle over the micro-powers, the genealogical analysis has paved the way for a new philosophical language about the Western space/place, arising from the assertion that "the problem of space assumes biopolitical significance," ruling both the body and space and spatial transformations where governmentality (biopolitical techniques) runs parallel to architecture and urbanism—where the cities are places of surveillance.[5]

Third, the schema that I have just laid out introduces a set of additional claims by cultural theorist Ian Buchanan and literary theorist Gregg Lambert that point to a promising terrain in the analysis of *space/place*. Citing Deleuze and Guattari, Buchanan and Lambert argue persuasively about the conceptual framework of "nonspace and nonplace" and the many ways our perception of space and place have been altered in the face of globalization, "which has evicted us from the world we thought we knew."[6] These reservations aside, contested spaces—such as the public perception of the Cordoba House/Park51 and the Moschea della Misericordia—have contributed to the critical intent with which space and place have been altered. The assumption is that "there can be no emancipation without certain ideological conflicts which underlie the controversies . . . in which spatial relations can be represented."[7]

Given the foregoing remarks, we can restate a key question: "What are the relations between knowledge . . . and power?"[8] A possible response can be found in Jean-Michel Brabant's statement that "every strategy of power has a spatial dimension." It might be added that Brabant's statement has spatial dimensions to which we can apply "a historical causal explanation [of the *place* of the mosque in the Western world] that is material, multiple and corporeal."[9] But at the same time, this maneuver restates the fact that the real lives of people—by allowing people to "be there" in that *place*—have become increasingly contested. "It is no doubt a geographical notion, but it is first of all a juridico-political one: the area controlled by a certain kind of power." However, the distinct facet of control and "the politico-strategic term is an indication of how [micro-powers] actually come to inscribe themselves both on a material soil and within forms of discourse."[10]

Our discussion in chapter 4 is a good example of what I have just described and of the geography of the Bible Belt and a certain kind of power wielded in Starkville, Mississippi, and Murfreesboro, Tennessee, and in the battle for place in Basking Ridge, New Jersey. First, "they are 'transversal' struggles . . . that is, they are not limited to one country"; by this we mean that the struggle is not limited to one political or economic system or form of government. Second, the struggle is about the micro-power effects as such—for example, the civil rights movement and the struggle for social justice (race, religion, and identity) and against institutional racism, exclusionary zoning, and similar oppressions. Third, as Foucault would argue, "these are 'immediate' struggles" to criticize the instances of power close to them and to question the status of an individual, a society, or a government.[11]

In this reading, then, sociologists Julie Elizabeth Gagnon and Annick Germain argue that "with regard to the development of religious establishments, municipalities can acquire tools to determine how many can be established on their territory, where and how. The main tools available to them for this are zoning by-laws and, to a lesser extent, site planning and architectural integration plans, which allow them to assess and subject the granting of a permit to certain more qualitative criteria relating to architecture and development."[12]

Note too that race, religion, and identity are "above all a matter of drawing boundaries around [*spaces/places*] of belonging and non-belonging."[13] In other words, prejudice—such as birtherism, the Muslim ban, and the xenophobic views of MAGA sycophants—"enables us to see that meaning is not something that we can produce as we will but rather the dimensions of an event [or action] within the shared historical realm in which we and our interpretations belong."[14]

Although much more can be said about the perpetrators who have forged these boundaries with the aim of exclusion, we know this behavior is not new. For example, in the post–World War II era, setbacks on racial identity and exclusion had already emerged in Levittown, New Jersey. The town ordinance was explicitly written to exclude Blacks, even Black vets, and their families—men and women who had just fought and died to defend America's freedom. One of Levittown's builders, Bill Levitt, "voiced his concerns that opening the doors to blacks would drive away the whites—and sales."[15] Similarly, *The Islamic Center v. The Boston Herald* is a most extreme example of controversy over *place*, if readers choose to pursue the details of the case. In short, the place of the mosque has as many complexities as possible and formations—including "assumed space of language . . . that is allowed to spread beyond the cannons of philosophy . . . thus creating a new space for contemplation and analysis."[16]

Finally, the distinct facets that I have employed were intended to critique the dismantling of ideologies—that is, the rights to space, subjugated knowledge and the biopolitical, and the "*subjective* elements of identity construction, processes of *identification* with particular groups, as well as responses to labels of identity and difference imposed from the outside."[17] That is to say, the difficulty in recognizing the place of the mosque has an adverse impact on the daily life—the quotidian practices—of the North American Muslim community. In other words, the spatial confine of *place* is significant to urban places. However, the inability of the micro-powers to consider the possibility of this dimension of place in urban and rural settings, in turn, makes them "blind to the numerous controversies that many urban and rural *places* seem to attract."[18]

Moreover, understanding the likelihood of this type of controversy, as intimated by Supreme Court Justice John Paul Stevens, requires observing and acknowledging the equivocal relationship of the Western world to Islam and the communities of the faithful who happen to reside there. In this connection, Justice Stevens provides a fitting response with the prudent use of his judicial experience and legal judgment. He argues that "many of the Muslims who pray in New York mosques may well have come to America to escape the intolerance of radicals like those who dominate the Taliban. Descendants of pilgrims who came to America in the seventeenth century to escape religious persecutions . . . should understand why American Muslims should enjoy the freedom to build their places of worship wherever permitted by local zoning laws."[19]

To restate the distinctiveness of the history of the present—that Foucault appears to adopt as a discursive strategy—I believe that architectural history, theory, and criticism are wracked by debate over historiographic ideologies. I add that few literati, if any, would support an interpretation that is mutually accepted to some ethnographic concept of the Moorish architectural tradition. Admittedly, the Ibero-Moorish world represents an ontological possibility and a historical reality that are mutually reinforcing to Islamic art and architecture and the aesthetic language that we find in the Alhambra, the Great Mosque of Córdoba, and other significant buildings in the North African foci. We are talking about the meeting of Ibero-Moorish aesthetics with the Western world. It is not a chance encounter. That is to say, unlike the willing public acceptance of the Fox Theatre, the Mosque Theater, and Opa-Locka city hall, "we can distinguish legitimate prejudice from those to be overcome and thus approach built-forms and cultures [that have their origins in the Ibero-Islamic world from] within their tradition and contexts."[20] Hispano-America has hosted these traditions through the artistic and architectural production.

Likewise in the Hispano-American world, R. Brooks Jeffery informs us that the specific knowledge and a plurality of references to the foci interweave both with the production of space and with the architectural work's means, materiality, and much more. The main thrust of his statement resides in a quotation by Cardinal Francisco Ximenez de Cisneros: "They lack our faith, but we lack their works."[21] Here Cisneros makes an avowal by referring to Moorish traditions, the craftsmen and builders, people of Muslim and Arab descent who traveled to the Hispano-American world during the colonial period, bringing with them the knowledge of ornamentation, architectural form, and public spaces.

Lest we forget, in the short but lucid *Dates, Names and Places*, Thomas Ballantine gives an account of how "Cisneros ruthlessly burned books of great value in a bonfire in the city center [of Granada] in 1501[and] two years later, books that were seized from private collections and had gold and silver bindings, as well as from public libraries, simply because they were written in Arabic on Islamic history, religion, and culture."[22]

Cisneros's actions follow a peculiar power/knowledge and biopolitical strategy—no different from the modern-day apartheid regimes that remain throughout the world, and no different from Hitler's *Kristallnacht* in Germany or than the destruction of private houses in occupied Palestine and the repeated desecration of Islam's third holiest site, al-Aqsa Mosque. These despotic practices are meant to exert control of *space/place*, the lives of people, and their quotidian practices. Granada, aside from Córdoba, was one of the cities around which the despotic edicts were applied by Cisneros with the help of his ecclesiastical assistant Diego de Deza. Similarly, the Pragmatica of 1529—an anti-Islamic campaign—reinforced laws implemented by royal decree to govern Muslim behavior both in public and in private, in cities, towns, and throughout the Iberian world.[23] It is for this reason that I began our discussion with the Mosque of Córdoba, by insisting that the place of the Córdoba Mosque matters; it opens the imagination to a discursive understanding of the place of the mosque in the Western world.

We might take another example to illustrate the construction of place and the coexistence of difficult spatial relationships in the Western world from the subject of resemblances. The premise marks the setting of place to understand *resemblances* and the specific binominal nature and etymology of words (the Confucian naming of things). This was the focus and the discursive analysis of the Fox Theatre, the Mosque Theater, and Opa-Locka city hall and the underlying dis/continuities, accidents, deviations, and reversals. In this regard, psychologist James Hillman writes that, like myths themselves, resemblances are "seminal substructures" wanting to be real while not being real; "they feel insubstantial. . . . But in their devotion to the other world—they are [at best insincere] missionaries of transcendence."[24]

Yves Grafmeyer makes similar claims regarding the coexistence of difficulties; this provides another opportunity for the retrieval of the surprising combination of resemblances. According to Grafmeyer, we must look "beyond the heterogeneity of these values' systems and the multiple points of friction around which these *coexistence of difficulties* can crystallize."[25] However, Grafmeyer's coexistence of difficulties must be further examined for at least two reasons: First, to emphasize the point that calling the cinema "the Mosque Theater" is an insolent misuse of the word *mosque*—highlighting the parturition of resemblances. I have chosen to adapt the term *ceci n'est pas une mosquee* to demarcate the temporal distinction between the "functional" *masjid* and the Mosque Theater. In this respect, does the Mosque Theater have ontological validity? I asked the question because I want the reader to understand that ontological meaning, as it is constituted in Ibero-Moorish traditions, is "a form of history which can account for the constitution of knowledges, discourses, [and the] domains of objects."[26]

Second, the Moorish tradition has been influential and serves as the primary architectural reference in North America for the Fox, the Mosque, and Opa-Locka, and the notable dichotomy about the naming of things (and the spatial ordering of things) is subsumed in another. In this way, the Fox, the Mosque, and Opa-Locka are a difficult set of resemblances for which no standard appellation exists—despite the common use of the term *Moorish*. At the same time, the lexicographical term *masjid* already exists in our vocabulary. The Islamic Center of Washington rightly affirms the distinction of an urban *masjid*, even though the aesthetic treatment for the edifice—the mixed-use vocabulary of resemblances—borrows heavily from Egypt's neo-Mamluk feature.[27]

Here lies another dilemma with which I have dealt by using the expression *the burden of the architect*. So, what exactly does architect Walter Gropius tell us about his intentions in his plans for the mosque at the University of Baghdad? In *Epistemologies of Aesthetics*, scholar of philosophy Dieter Mersch argues that "knowledge cannot be reduced to any other form of knowledge, neither to the hermeneutic knowledge of interpretation." Mersch's claim presents yet another dichotomy: it suggests that "aesthetic paradoxes are based on contrasts . . . [that are] literally acts of standing out against or setting against one another and have a particular simultaneity showing both sides of this standing out."[28]

But, then, how does Gropius's mosque ground itself if the anomaly points to the absence of knowledge—apart from the fact that tradition and meaning have gone away? This leaves us to conclude that all we are left with are resemblances—the condition of architectural indeterminacy. In other words, we are left with a heterotopic condition, which corresponds to the very thing Foucault vigorously tried to undermine in his writing on visual spaces and the subject of genealogy.[29] What is being argued is that polysemic meaning is a dense, palimpsestic juxtaposition of architectural form and visual elements. In other words, with the failure of architectural judgment, the edifice may incite, but the paradox abruptly calls forth a heterotopic condition—the visual disorder. And according to René Magritte's 1929 article for *La révolution surréaliste*, "Les mots et les images," "an object encounters its image, an object encounters its name."[30] Yet as we consider Magritte's assertion, it must become quite apparent that the aesthetic apparatus does not represent tradition or hermeneutics, "seeking the *chimera* of objective meaning as traditional approaches do, or shared polyvalent meanings, as hermeneutics does."[31]

Another aspect of Grafmeyer's coexistence of difficulties pertains to the Qaytbay complex that was restaged as the Cairo Street exhibition at Chicago's 1893 World's Fair. I have argued against the idea of accepting the Qaytbay as the first urban mosque in North America, as doing so would imply that the building "is grounded in [local knowledge and production] processes that bring together emotions and affects, and their varying intensities while also reflecting on the act of creation itself."[32] Professor Zeynep Çelik's *Displaying the Orient* explains the problem that we face with the Qaytbay complex in lucid terms. "The indispensable Cairo Street put on its show in Chicago," she writes. "Its facade on the Midway had 'nothing artistic' about it; passersby had no clue to the life of the street from the plastered exterior wall. But once inside the gate, visitors saw a lively array of shops and houses, a cafe, the 'solemn spectacle' of [the Qaytbay] mosque, two obelisks, a 'Temple of Luxor,' and a much talked-about theater where the belly dance was performed. The street itself was just as crooked as one has a right to expect in a Cairo thoroughfare."[33]

I have argued that simulacra are omnipresent at the Cairo Street exhibition and that we can understand resemblance simply as a demarcation of place—that is, without retracing the history of the real Qaytbay complex and the medieval "Street in Cairo"—which intimates the heterotopic condition without achieving the status of the "real."[34] Foucault describes this condition and the demarcation in another way: "One could say, by way of retracing this history of space very roughly . . . [that] there was a hierarchic ensemble of places; sacred spaces and profane spaces; protected places and open, exposed places, urban places and rural places."[35] With Grafmeyer's coexistence of difficulties and Foucault's hierarchic ensemble of other spaces, we may conclude that *place* has a variety of meanings pertinent to fractured architectural histories, the production of space, marginal contexts, and public discourses.

At this point, these descriptive markers of place continue to mirror temporal existence, in which human experience of the world is important such that resemblances would seem wholly relevant to a full reversal of genealogical positions. Thus, with the ontological discourse, we have attempted to demonstrate that with the axis of prayer—the *qibla*—we can see why architecture and ontology are appropriate and how the practice of facing the *Ka'ba* offers a wellspring of contemplation. The practice confirms an ethos whereby the *Ka'ba* retains its own symbolic rhythms—the rhythms of incessant circumambulation, at the heart of the sacred mosque—al-Masjid al-Haram.

The ethos fuses temporal distinctions of sacred space with historical knowledge and the geography of the city of Makkah; it is here more than anywhere else in the world that devotees are the inheritors of knowledge and that adherents of the faith have the right to the city. In other words, Makkah represents a symbolic locus wherein memory, body, and space are attached to the ontological nature of the *Ka'ba*—wherein the devotional act gives blessing—*baraka*—and exalted serenity to the everyday devotee and the pilgrim alike. At the foundation of this concept lies the Qur'anic acclaim, "Nay, I swear by this city [Makkah]; and you are free to dwell in this city" (Q. 90:1–2). Pilgrims exercise that right during the hajj season, when the city is penetrated with audible rhythms and declarations of the faithful as they stridently repeat the *talbiya*: *I respond to your call, O Allah! I respond to your call!*[36] These interactions *concern the real life of people* and make it clear that the city is open to all forms of connectedness, human agency, and ontological frameworks.

To keep the question of place open, I hope that the previous remarks have demonstrated that place is also dependent on specific configurations of space to invent, to disguise, or to replace their origins and meanings. The making and remaking of a discourse—taking the contestation of sites—hint at different moments of the reappraisal of knowledge and the effects intrinsic to power as well as to changing forms of architectural production. A worthy example is the binominal status of the Hagia Sophia—Church of the Holy Wisdom or Church of the Divine Wisdom (figure 5.1).[37] Rather, in this case, the centrally

Figure 5.1 The Hagia Sophia, c. 1890–1900. Photograph. Source: Library of Congress.

planned space of the edifice was designed by mathematician Anthemios of Tralles and engineer Isidoros of Miletus between 532 and 537 to facilitate the Christian liturgy. With the conquest of Constantinople in 1453, the building was repurposed by Mehmed II, with the addition of a wooden minaret (on the exterior, which did not survive), a *mihrab*, and a *minbar*. The red minaret that stands on the southeast corner of the structure was either erected by Mehmed II or his son, Bayezid II. Bayezid II also erected the slender white minaret on the northeast side of the edifice, and "the two identical minarets on the western side were likely commissioned by Selim II or Murad II and built by renowned Ottoman architect Sinan in the 1500s."[38]

The Hagia Sophia has been a museum since 1934, and in 1985 it became a UNESCO World Heritage Site. Considering the July 2020 decree of the Council of State, Turkey's highest administrative court, that transformed the edifice from a museum to a mosque, we must now ask, Is the transformation brought about by power relations? Scholar of architecture Ziad Jamaleddine argues that "clearly the decision was politically calculated, an opportunistic bid that underscores the country's ambition to play a central geopolitical role in the Middle East. Having been denied membership in the European Union for decades, Turkey has turned instead towards the East."[39]

According to Jamaleddine, "since 2016 there has been a full-time Imam" and "the call to prayer has been sung . . . five times daily, to the pleasure of tourists and locals alike. Thus Hagia Sophia was already . . . 'functioning as both a museum and a mosque.'" Disagreement over the decree is omnipresent, and "the negative response has been no less problematic. . . . Over the centuries thousands of mosques in Spain and Greece have been converted into churches or repurposed for other uses—a history that has been largely ignored by Western authorities."[40]

If there is a linkage between power and the Hagia Sophia, it is also a discursive statement about the indeterminate status of a religious edifice. The issue here is that the statement is "essentially based on the constitution of political power." In which case, we need to expand the subject of power to effectively include concrete spaces. But, in the end, we are confronted with the production of truth and the manifold relations of power.[41] While sincere academic interpretation of place as it pertains to the Hagia Sophia remains inherently conventional, it also threatens our understanding of the will to truth, the will to challenge this significance and to examine further without the fear of corrupting what we already know. This brief characterization of the status of the Hagia Sophia and the public *esthesis*—feeling, experience, or felt experience—indicates the difficulty that underpins space, knowledge, and power that we have attempted to critique in the foregoing chapters.

I wish to make several comments in closing. First, the Foucauldian hypothesis suggests another challenging proposition: "There can be no possible exercise of power without the production of certain . . . discourses of truth which operate through and on the basis of this association."[42] Just so, there is a growing body of literature on the topic of the American mosque—for example, *Making Moderate Islam: Sufism, Service, and the "Ground Zero Mosque" Controversy*.[43] In addition, readers interested in pursuing critical theory and the related discourse can explore *The Transnational Mosque: Architecture and Historical Memory in the Contemporary Middle East* and a number of related texts.[44] Obviously these sources and others that critique the mosque in the modern world allow for a direct comparison of tradition, lost meanings, and the recovery of meanings.[45]

The second point I wish to drive home in closing is that, in this context, "Foucault thought that the modern pursuit of the question of origins has contributed to the understanding of the ontological significance of time. He challenged the significance and the examination that led to space as a relevant intellectual category."[46] This form of resolution is wholly appropriate to the architect who does not believe in the beneficial nature of history and tradition (that is, who believes not merely in the beauty or aesthetics of art and architecture but in the truth or falsity of the judgements that challenge the place of the mosque). Or, to put it somewhat differently, society is enriched by the existential meaning of place, its cultural diversity, its history, and its tradition.

This view of cultural diversity was notable at Venice's Biennale Architettura 2021, with its provocative theme, "How will we live together?" The Biennale, with the Victoria and Albert Museum, exhibited *Three British Mosques*: "collaborating with author and architect Shahed Saleem, the Pavilion looks at the self-built and often undocumented world of adapted mosques. The three case studies . . . examine the Brick Lane mosque, a former Protestant chapel then Synagogue; Old Kent Road mosque housed in a former pub; and Harrow Central mosque, a purpose-built space that sits next door to the converted terraced house it used to occupy" (figures 5.2, 5.3, and 5.4). The carpeted pavilion, designed to resemble the floor of a mosque where prayers are performed daily, was meant to "be explored through 3D architectural reconstructions, filmed interviews and photographs."[47]

On the one hand, the exhibit afforded viewers insight into the transformation of space/place and the life of Muslims in urban Britain. On the other hand, *Three British Mosques* forces us to ask, "How will we live together?" But above all, this question allows us to revisit the religious prejudice and alienating rejection that plagued Christoph Buchel's *Moschea della Misericordia*, exhibited at the 2015 Biennale.

While I have attempted to trace such disruptions in the book's chapters to show that place embodies the historical, juridical, and discursive analysis of space, our discussion has largely excluded the recent emergence of the women's mosque or oppositional discourses about space and gender across

Figure 5.2 Brick Lane mosque. Photograph. Source: ©Guy Sinclair, Fabrication Lab, University of Westminster, 2021.

other critical theories and disciplines. This treatment is needed as part of the discourse to remedy the repositioning of spatial equity for women. The first women-only mosque in the United States, the Women's Mosque of America, opened in Los Angeles in 2015, mirroring women-only mosques that have existed among the Hui community in China for several hundred years.[48] In short, several verses in the Qur'an preserve the identity of the mosque—the *masjid*. For instance, "The places of worship [masajid] belong to God" (Q.

Figure 5.3 Old Kent Road mosque. Photograph. Source: ©Guy Sinclair, Fabrication Lab, University of Westminster, 2021.

72:18). This verse is one of several that protect the hermeneutical and ontological sanctity of the *masjid*; implicitly, it safeguards the edifice from the possibility of excluding a male or female worshipper.

Finally, if in our exploration herein my general interpretation of the triad has leaned too heavily on the genealogical framework, it is because Foucault's genealogy writes the history of these instances, of irony and ambiguity, the mistaken beliefs and misconceptions and their transformation. For instance, "even with the arrival of the Renaissance, Christian Europe continued to give the word—religious revelation—precedence over both reason and evidence of the senses and the final index of the real."[49] In other words, "what makes these unusual spaces special is the fact that Foucault's [discursive analysis] provide[s] sense to this complex geography, endowing it with the possibility for the next action or a fresh thought."[50]

Foucault's texts can be read and studied and interpreted by architects and professional educators like myself, but it also seems to me that any text can

Figure 5.4 Harrow Central mosque. Photograph. Source: ©Guy Sinclair, Fabrication Lab, University of Westminster, 2021.

open up a fresh discourse about space, knowledge, and power with the intent to propose a genealogical turn. At the same time, my final admonition is to incite readers to pursue a different methodology by attending to the way *place* has been understood and to tease out the concept of space, knowledge, and power. Moreover, some may not see this urging as exhaustive of the whole issue of place; however, it could be regarded as a starting point for the "next action or fresh thought." Additionally, the modalities of space/place are not a question that we can fully answer in one volume, since "new findings, new positions and changed perspectives are always possible—and always compromise the unforeseeable."[51]

NOTES

1. See Michel Foucault, "Of Other Spaces," trans. Jay Miskowiec, *Diacritics* 16, no. 1 (Spring 1986): 22.

2. See George Lakoff, "Cognitive Semantics," in *Meaning and Mental Representations*, Advances in Semiotics series, ed. Umberto Eco, Marco Santambrogio, and Patrizia Violi (Bloomington: Indiana University Press, 1988), 119–54.

3. Faubion, *Essential Works*, xxix.

4. Fontana-Giusti, *Foucault for Architects*, 161.

5. D'Ascoli, *Public Space*, 22.

6. Buchanan and Lambert, *Deleuze and Space*, 6–7.

7. King, *Emancipating Space*, 220.

8. Jeremy W. Crampton and Stuart Elden, eds., *Space, Knowledge and Power Foucault and Geography* (Aldershot, Eng.: Ashgate, 2007), 3.

9. Brabant as analyzed in Crampton and Elden, *Space, Knowledge and Power*, 25 and then 47.

10. Elden "Land, Terrain, Territory," 807 and then 807.

11. Foucault, "The Subject and Power," 780.

12. Gagnon and Germain, "Espace urbain et religion," 152, my translation from the original French.

13. Rattansi, *Racism*, 88.

14. Mugerauer, *Interpreting Environments*, xxxi. *Birtherism* is the discredited claim that Barack Obama is not a natural-born US citizen. The Muslim ban is the informal name for a Trump administration policy in which foreign nationals of primarily Muslim nations were banned entry into the United States. And during his campaign for the US presidency, Donald Trump's campaign promise was to "Make America great again"—or *MAGA*, as it has come to be known.

15. David Kushner, *Levittown: Two Families, One Tycoon, and the Fight for Civil Rights in America's Legendary Suburb* (New York: Walker and Co., 2009), 185.

16. Fontana-Giusti, *Foucault for Architects*, 160.

17. Rattansi, *Racism*, 88–89, emphasis original.

18. Gagnon and Germain, "Espace urbain et religion," 144, my translation from the French.

19. John Paul Stevens, remarks delivered at the National Japanese American Memorial Foundation 10th Anniversary Gala Celebration, Washington, D.C., November 4, 2010, text archived at https://www.supremecourt.gov/publicinfo/speeches/sp_11-04-10.pdf.

20. Mugerauer, *Interpreting Environments*, xxix.

21. Jeffery, "From Azulejos to Zaguanes," 289.

22. Thomas Ballantine Irving, *Dates, Names and Places: The End of Islamic Spain* (Cedar Rapids, IA: Mother Mosque Foundation, 1990), 3.

23. Irving, *Dates, Names and Places*, 3, 6.

24. James Hillman, *The Soul's Code: In Search of Character and Calling* (New York: Ballantine Books, 2017), 283.

25. Yves Grafmeyer quoted in Gagnon and Germain, "Espace urbain et religion," 144, my translation from the French. And see Yves Grafmeyer, "La coexistence en milieu urbain: Échanges, conflits, transactions," *Recherches Sociologiques* 30, no. 1 (1999): 175, emphasis original, my translation from the original French, available online at https://sharepoint.uclouvain.be/sites/rsa/Articles/1999-XXX-1_11.pdf.

26. Foucault, *Power/Knowledge*, 117.

27. Norberg-Schulz, *Intentions in Architecture*, 16.

28. Mersch, *Epistemologies of Aesthetics*, 20, 173.

29. Johnson, "Foucault and Visual Art's Adventurous Spaces," 21.

30. As quoted in Mersch, *Epistemologies of Aesthetics*, 167.

31. Mugerauer, *Interpreting Environments*, xl, emphasis original.

32. Mersch, *Epistemologies of Aesthetics*, 25.

33. Çelik, *Displaying the Orient*, 83.

34. Mersch, *Epistemologies of Aesthetics*, 23.

35. Foucault, "Of Other Spaces," 22.

36. The original text is "Labbaik Allahumma labbaik. Labbaik la sharika laka labbaik. Innal-hamda wa-nimata laka wal-mulk, la sharika laka." The English translation of this is "I respond to Your call, O Allah! I respond to Your call. You have no partner. I respond to Your call. All praise, thanks, and blessings are for You. All sovereignty is for You. And You have no partners with You."

37. Hagia Sophia, *Ayasofya* (Turkish), *Sancta Sophia* (Latin).

38. Editors of Encyclopedia Britannica, "Hagia Sophia," *Encyclopedia Britannica*, accessed February 28, 2021, https://www.britannica.com/topic/Hagia-Sophia. Sinan's work demonstrates myriad examples of geometric eloquence with the dome. Essentially, he developed the principles of dome geometry as an ordering element for redefining a spatial conception—and beyond the standards that had already been established in the Hagia Sophia.

39. Ziad Jamaleddine, "Hagia Sophia Past and Future," *Places*, August 2020, https://placesjournal.org/article/hagia-sophia-past-and-future/.

40. Jamaleddine, "Hagia Sophia Past and Future."

41. Foucault, *Power/Knowledge*, 88–89.

42. Foucault, *Power/Knowledge*, 93.

43. Rosemary R. Corbett, RaceReligion series (Stanford: Stanford University Press, 2016).

44. Kishwar Rizvi (Chapel Hill: The University of North Carolina Press, 2015).

45. Mugerauer, *Interpreting Environments*, 122.

46. Fontana-Giusti, *Foucault for Architects*, 134.

47. Biennale di Venezia, "*Three British Mosques*: Sale d'Armi A, Arsenale," Biennale Architettura 2021, Special Project Pavilion of Applied Arts, in collaboration with the Victoria and Albert Museum, London, 2021, https://www.labiennale.org/en/architecture/2021/pavilion-applied-arts.

48. Visit the Women's Mosque online at https://womensmosque.com. And see Maria Jaschok and Jingjun Shui, *The History of Women's Mosques in Chinese Islam: A Mosque of Their Own* (Richmond: Routledge Curzon, 2000).

49. Foucault, *This Is Not a Pipe*, 7.

50. Fontana-Giusti, *Foucault for Architects*, 133.

51. Dieter Mersch, *Epistemologies of Aesthetics*, 174–75.

Appendix

FURTHER READING

Bagby, Ihsan, Paul M. Pearl, and Bryan T. Froehle. *The Mosque in America: A National Portrait; A Report from the Mosque Study Project*. Coordinated by Carl Dudley and David Rooze. Washington DC: Council on American-Islamic Relations, 2001.

Becket. "Christians, Jews, Sikhs, Hindus Defend New Jersey Mosque." Press release. BecketLaw.org, May 11, 2016. https://www.becketlaw.org/media/christians-jews-sikhs-hindus-defend-new-jersey-mosque/.

———. "Mosque Wins Equal Treatment, $3.25 Million Settlement." Press release. BecketLaw.org, May 30, 2017. https://www.becketlaw.org/media/mosque-wins-equal-treatment-3-25-million-settlemen/.

———. "Mosque Wins Right to Meet, Drops Lawsuit." Press release. BecketLaw.org, July 28, 2014. https://www.becketlaw.org/media/mosque-wins-right-meet-drops-lawsuit/.

———. "Supreme Court Rejects Attempt to Shut Down Mosque." Press release. BecketLaw.org, June 2, 2014. https://www.becketlaw.org/media/supreme-court-rejects-attempt-shut-mosque/.

Gutting, Gary, and Johanna Oksala. "Michel Foucault." *Stanford Encyclopedia of Philosophy Archive*, Spring 2019 ed. Edited by Edward N. Zalta. Last modified May 22, 2018. https://plato.stanford.edu/archives/spr2019/entries/foucault/.

Harvard Law Review. "Religious Land Use in the Federal Courts under RLUIPA." Note. Harvardlawreview.org, 120, no. 8 (June 2007): 2718–99. https://harvardlawreview.org/wp-content/uploads/pdfs/religious_land_use.pdf.

Hertzberg, Hendrik. "Cordoba and the Carmelites." News Desk. *The New Yorker*, August 13, 2010. https://www.newyorker.com/news/hendrik-hertzberg/cordoba-and-the-carmelites.

Mawani, Rizwan, *Beyond the Mosque: Diverse Spaces of Muslim Worship*, London: I. B. Taurus, 2019.

Marzouki, Nadia, *Islam: An American Religion,* Translated by C. Jon Delogu. New York: Columbia University Press, 2017.

Glossary

Allah: Arabic for (God) the Creator of the universe, the sole deity that Muslims must worship.
basmala: the statement at the beginning of each *sura* of the Qur'an (except *sura* 9)—"In the Name of Allah the Merciful, the Compassionate," also used by Muslims as an invocation.
adhan: the call to prayer.
ahkam: (pl. *hukum*) laws, values, ordinances.
aql: intellect, rationality, reason.
din: a dogma or religious system, used in the Qur'an to refer to specific beliefs and practices.
du'a: informal supplication.
fatwa: an authoritative legal opinion contrived by a *mufti* who is a jurist qualified to make legal decisions in matters affecting the *ummah* (community of believers).
fiqh: jurisprudence, the science of Islamic law, which falls under the purview of the jurists or *fuqaha* (sing. *faqih*).
hadith: a tradition, saying, narrative or written report of actions attributed to the Prophet Muhammad, being the source of material for the *sunnah*. Regarded as a source of Islamic law.
hajj: the Pilgrimage to Makkah performed during the 12th month of the Islamic lunar calendar; one of the five pillars of Islam.
halal: that which is beneficial or not forbidden by Islamic law.
Hanafi madhhab: a *sunni* canonical school of law, which gets its eponym from the founder of the school, Abu Hanifah (d. 147/767).
Hanbali madhhab: a *sunni* canonical school of law, which gets its eponym from the founder of the school, Ibn Hanbal (d. 241/855).
haram: acts which are forbidden by Islamic Law.
ijtihad: lit. Exertion and technically the effort a jurist makes in order to deduce the law which is not self-evident from its sources.
Islam: submission to divine will or purpose.

iktilaf: juristic disagreement.

ilm: religious science, knowledge.

Ja'fari madhhab: the primary Shi'i canonical school of law.

jami: (lit. what brings together); congregational mosque where the Friday prayer is performed.

ijma: consensus.

imam: a prayer leader who is designated to lead any of the formal prayers; In America, a director of the *masjid* or Islamic center.

Ka'ba: the sacred black cube-shaped structure located in the mosque at Makkah. Abraham and Ismail rebuillt the *Ka'ba* after Adam as a symbol of monotheism.

khatib: the speaker who delivers the *khutba* (exhortation) at the time of congregational worship on Fridays.

khatt: Arabic calligraphy using one or more of the six major styles: *Kufic, Naskh, Diwan, Thuluth, Riqah, Maghribi,* etc.

madhhab: (pl. *madhahib*) a juristic or theological school.

maslahah: consideration of public interest.

madrasa: a school for teaching religious as well as secular subjects.

masjid: mosque, a place of congregational gathering, education and religious activities.

markaz al-Islami: Islamic Center, a building complex which consists of a mosque, classrooms, book store, cultural center, library, religious center and ancillary facilities. For example, Islamic Cultural Center of New York and Washington DC.

Maliki madhhab: a *sunni* canonical school of law, which gets its eponym from the founder of the school, Imam Malik (d. 179/795).

musalla: a designated extra-muros (or intra-muros) prayer space or area that is not a formal *masjid*; In America it is sometimes used to designate the prayer area in an Islamic center.

Muslim: one who submits to the will of Allah, one who accepts, professes, and practices Islam.

mujtahid: a mufti who is qualified to practice independent reasoning or *ijtihad*.

mihrab: the prayer niche indicating the direction of Makkah.

minbar: (also pronounced *mimbar*) a rostrum or platform of three or more steps upon which the *khatib* stands to deliver the exhortation on Fridays.

minaret: an elevated tower integrated in the architecture of a mosque, in earlier times, from where the call to prayer was pronounced. Today a public address system is used.

Orientalist: those who study the orient, specifically those who study the Islamic World.

al-Qu'ran: the sacred text of Islam, literally translated as "recitation" or "reading."

qadi: a judge who makes decisions on the basis of the *shari'ah*.

qibla: the direction of the *Ka'ba* and Makkah, which a worshipper must face Makkah during the ritual performance of prayer; all mosques have a *mihrab* which indicates the direction of Makkah.

qiyas: juridical analogy; analogical reasoning.

Rak'a: the cycles of postures of prayer (*salat*), such as standing, bowing, prostration, sitting.

riwaq: trabeated hall with regular spaced columns and arches.

salat al-juma: the Friday congregational prayer.

Shafi'i madhhab: a *sunni* canonical school of law, which gets its eponym from the founder of the school, Imam Shafi'i (d. 204/819).

shirk: polytheism, the opposite of monotheism.

shahada: the declaration of faith: "There is no God except Allah and Muhammad is the Prophet of Allah." One of the five pillars of Islam.

shari'ah: the religious law derived from four sources of law in Sunni Islam: (*Qur'an, sunnah, qiyas,* and *ijma*).

store front masjid: a small mosque or *musalla* which can accommodate a small local or neighborhood gathering.

sujud: derived from the Arabic verb *sa ja da*, to prostrate; hence the noun *masjid* often translates as mosque.

tauhid: the Islamic principle of monotheism, which acknowledges Allah as the sole creator of the universe.

tafsir: also (ta'wil) exegesis, interpretation, commentary of the Qur'an concerning matters of grammar, clarifying textual allegorical meaning, including the study of philology, lexicography, and so on.

urf: custom, habit and agreement.

ulama: (sing. *alim*) jurists, doctors of law and Qur'anic sciences, including specialists in theology, *hadith* and other categories of scholarship.

Wudu: ablutions performed by a worshipper before performing the prayer.

Bibliography

Abdul-Rauf, Muhammad. *History of the Islamic Center: From Dream to Reality.* Washington, DC: Colortone Press, 1978.

Abi-Habib, Maria, and Sameer Yasir. "Court Backs Hindus on Ayodhya, Handing Modi Victory in His Bid to Remake India." *New York Times*, November 8, 2019. https://www.nytimes.com/2019/11/08/world/asia/ayodhya-supreme-court-india.html.

Adamson, Peter. "Fakhr al-Dīn Al-Rāzī on Place." *Arabic Sciences and Philosophy* 27, no. 2 (2017): 205–36.

Al-Azraqi, Muhammad ibn 'Abd Allah. *Kitab Akhbar Makkah*. Edited by Abdul Malik Dahesh. Maktabat al-Asadi: N.p., [9th century] 2003.

Al-Ġazzālī, Abū-Ḥāmid Muḥammad Ibn-Muḥammad. *The Niche of Lights: A Parallel English-Arabic Text.* Translated, introduction, and annotated by David Buchman. Provo, UT: Brigham Young University Press, 1998.

al-Harithy, Howayda. "The Concept of Space in Mamluk Architecture." *Muqarnas* 18 (2001): 73–93.

Al Jazeera. "China Committing Genocide against Uighurs, Says Report." AlJazeera.com, March 10, 2021. https://www.aljazeera.com/news/2021/3/10/china-committed-genocide-against-uighurs-in-xinjiang-says-report.

al-Rāzī, Fakhr al-Dīn. *The Great Exegesis: Vol. 1, The Fātiha.* Translated by Sohaib Saeed. Cambridge: The Royal Aal al-Bayt Institute for Islamic Thought and the Islamic Texts Society, 2018.

Altria Theater. "History," AltriaTheater.com, accessed June 30, 2020. https://www.altriatheater.com/about-us/history.

Arce-Sainz, Fernando. "La supuesta basílica de San Vicente en Córdoba: de mito histórico a obstinación historiográfica/The Alleged Basilica of Saint Vincent of Córdoba: From a Historical Myth to an Obstinacy of Historiography." *Al-Qanṭara* 36, no. 1 (2015): 11–44. https://al-qantara.revistas.csic.es/index.php/al-qantara/article/view/337/329.

Archer, Isabella. "(Re)Envisioning Orientalist North Africa: Exploring Representations of Maghrebian Identities in Oriental and Occidental Art, Museums, and Markets." *intersections* 11, no. 2, (2010): 67–107. http://depts.washington.edu/chid/

intersections_Autumn_2010/Isabella_Archer_%28Re%29Envisioning_Orientalist_North_Africa.pdf.
Austin, Allan D. *African Muslims in Antebellum America: Transatlantic Stories and Spiritual Struggles*. New York: Routledge, 1997 [1984].
Barnard, Anne. "In Lower Manhattan, 2 Mosques Have Firm Roots." *New York Times*, August 13, 2010. https://www.nytimes.com/2010/08/14/nyregion/14mosque.html.
Barthes, Roland. *Mythologies*. New York: Noonday Press, 1991.
Baudrillard, Jean. *Simulacra and Simulation*. Translated by Sheila Faria Glaser. Ann Arbor: University of Michigan Press, 1994.
BBC News. "Myanmar Rohingya: What You Need to Know about the Crisis." BBC.com, January 23, 2020. https://www.bbc.com/news/world-asia-41566561.
———. "Who Are the Uyghurs and Why Is China Being Accused of Genocide?" BBC.com, June 21, 2021. https://www.bbc.com/news/world-asia-china-22278037.
Behiery, Valerie. Review of *Art of Islam, Language and Meaning* by Titus Burckhardt. *Journal of Shi'a Islamic Studies* 4, no. 2 (2011): 225–27. Archived at https://static1.squarespace.com/static/5b2d2b3450a54f8020389343/t/5b45129703ce64cf6ce58d75/1531253425998/Art+of+Islam.pdf.
Behrens-Abouseif, Doris. *Islamic Architecture in Cairo: An Introduction*. Cairo: American University in Cairo Press, 1989.
Belsey, Catherine. *Poststructuralism: A Very Short Introduction*. Oxford: Oxford University Press, 2002.
Bernstein, Gerald Steven. "In Pursuit of the Exotic: Islamic Forms in Nineteenth-Century American Architecture." PhD diss., University of Pennsylvania, 1968.
Besirevic-Regan, Jasmina. "Yugoslavia." Yale University, Genocide Studies Program, accessed November 18, 2021. https://gsp.yale.edu/case-studies/yugoslavia-former.
Bevan, Robert. *The Destruction of Memory: Architecture at War*. London: Reaktion Books, 2006.
Beydoun, Khaled A. *American Islamophobia: Understanding the Roots and Rise of Fear*. Oakland: University of California Press, 2018.
Bhabha, Homi K. *The Location of Culture*. London: Routledge, 2004.
Bialasiewicz, Luiza. "'That Which Is Not a Mosque': Disturbing Place at the 2015 Venice Biennale." *City* 21, nos. 3–4 (2017): 367–87. https://www.tandfonline.com/doi/pdf/10.1080/13604813.2017.1325221.
Biennale di Venezia. "*Three British Mosques*: Sale d'Armi A, Arsenale." Biennale Architettura 2021, Special Project Pavilion of Applied Arts, in collaboration with the Victoria and Albert Museum, London, 2021. https://www.labiennale.org/en/architecture/2021/pavilion-applied-arts.
Bier, Carol. "Geometry in Islamic Art," *Encyclopaedia of the History of Science, Technology, and Medicine in Non-Western Cultures* (2015): 1–21
Borsi, Katharina, Tarsha Finney, and Pavlos Philippou. "Architectural Type and the Discourse of Urbanism." *The Journal of Architecture* 23, nos. 7–8 (October 2018): 1093–103. https://www.tandfonline.com/doi/pdf/10.1080/13602365.2018.1513478.
Bosco, Robert M., and Lori Hartmann-Mahmud. "The Securitization of Park51." *Peace Review: A Journal of Social Justice* 23, no. 4 (2011): 530–36.

Boundaoui, Assia, dir. *The Feeling of Being Watched: Surveillance in a US-Arab Community*. Distributed in the United States by Women Make Movies, 2018.

Brabant, Jean-Michel. "Response." Translated by Gerald Moore. In *Space, Knowledge and Power: Foucault and Geography*. Edited by Jeremy W. Crampton and Stuart Elden, 25–28. Aldershot, Eng.: Ashgate, 2007.

Bridge Initiative Team. "Factsheet: The NYPD Muslim Surveillance and Mapping Program." Georgetown.edu, May 11, 2020. https://bridge.georgetown.edu/research/factsheet-the-nypd-muslim-surveillance-and-mapping-program/.

Brown v. Board of Education of Topeka, 347 U.S. 483 (1954).

Brown v. City of Richmond, 204 Va. 471 (1963).

Buchanan, Ian, and Gregg Lambert, eds. *Deleuze and Space*. Edinburgh: Edinburgh University Press, 2005.

Burckhardt, Titus. *The Art of Islam: Language and Meaning*. Foreword by Seyyed Hossein Nasr, introduction by Jean-Louis Michon. Bloomington, IN: World Wisdom, 2009.

Burgen, Stephen. "Córdoba Rejects Catholic Church's Claim to Own Mosque-Cathedral." *The Guardian*, March 13, 2016. https://www.theguardian.com/world/2016/mar/13/cordoba-catholic-churchs-claim-mosque-cathedral.

Catholic New Agency. "Bishop Requests Historic Cathedral No Longer Be Referred to as Mosque." November 5, 2010. https://www.catholicnewsagency.com/news/bishop-requests-historic-cathedral-no-longer-be-referred-to-as-mosque.

Çelik, Zeynep. *Displaying the Orient: Architecture of Islam at Nineteenth-Century World's Fairs*. Comparative Studies on Muslim Societies 12. Berkeley and Los Angeles: University of California Press, 1992.

Central Hudson Gas & Electric Corp. v. Public Service Commission, 447 U.S. 557 (1980).

Chao, Jenifer. "Oppositional Banality: Watching Ordinary Muslims in 'Little Mosque on the Prairie.'" *NECSUS/European Journal of Media Studies*, no. 1 (2015): 27–45. https://necsus-ejms.org/oppositional-banality-watching-ordinary-muslims-in-little-mosque-on-the-prairie/.

Chittick, William C. "Time, Space, and Objectivity of Ethical Norms: The Teachings of Ibn Al-'Arabī." *Islamic Studies* 39, no. 4 (Winter 2000): 581–96. Reprinted in http://www.iqbalcyberlibrary.net/files/009/IRE-OCT-2004.pdf.

Chorbachi, W. K. "In the Tower of Babel: Beyond Symmetry in Islamic Design, *Computers & Mathematics with Applications*, vol. 17, 4:6 (1989): 751–89;

City of Atlanta, Georgia (website). "Fox Theatre." City Planning/Historic Preservation/Property & District Information, Atlanta.gov, accessed October 27, 2021. https://www.atlantaga.gov/government/departments/city-planning/office-of-design/urban-design-commission/fox-theatre.

Clark, Emma. *The Art of the Islamic Garden*. Ramsbury, Marlborough, and Wiltshire, UK: The Crowood Press, 2010.

Clark, Gordon L. *Judges and Cities: Interpreting Local Autonomy*. Chicago: University of Chicago Press, 1985.

Clark, Laura Blackwell, and Barbra Newman Young. "The Murfreesboro Mosque: To Build or Not to Build?" *Forum on Public Policy* 2012, no. 2 (2012). https://

4e429266-b6af-4a71-83d3-81ca05731064.filesusr.com/ugd/553e83_91272a6d006
444b49636f87f89e9e589.pdf.

Corbett, Rosemary R. *Making Moderate Islam: Sufism, Service, and the "Ground Zero Mosque" Controversy*. RaceReligion series. Stanford: Stanford University Press, 2016.

Cordes, Mark W. "Where to Pray? Religious Zoning and the First Amendment." *University of Kansas Law Review* 35, no. 4 (1987): 697–762. https://commons.lib.niu.edu/bitstream/handle/10843/16450/Cordes%2035%20U%20Kan%20L%20Rev%20697%201987-HeinArticle.pdf.

Crampton, Jeremy W., and Stuart Elden, eds. *Space, Knowledge and Power: Foucault and Geography*. Aldershot, Eng.: Ashgate, 2007.

Crang, Mike, and Nigel Thrift. "Introduction." In *Thinking Space*, edited by Mike Crang and Nigel Thrift, 1–30. London: Routledge, 2000.

Curtin, Philip D., ed. *Africa Remembered: Narratives from the Era of the Slave Trade*. Introductions and annotations by Philip D. Curtin and others. Madison: University of Wisconsin Press, 1967.

Darr, Robert Abdul Hayy. "The Palace of Blessing and Grace: Discovering Spiritual Symbolism in the Court of Lions at the Alhambra in Spain." Sufi Garden (website), 2004. http://www.sufigarden.com/images/documents/2004_The-Palace-of-Grace.pdf.

D'Ascoli, Angela. *Public Space: Henri Lefebvre and Beyond*. Architecture 3. Milan: Mimesis International, 2018.

de Ruijter, A. "The Structuralism of Lévi-Strauss: Problems and Prospects." Translated by Jan de Wolf. *JASO—Journal of the Anthropological Society of Oxford* 14, no. 3 (1983): 273–91. https://www.anthro.ox.ac.uk/sites/default/files/anthro/documents/media/jaso14_3_1983_273_291.pdf.

Dickie, James. "The Works of Mario Rossi at Alessandria." Amate Sponde . . . Presence of Italy in the Architecture of the Islamic Mediterranean. *Environmental Design: Journal of the Islamic Environmental Design Research Centre*. Nos. 9–10 (1990): 94–101. https://s3.us-east-1.amazonaws.com/media.archnet.org/system/publications/contents/3237/original/DPC0789.pdf.

Dodds, Jerrilynn D., ed. *Al-Andalus: The Art of Islamic Spain*. Publication issued in conjunction with the exhibition, Metropolitan Museum of Art, New York, July 1–September 27, 1992. New York: Abrams, 1992. Online at https://books.google.com/books?id=lLAryx8bC8UC&printsec=frontcover#v=onepage&q&f=false.

Donadio, Rachel. "Name Debate Echoes Old Clash of Faiths." *New York Times*, November 4, 2010. https://www.nytimes.com/2010/11/05/world/europe/05cordoba.html.

Douglass, Frederick. "West India Emancipation." Speech delivered at an event celebrating the twenty-third anniversary of the emancipation of West India, Canandaigua, New York, August 3, 1857. Text archived at https://rbscp.lib.rochester.edu/4398.

Eco, Umberto. *The Limits of Interpretation*. Advances in Semiotics. Bloomington: Indiana University Press, 1990.

Editors of Encyclopedia Britannica. "Hagia Sophia." *Encyclopedia Britannica*, accessed February 28, 2021. https://www.britannica.com/topic/Hagia-Sophia.

Ekins, Emily. "The State of Free Speech and Tolerance in America." Cato Institute, October 31, 2017. https://www.cato.org/survey-reports/state-free-speech-tolerance-america.

Elden, Stuart. "Land, Terrain, Territory." *Progress in Human Geography* 34, no. 6 (2010): 799–817.

Erzen, Jale Nejdet. "Aesthetics and Aisthesis in Ottoman Art and Architecture." *Journal of Islamic Studies* 2, no. 1 (1991): 1–24.

Evans, G. S. "This Could Be a Pipe: Foucault, Irrealism and *Ceci n'est pas une pipe*." *irreal (re)views*, last modified 2013. http://cafeirreal.alicewhittenburg.com/review5.htm.

Faubion, James D. *The Essential Works of Foucault, 1954–1984: Aesthetics, Method, and Epistemology*, vol. 2. Translated by Michael Hurley et al. New York: The New Press, 1994.

———. "Michel Foucault." *Britannica.com*. Last modified October 11, 2021. https://www.britannica.com/biography/Michel-Foucault/Foucaults-Ideas.

Fleming, Walter Millard, and William S. Paterson. *Mecca Temple: Ancient Arabic Order of the Nobles of the Mystic Shrine; Its History and Pleasures, Together with the Origin and History of the Order*. New York: Press of Andrew H. Kellogg, 1894.

Fontana-Giusti, Gordana. *Foucault for Architects*. Oxon: Routledge, 2013.

Foucault, Michel. *The Archeology of Knowledge: And the Discourse on Language*. Translated by A. M. Sheridan Smith. New York: Pantheon Books, 1972.

———. "Des espaces autres." From a talk given at Conférence au Cercle d'études architecturales, Paris, March 14, 1967. Published in *Architecture/Mouvement/Continuité*, no. 5 (October 1984): 46–49. Translated by Jay Miskowiec as "Of Other Spaces: Utopias and Heterotopias." Published in English as "Of Other Spaces," *Diacritics* 16, no. 1 (Spring 1986): 22–27. Text available at https://web.mit.edu/allanmc/www/foucault1.pdf.

———. *The Hermeneutics of the Subject: Lectures at the Collège de France, 1981–1982*. Vol. 3. Edited by Frédéric Gros, translated by Graham Burchell. English series edited by Arnold I. Davidson. New York and Basingstoke: Palgrave-Macmillan, 2005.

———. "Nietzsche, Genealogy, History." Translated by Donald F. Bouchard and Sherry Simon, edited by Donald F. Bouchard. In *The Foucault Reader*, compiled, edited, and introduced by Paul Rabinow, 76–100. New York: Pantheon Books, 1984.

———. *Power/Knowledge: Selected Interviews and Other Writings, 1972–1977*. Edited by Colin Gordon, translated by Colin Gordon, Leo Marshall, John Mepham, and Kate Soper. New York: Vintage Books, 1980.

———. *Society Must Be Defended: Lectures at the Collège de France, 1975–76*. Edited by Mauro Bertani, translated by David Macey. New York: Picador, 2003.

———. "The Subject and Power." *Critical Inquiry* 8, no. 4 (Summer 1982): 777–95.

———. *This Is Not a Pipe*. With illustrations and letters by René Magritte, translated and edited by James Harkness. Berkeley: University of California Press, 1982.

———.*The Will to Knowledge: The History of Sexuality*. Translated by Robert Hurley. London: Penguin Books, 1998.

Frampton, Kenneth. "Towards a Critical Regionalism: Six Points for an Architecture of Resistance." In *Anti-aesthetic: Essays on Postmodern Culture; A Reader*, ed. and intro. Hal Foster, 16–30. Seattle: Bay Press, 1983. Text available at https://www.modernindenver.com/wp-content/uploads/2015/08/Frampton.pdf.

Friedman, Kenneth S. *Myths of the Free Market*. New York: Algora Publishing, 2003.

Fuchs, Dale. "Mass versus Minarets: The Cordoba Controversy." *The Independent*, October 23, 2011. Cached at https://www.independent.co.uk/news/world/europe/mass-versus-minarets-the-cordoba-controversy-2108224.html.

Gagnon, Julie Elizabeth, and Annick Germain. "Espace urbain et religion: Esquisse d'une géographie des lieux de culte minoritaires de la région de Montréal." *Cahiers de géographie de Québec* 46, no. 128 (January 2002): 143–61. https://www.erudit.org/fr/revues/cgq/2002-v46-n128-cgq2700/023038ar/.

Giedion, Sigfried. *The Eternal Present: The Beginnings of Art*. Oxford: Oxford University Press, 1962.

———. *Space, Time and Architecture*. 5th ed. Cambridge, MA: Harvard University Press, 1967.

Giese, Francine, and Ariane Varela Braga. "The Protagonists of the Moorish Revival: Translating Ibero-Islamic Heritage in Eighteenth-and Nineteenth-Century Europe." *Art in Translation* 11, no. 2 (2019): 119–23. https://www.tandfonline.com/doi/epub/10.1080/17561310.2019.1703333.

Gingrich, Newt. "Newt's Statement on the Proposed 'Cordoba House' Mosque at Ground Zero." *Gingrich 360* (website), July 22, 2010. Archived at https://web.archive.org/web/20190930005239/https://www.gingrich360.com/2010/07/mosquestatement/.

Glass, Andrew. "Eisenhower Dedicates D.C. Islamic Center, June 28, 1957." *Politico*, June 28, 2018. https://www.politico.com/story/2018/06/28/eisenhower-dedicates-dc-islamic-center-june-28-1957-667325.

Glass, Philip. "From Egypt." No. 16, a recording of the Azan, in the soundtrack for *Powaqqatsi: Life in Transformation*, dir. Godfrey Reggio, dist. United States, the Cannon Group, 1988. Available online at https://www.youtube.com/watch?v=ZVE-a-24prE.

Grabar, Oleg. "Upon Reading Al-Azraqi." *Muqarnas* 3 (1985): 1–7.

Grafmeyer, Yves. "La coexistence en milieu urbain: Échanges, conflits, transactions." *Recherches Sociologiques* 30, no. 1 (1999): 157–76. Available online at https://sharepoint.uclouvain.be/sites/rsa/Articles/1999-XXX-1_11.pdf.

Gril, Denis. "Love Letters to the Ka'ba: A Presentation of Ibn 'Arabi's *Tâj al-Rasâ'il*." *Journal of the Muhyiddin Ibn Arabi Society* 17 (1995). https://ibnarabisociety.org/love-letters-to-the-kaaba-denis-gril/.

Gruber, Christiane. "The Missiri of Fréjus as Healing Memorial: Mosque Metaphors and the French Colonial Army (1928–64)," *International Journal of Islamic Architecture*, 1:1 (2012): 25–60.

Gutleben, Christian. "'Urban Palimpsests': When Novelistic and Architectural Languages Merge in Penelope Lively's *City of the Mind*." *Études britanniques contemporaines* 52 (2017). https://journals.openedition.org/ebc/3545.

Gutterman, David S., and Andrew R. Murphy. "The 'Ground Zero Mosque': Sacred Space and the Boundaries of American Identity." *Politics, Groups, and Identities* 2, no. 3. (2014): 368–85.

Gutting, Gary. *Foucault: A Very Short Introduction*. Oxford: Oxford University Press, 2005. Available online at https://issuu.com/376746/docs/foucault__a_very_short_introduction__very_short_in

Haider, Gulzar. "'Brother in Islam, Please Draw Us a Mosque': Muslims in the West; A Personal Account." In *Expressions of Islam in Buildings*, ed. Hayat Salam, 155–66. Singapore: Concept Media/The Aga Khan Award for Architecture, 1990.

Hampson, Rick. "Ground Zero Cross a Powerful Symbol for 9/11 Museum." *USA Today*. Last modified May 15, 2014. https://www.usatoday.com/story/news/nation/2014/05/13/911-ground-zero-museum-cross-world-trade-center/8907003/.

Haskins, Ekaterina V., and Justin P. DeRose. "Memory, Visibility, and Public Space: Reflections on Commemoration(s) of 9/11." *Space and Culture* 6, no. 4 (November 2003): 377–93.

Helm, Joan. "Erec and Enide: Cosmic Measures in Nature and the Hebrew Heritage." In *Medieval Numerology: A Book of Essays*, edited by Robert Leo Surles, 53–76. New York: Garland Publishing, 1993.

Hejduk, John. *Mask of Medusa*. Edited by Kim Shkapich. New York: Rizzoli, 1989.

Hier, Sean P., and B. Singh Bolaria, eds. *Identity and Belonging, Rethinking Race and Ethnicity in Canadian Society*. Toronto: Canadian Scholars Press, 2006.

Hillenbrand, Robert. "Occidental Oriental: Islamic Influences in the Art of Britain and America." Review of *The Oriental Obsession, Islamic Inspiration in British and American Art and Architecture, 1500–1920*, John Sweetman. *Oriental Art* 35, no. 4 (Winter 1989–90): 218–25. Available online at https://www.academia.edu/33212137/Robert_Hillenbrand_Oriental_Occidental_Islamic_influences_in_the_art_of_Britain_and_America_Oriental_Art_N_S_XXXV_4_1989_218_25.

Hillman, James. *The Soul's Code: In Search of Character and Calling*. New York: Ballantine Books, 2017.

Hirst, Paul Q. "Foucault and Architecture." *AA Files*, no. 26 (Autumn 1993): 52–60.

———. *Space and Power: Politics, War, and Architecture*. Cambridge, MA: Polity Press, 2005.

Hoeveler, Diane Long, and Jeffrey Cass. "Introduction: Mapping Orientalism; Representations and Pedagogies." In *Interrogating Orientalism Contextual Approaches and Pedagogical Practices*, ed. Diane Long Hoeveler and Jeffrey Cass, 1–22. Columbus: The Ohio State University Press, 2015.

Holt, Jaan. "Architecture and the Wall Facing Mecca." *Via: The Journal of the Graduate School of Fine Arts University of Pennsylvania*, 5, Determinants of Form 5 (1982): 24–28.

Hook, Derek. "Genealogy, Discourse, 'Effective History': Foucault and the Work of Critique." *Qualitative Research in Psychology* 2, no. 1 (2005): 3–31.

Hotel Viento 10. "Muhammad Iqbal: Probably the First and Only Muslim in Eight Centuries to Have Prayed in the Mezquita." Blog, September 20, 2018. https://hotelviento10.es/en/?view=article&id=126:posiblemente-el-unico-musulman-que-ha-rezado-en-la-mezquita-en-los-ultimos-ocho-siglos.

Howell, Sally. "Laying Groundwork for American Muslim Histories: 1865–1965." In *The Cambridge Companion to American Islam*, ed. Juliane Hammer and Omid Safi, 45–64. New York: Cambridge University Press, 2013.

Hyussen, Andreas. *Present Pasts: Urban Palimpsests and the Politics of Memory*. Stanford: Stanford University Press, 2003.

ibn ʿAbd al-ʿAzīz, Muḥammad, Muḥammad al-Ḥabīb Hīlah ibn Fahd, and ʿUmar ibn Muḥammad Ibn Fahd. *Kitāb Nayl al-muná bi-dhayl bulūgh al-qirá li-takmilat Itḥāf al-wará: tārīkh Makkah al-Mukarramah min sanat 922 H ilá 946 H*. 2 vols. Edited by Abdul Malik Dahesh. London: Muʾassasat al-Furqān lil-Turāth al-Islāmī, Farʿ Mawsūʿat Makkah al-Mukarramah wa-al-Madīnah al-Munawwarah, 2003.

Iqbal, Muhammad. "Masjid-e-Qurtaba" (The Mosque of Córdoba). In *Bāl-e Jibrīl* (*The Wing of Gabriel*). Lahore: Taj, 1935.

Iqbal Urdu (blog). "(Bal-e-Jibril-124) Masjid-e-Qurtaba (مسجد طرقبہ) The Mosque of Córdoba." Allama Iqbal Poetry مالک ‏مع‏ال‏م حمد اقبال. April 2011. http://iqbalurdu.blogspot.com/2011/04/bal-e-jibril-124-masjid-e-qurtaba.html.

Irving, Thomas Ballantine. *Dates, Names and Places: The End of Islamic Spain*. Cedar Rapids, IA: Mother Mosque Foundation, 1990.

Islamic Center of Mississippi, Inc., et al., Plaintiffs-appellants, v. City of Starkville, Mississippi, Defendant-appellee, 840 F.2d 293 (5th Cir. 1988).

Islamic Center of Mississippi, Inc., et al., Plaintiffs-appellants, v. City of Starkville, Mississippi, Defendant-appellee, 876 F.2d 465 (5th Cir. 1989).

Islamic Center of Murfreesboro and Dr. Ossama Bahloul v. Rutherford County, Tennessee. "Plaintiffs' Memorandum of Law in Support of Plaintiffs' Application for a Temporary Restraining Order or Preliminary Injunction," United States District Court, Middle District of Tennessee, Nashville Decision, July 18, 2012. Available at https://becketpdf.s3.amazonaws.com/Memo-in-Support-of-TRO-07.18.12.pdf.pdf.

The Islamic Society of Basking Ridge et al v. Township of Bernards et al., No. 3:2016cv01369, Document 81 (D.N.J. 2016). https://becketpdf.s3.amazonaws.com/ISBR-v.-Twp-of-Bernards-et-al_Complaint.pdf. https://law.justia.com/cases/federal/district-courts/new-jersey/njdce/3:2016cv01369/330708/81/.

The Islamic Society of Basking Ridge, et al., v. Township of Bernards et al. Civil action no. 16–1369 (MAS) (LHG). Case 3:16-cv-01369-MAS-LHG. Document 93. Opinion. Filed in the US District Court, District of New Jersey, December 31, 2016. https://www.govinfo.gov/content/pkg/USCOURTS-njd-3_16-cv-01369/pdf/USCOURTS-njd-3_16-cv-01369-1.pdf.

Jamaleddine, Ziad. "Hagia Sophia Past and Future." *Places*, August 2020. https://placesjournal.org/article/hagia-sophia-past-and-future/.

James, Nickolas. "Law and Power: Ten Lessons from Foucault." *Bond Law Review* 30, no. 1 (2018): 31–42. https://pure.bond.edu.au/ws/portalfiles/portal/27624577/Law_and_Power_Ten_Lessons_From_Foucault.pdf.

Jaschok, Maria, and Jingjun Shui. *The History of Women's Mosques in Chinese Islam: A Mosque of Their Own*. Richmond: Routledge Curzon, 2000.

J G and Margaret. "Córdoba's Cathedral Is a Mosque!" *Spain Then and Now*. Accessed June 7, 2020. http://www.spainthenandnow.com/spanish-architecture/cordobas-cathedral-is-a-mosque.

Jeffery, R. Brooks. "From Azulejos to Zaguanes: The Islamic Legacy in the Built Environment of Hispano-America." *Journal of the Southwest* 45, nos. 1–2 (Spring–Summer 2003): 289–327.

Johnson, Peter. "Foucault and Visual Art's Adventurous Spaces." *Heterotopian Studies* (website), November 2015. http://www.heterotopiastudies.com/wp-content/uploads/2015/06/Foucault-and-art-article-pdf.pdf.

Jones, Lindsay. "The Hermeneutics of Sacred Architecture: A Reassessment of the Similitude between Tula, Hidalgo and Chichen Itza, Yucatan, Part I." *History of Religions* 32, no. 3 (1993): 207–32.

Kahera, Akel Ismail. "The Accuracy of the Qibla Axis (*Inhiraf al-Qibla*): A Legal Debate." *Al-Shajarah: Journal of the International Institute of Islamic Thought and Civilization* 8, no. 2 (2003): 191–212.

———. *Deconstructing the American Mosque: Space, Gender, and Aesthetics*. Austin: University of Texas Press, 2002.

———. "'God's Dominion': Omar Ibn Said's Use of Arabic Literacy as Opposition to Slavery Disposition." *The South Carolina Review* 46, no. 2 (2014): 126–34. https://tigerprints.clemson.edu/cgi/viewcontent.cgi?article=1000&context=archetecture_pubs.

———. "Image, Text, and Form: Complexities of Aesthetics in an American *Masjid*." *Studies in Contemporary Islam* 1, no. 2 (Fall 1999): 73–84. Text available at https://www.academia.edu/37564285/Image_Text_and_Form_Complexities_of_Aesthetics_in_an_American_Masjid.

———. *Reading the Islamic City: Discursive Practices and Legal Judgment*. Lanham, MD: Lexington Books, 2012.

———. "Towards an 'Integrated' Design Pedagogy: Exploring Architectural Displacements and the Location of Culture Beyond the Bauhaus Tradition." In *Not White: Proceedings of the 20th National Conference on the Beginning Design Student; April 1–3, 2004, Hampton University Department of Architecture*, edited by Shannon Chance, 109–14. Hampton, VA: Hampton University Urban Institute, 2006. http://ncbds.la-ab.com/20_Proceedings.pdf.

Kahera, Akel Ismail, and Bakama Bakamanume. "Houston Mosques: Space, Place and Religious Meaning." In *The Changing World Religion Map: Sacred Places, Identities, Practices and Politics*, ed. Stanley D. Brunn, 2353–76. Dordrecht: Springer Netherlands, 2015.

Kakutani, Michiko. "The Right Architect with the Wrong Name." *New York Times*, August 15, 2011. https://www.nytimes.com/2011/08/16/books/the-submission-by-amy-waldman-review.html.

Kali, Andrea, and Bill Duke, dirs. *Prince Among Slaves*. Film. Unity Productions Foundation, 2008. Watch at https://www.upf.tv/films/prince-among-slaves/watch/.

Kennedy, Randy. "Mosque Installed at Venice Biennale Tests City's Tolerance." *New York Times*, May 6, 2015. https://www.nytimes.com/2015/05/07/arts/design/mosque-installed-at-venice-biennale-tests-citys-tolerance.html.

Kent Law School, University of Kent. "Foucault's Biopolitics and State Racism," *Law and the Humanities LLM* (blog), February 15, 2019. https://blogs.kent.ac.uk/lawandthehumanities/2019/02/15/foucaults-biopolitics-and-state-racism/.

Khalidi, Omar. "Approaches to Mosque Design in North America." In *Muslims on the Americanization Path*, ed. Yvonne Yazbeck Haddad and John L. Esposito, 399–424. New York: Oxford University Press, 1998.

Khoury, Nuha N. N. "The Mihrab: From Text to Form." *International Journal of Middle East Studies* 30, no. 1 (1998): 1–27.

———. "The Mihrab Image: Commemorative Themes in Medieval Islamic Architecture." In *Muqarnas: An Annual on Islamic Art and Architecture*, vol. 9, ed. Oleg Grabar, [11]–29. Leiden: E. J. Brill, 1992.

Kilde, Jeanne Halgren. "The Park 51/Ground Zero Controversy and Sacred Sites as Contested Space." *Religions* 2, no. 3 (2011): 297–311. Text available at https://www.mdpi.com/2077-1444/2/3/297/htm.

King, David A. "The Sacred Direction in Islam: A Study of the Interaction of Religion and Science in the Middle Ages Article." *Interdisciplinary Science Reviews* 10, no. 4 (1985): 315–28.

King, Ross. *Emancipating Space: Geography, Architecture, and Urban Design*. London: Guilford Press, 1996.

Kuo, Lily. "Revealed: New Evidence of China's Mission to Raze the Mosques of Xinjiang." *The Guardian*, May 6, 2019. https://amp.theguardian.com/world/2019/may/07/revealed-new-evidence-of-chinas-mission-to-raze-the-mosques-of-xinjiang.

Kushner, David. *Levittown: Two Families, One Tycoon, and the Fight for Civil Rights in America's Legendary Suburb*. New York: Walker and Co., 2009.

Lakoff, George. "Cognitive Semantics." In *Meaning and Mental Representations*, Advances in Semiotics series, ed. Umberto Eco, Marco Santambrogio, and Patrizia Violi, 119–54. Bloomington: Indiana University Press, 1988.

Landy, Frédéric. "Conception of National Territory and Grain Circulation: The Indian Public Distribution System (PDS)." *Annales de géographie* 677, no. 1 (2011): 26–49. Text available at https://www.cairn-int.info/article-E_AG_677_0026--conception-of-national-territory-and.htm.

Larsonneur, Claire. "Location, Location, Location." *Études britanniques contemporaines* 37 (2009): 141–52. Text available at https://journals.openedition.org/ebc/3692.

Leach, Neil, ed. *Rethinking Architecture: A Reader in Cultural Theory*. London: Routledge, 1997.

Lefebvre, Henri. *Éléments de rythmanalyse* (*Rhythmanalysis*). Paris: Éditions Syllepse, 1992.

———. *The Production of Space*. Translated by Donald Nicholson-Smith. Oxford: Blackwell, 1991.

Leviter, Lee. "The Myth of Christian Innocence Reinforces Anti-Semitism." *Sojourners*, April 30, 2020. https://sojo.net/articles/myth-christian-innocence-reinforces-anti-semitism.

Lévi-Strauss, Claude. *Structural Anthropology*. Translated by Claire Jacobson and Brooke Grundfest Schoepf. New York: Basic Books Inc., 1963.

Lindenberg, David Meyer. "In New Jersey, a Long-Overdue Mosque Will Finally Be Built." *Mimesis Law*, January 9, 2017. http://mimesislaw.com/fault-lines/new-jersey-long-overdue-mosque-will-finally-built/15248.

Llewellyn, Karl N. "On the Good, the True, the Beautiful, in Law." *The University of Chicago Law Review* 9, no. 2 (1942): 224–65. https://chicagounbound.uchicago.edu/cgi/viewcontent.cgi?article=1983&context=uclrev.

Lochner v. New York, 198 U.S. 45 (1908).

Lugo, Karen. *Mosques in America: A Guide to Accountable Permit Hearings and Continuing Citizen Oversight*. N.p.: CreateSpace Independent Publishing Platform, 2016. Available at https://centerforsecuritypolicy.org/wp-content/uploads/2016/12/Mosque_in_America.pdf.

Lukermann, Fred E. "The Concept of Location in Classical Geography." *Annals of the Association of American Geographers* 51, no. 2 (June 1961): 194–210.

Malpas, Jeff E. "Building Memory." *Interstices: Journal of Architecture and Related Arts* 13 (2012): 11–21.

———. *Place and Experience: A Philosophical Topography*. Cambridge: Cambridge University Press, 1999. Available online at http://assets.cambridge.org/97805216/42170/sample/9780521642170web.pdf.

———. "Putting Space in Place: Philosophical Topography and Relational Geography." *Environment and Planning: Society and Space* 30, no. 2 (2012): 226–42.

Martin, Catherine Gimelli. "Reversible Space, Linear Time: Andrew Marvell's 'Bermudas.'" *Comitatus: A Journal of Medieval and Renaissance Studies*, 21, no. 1 (1990): 72–89. Available at https://escholarship.org/uc/item/8k96m653.

Melhuish, Fiona. "The Grammar of Ornament." Featured item. Special Collections Services, University of Reading, February 2009. https://www.reading.ac.uk/web/files/special-collections/featurejonesgrammar.pdf.

Merleau-Ponty, Maurice. *Phenomenology of Perception*. Translated by Donald A. Landes. London: Routledge, 2012.

Merriam-Webster.com. "Mimesis.' Accessed May 21, 2020. https://www.merriam-webster.com/dictionary/mimesis.

———. "Simulacrum." Accessed May 21, 2020. https://www.merriam-webster.com/dictionary/simulacrum.

Mersch, Dieter. *Epistemologies of Aesthetics*. Translated by Laura Radosh. Zurich and Berlin: diaphanes, 2015.

Metcalf, Barbara Daly, ed. *Making Muslim Space in North America and Europe*. Comparative Studies on Muslim Societies series 22. Berkeley: University of California Press, 1996.

Midavaine, Bree. "Henri Matisse and the Alhambra." Term paper for HA 511, "Picasso/Matisse Seminar." Pratt Institute, New York, spring 2014. Available online at https://www.academia.edu/24561900/Henri_Matisse_and_the_Alhambra.

Millard, Bill. "The Mosque that Might Have Been." Center for Architecture (website), May 9, 2012. https://www.centerforarchitecture.org/news/the-mosque-that-might-have-been/.

Moffat, Chris. Review of *Expertise and Architecture in the Modern Islamic World*, ed. Peter Christensen. *Reviews in History* (February 2019). https://reviews.history.ac.uk/review/2306.

Moore, Kathleen M. *Al-Mughtaribūn: American Law and the Transformation of Muslim Life in the United States*. SUNY Series in Middle Eastern Studies. Albany: State University of New York, 1995.

Mugerauer, Robert. *Interpreting Environments: Tradition, Deconstruction, Hermeneutics*. Austin: University of Texas Press, 1995.

Mustafa, Sulaiman Ahmed. "Baghdad University Design." Working paper, South Dakota State University, May 2015. https://www.researchgate.net/publication/303868738_Baghdad_University_Design.

National Park Service. "Fox Theatre Historic District." *Atlanta: A National Register of Historical Places Travel Itinerary* (website), accessed July October 27, 2021. https://www.nps.gov/nr/travel/atlanta/fox.htm.

———. "National Register of Historic Places—Registration Form." Listing for Liberty Corner Historic District, Somerset County, New Jersey, August 6, 1991. 4 pages. Available online through the NP Gallery: Digital Asset Management System (website), US Department of the Interior, accessed October 15, 2021. https://npgallery.nps.gov/GetAsset/93096fd2-00f5-42ac-980f-9267ff3ae80d.

———. "National Register of Historic Places: Inventory—Nomination Form." Listing for Fox Theatre, Atlanta, GA, May 17, 1974. Available through the US National Archives Catalog (website), accessed July 1. 2020. https://catalog.archives.gov/id/93208180.

———. "National Register of Historic Places: Inventory—Registration Form." Listing for Opa-Locka Thematic Resource Area, Opa-Locka, Florida, March 22, 1982. Available through the NP Gallery: Digital Asset Management System (website), US Department of the Interior, accessed August 31, 2020. https://npgallery.nps.gov/NRHP/GetAsset/NRHP/64000117_text.

Norberg-Schulz, Christian. *Intentions in Architecture*. Cambridge MA: MIT Press, 1968.

The North Jersey Vineyard Church v. Township of South Hackensack et al., no. 2:2015cv08369, document 30 (D.N.J. 2016).

The North Jersey Vineyard Church v. South Hackensack, New Jersey, United States District Court, New Jersey Division, case no. 14–07759 WJM-MF.

Olbermann, Keith. "Olbermann: 'There Is No Ground Zero Mosque.'" *NBC News*, August 16, 2010. https://www.nbcnews.com/id/wbna38720233.

Ormos, István. "Between Stage Décor and Reality: The Cairo Street at the World's Columbian Exposition of 1893, Chicago." In *Studies in Memory of Alexander Fodor*, Arabist series 37, ed. Kinga Dévényi, 116–34. Budapest: Csoma de Kőrös

Society, 2016. Text available at https://www.academia.edu/36405172/Between_Stage_Décor_and_Reality_The_Cairo_Street_at_the_Worlds_Columbian_Exposition_of_1893_at_Chicago_Studies_in_Memory_of_Alexander_Fodor_The_Arabist_Budapest_Studies_in_Arabic_37_Budapest_2016_pp_115_134_2016_.

———. "Cairo Street at the World's Columbian Exposition of 1893 in Chicago: A New, Fresh Reading." In *Dialogues artistiques avec les passés de l'Égypte: Une perspective transnationale et transmédiale*, ed. Mercedes Volait and Emmanuelle Perrin. Paris: Publications de l'Institut national d'histoire de l'art, 2017. Text available at https://books.openedition.org/inha/7201.

Pervanić, Kemal. "'With their mosques, you must not just break the minarets,' he said. 'You've got to shake up the foundations because that means they cannot build another. Do that, and th . . .'" @kemalpervanic, Twitter, June 9, 2020. https://twitter.com/kemalpervanic/status/1270481037286653960.

Pew Research Center. "Controversies Over Mosques and Islamic Centers Across the U.S." PewForum.org, September 27, 2012. https://assets.pewresearch.org/wp-content/uploads/sites/11/2012/09/2012Mosque-Map.pdf.

Philadelphia Museum of Art. "*The Moorish Chief*: 1878; Eduard Charlemont, Austrian, 1848–1906." Accessed July 6, 2020. https://www.philamuseum.org/collections/permanent/102792.html, text archived at https://www.flickr.com/photos/rverc/38390338456.

Pinkus, Jenny. "Foucault." Massey University (website), August 1996. https://www.massey.ac.nz/~alock/theory/foucault.htm.

Plessy v. Ferguson, 163 U.S. 537 (1896).

Poole, Steven. "The Impossible World of M. C. Escher." *The Guardian*, June 20, 2015. https://www.theguardian.com/artanddesign/2015/jun/20/the-impossible-world-of-mc-escher.

Rattansi, Ali. *Racism: A Very Short Introduction*. Oxford: Oxford University Press, 2007.

Raza, Syed Wajid, and Abdul Baseer. "Iqbal in Masjid-e-Qartaba." *Allama Iqbal* (blog), last modified April 7, 2003. http://www.allamaiqbal.com/webcont/406/web_pages/cordova_mosque.htm.

Reggio, Godfrey, dir. *Koyaanisqatsi: Life Out of Balance*. Film. Distributed in the United States by Island Alive, New Cinema, 1983.

———. *Powaqqatsi: Life in Transformation*. Film. Distributed in the United States by the Cannon Group, 1988.

The Religious Land Use and Institutionalized Persons Act of 2000 (RLUIPA). Public Law 106–274. U.S. Statutes at Large 114 (2000): 803–807. https://www.govinfo.gov/content/pkg/STATUTE-114/pdf/STATUTE-114-Pg803 pdf.

Rice, Andrew. "The Fight for the Right to Be a Muslim in America." *The Guardian*, February 8, 2018. https://www.theguardian.com/news/2018/feb/08/how-to-stop-a-mosque-the-new-playbook-of-the-right.

Richardson, Pedro. "Visiting the Museum of Islamic Art Doha, Qatar." *Travel with Pedro* (blog), accessed October 15, 2021. https://www.travelwithpedro.com/visiting-the-museum-of-islamic-art-doha-qatar/.

Rizvi, Kishwar. *The Transnational Mosque: Architecture and Historical Memory in the Contemporary Middle East.* Chapel Hill: The University of North Carolina Press, 2015.

Roseberry, Cecil R. *Glenn Curtiss: Pioneer of Flight.* Garden City, NY: Doubleday, 1972.

Rothstein, Richard. *The Color of Law: A Forgotten History of How Our Government Segregated America.* New York: Liveright Publishing Corporation, 2018.

Rubinowicz, Pawel. "Chaos and Geometric Order in Architecture and Design." *Journal for Geometry and Graphics* 4, no. 2 (2000): 197–207. Available at https://www.heldermann-verlag.de/jgg/jgg01_05/jgg0418.pdf.

Saad, Saidah, Naomi Salim, Hakim Zainal, and Shahrul Azman Mohd Noah. "A Framework for Islamic Knowledge via Ontology Representation." Paper presented at the International Conference on Information Retrieval and Knowledge Management (CAMP), Shah Alam, Selangor, Malaysia, March 16–18, 2010, 310–14. Available at https://www.researchgate.net/publication/224138969_A_framework_for_Islamic_knowledge_via_ontology_representation.

Said, Edward W. *Covering Islam.* London: Routledge and Kegan Paul, 1981.

———. *Orientalism.* New York: Vintage Books, 1979.

Salingaros, Nikos A. "Cognitive Dissonance and Non-adaptive Architecture: Seven Tactics for Denying the Truth." *Doxa* 11 (January 2014): 100–17. Text archived at https://applied.math.utsa.edu/~yxk833/CognitiveDissonanceandNonadaptiveArchitecture.html. Revised from an earlier version published online by *P2PF Wiki*, last modified February 3, 2011, https://wiki.p2pfoundation.net/Cognitive_Dissonance_and_Non-adaptive_Architecture.

Sani, Hanisah Binte Abdullah. "Corporeal Poetics of Sacred Space: An Ethnography of *Jum'ah* in a Chapel." *Space and Culture* 18, no. 3 (2015): 298–310.

Schad v. Borough of Mount Ephraim, 452 U.S. 61 (1981).

Schleifer, James T. "Tocqueville, Religion, and Democracy in America: Some Essential Questions." *American Political Thought* 3, no. 2 (2014): 254–72.

Sembou, Evangelia. *Hegel's Phenomenology and Foucault's Genealogy.* Abingdon, UK: Routledge, 2016.

Shapiro, Fred R., ed. *The Yale Book of Quotations.* Foreword by Joseph Epstein. New Haven, CT: Yale University Press, 2006.

Sheller, Mimi. "Theorising Mobility Justice." *Tempo Social* 30, no. 2 (2018): 17–34. https://www.revistas.usp.br/ts/article/view/142763/142049.

Sinding-Larsen, Staale. *The Burden of the Ceremony Master: Image and Action in San Marco, Venice, and in an Islamic Mosque; The Rituum Cerimoniale of 1564.* Rome: G. Bretschneider, 2000. Text available at https://folk.ntnu.no/staalesl/BurdenNet.pdf.

Smietana, Bob. "Murfreesboro Mosque Fight Laid to Rest after Supreme Court Ruling." *Washington Post*, June 3, 2014. https://www.washingtonpost.com/national/religion/murfreesboro-mosque-fight-laid-to-rest-after-supreme-court-ruling/2014/06/03/0da487c0-eb49-11e3-b10e-5090cf3b5958_story.html.

Smith, G. E. Kidder. *Source Book of American Architecture: 500 Notable Buildings from the 10th Century to the Present*. New York: Princeton Architectural Press, 1996.

Sørensen, Mathias Klitgård. "Foucault on Power Relations." Irenees.net, September 2014. http://www.irenees.net/bdf_fiche-notions-242_en.html.

Stevens, John Paul. Remarks delivered at the National Japanese American Memorial Foundation 10th Anniversary Gala Celebration, Washington, D.C., November 4, 2010. Text archived at https://www.supremecourt.gov/publicinfo/speeches/sp_11-04-10.pdf.

Taylor, Laurie. "Foucault and the Power of Texts." *The Social Construction of Literature* (blog), October 12, 2014. Rutgers.edu. https://soclit14.blogs.rutgers.edu/2014/10/foucault-and-the-power-of-texts/.

Toman, Rolf, ed. *The Art of the Italian Renaissance: Architecture, Sculpture, Painting, Drawing*. Königswinter, Ger.: Tandem Verlag GmbH, 2005.

Treene, Eric W. "RLUIPA and Mosques: Enforcing a Fundamental Right in Challenging Times." *First Amendment Law Review* 10, no. 2 (Winter 2012): 330–62. https://scholarship.law.unc.edu/cgi/viewcontent.cgi?article=1147&context=falr.

———. "Zoning and Mosques: Understanding the Impact of the Religious Land Use and Institutionalized Persons Act." *The Public Lawyer* 23, no. 1 (Winter 2015): 2–7. Archived at https://docplayer.net/46988863-Zoning-and-mosques-the-public-lawyer-winter-2015.html.

Tremlett, Giles. "Two Arrested after Fight in Cordoba's Former Mosque." *The Guardian*, April 1, 2010. https://www.theguardian.com/world/2010/apr/01/muslim-catholic-mosque-fight.

Turchiarulo, Mariangela. "The Construction of Al-Mursi Abou al-'Abbas Mosque, Alexandria." Paper presented at the 2nd International Balkans Conference on Challenges of Civil Engineering, BCCCE, Epoka University, Tirana, Albania, May 23–25, 2013, pp. 1084–92. Text available at https://core.ac.uk/download/pdf/152489497.pdf.

Twain, Mark [Samuel L. Clemens]. *The Innocents Abroad, or The New Pilgrims' Progress*. Hartford, CT: American Publishing Company, 1869.

UNESCO. "UNESCO Announces Winning Architectural Design of Competition to Rebuild Al-Nouri Mosque Complex in Mosul." UNESCO.org, April 15, 2021. https://en.unesco.org/news/unesco-announces-winning-architectural-design-competition-rebuild-al-nouri-mosque-complex-mosul.

United States v. Bernards Township (D.N.J. 2016) 16-cv-1369. Archived at https://becketpdf.s3.amazonaws.com/Bernards-Township-Complaint.pdf.

United States v. Rutherford County, Tennessee, No. 3:12-cv-00737, 2012, WL 2930076 (M.D. Term, filed July 18, 2012.

US Department of Justice. "Justice Department Files Lawsuit Requiring Rutherford County, Tenn., to Allow Mosque to Open in City of Murfreesboro." Press release. Justice.gov, July 18, 2012. https://www.justice.gov/opa/pr/justice-department-files-lawsuit-requiring-rutherford-county-tenn-allow-mosque-open-city.

———. "Report on the Twentieth Anniversary of the Religious Land Use and Institutionalized Persons Act." Justice.gov, September 22, 2020. https://www.justice.gov/crt/case-document/file/1319186/download.

Village of Euclid, Ohio v. Ambler Realty Co., 272 U.S. 365 (1926).

Waldman, Amy. *The Submission: A Novel*. New York: Farrar, Straus and Giroux, 2011.

Weedon, Chris. *Feminist Practice and Poststructuralist Theory*. Oxford: Basil Blackwell, 1987.

Wheeler, H. Sayre. "Opa-Locka, Created from *The Arabian Nights*." *Journal of the American Institute of Architects* (April 1928): 157–60.

Whelan, Estelle. "The Origins of the *Mihrāb Mujawwaf*: An Interpretation." *International Journal of Middle East Studies* 18, no. 2 (May 1986): 205–23.

Wikipedia. "Fox Theatre Atlanta." Last modified September 25, 2021. https://en.wikipedia.org/wiki/Fox_Theatre_(Atlanta).

———. "Islamic Center of Murfreesboro." Last modified October 27, 2021. https://en.wikipedia.org/wiki/Islamic_Center_of_Murfreesboro.

———. "List of the Last Surviving American Enslaved People." Last modified October 21, 2021. https://en.wikipedia.org/wiki/List_of_last_surviving_American_enslaved_people.

———. "Lochner era." Last modified July 26, 2021. https://en.wikipedia.org/wiki/Lochner_era.

———. "National September 11 Memorial and Museum." Last modified October 12, 2021. https://en.wikipedia.org/wiki/National_September_11_Memorial_%26_Museum.

———. "Opa-Locka, Florida." Last modified October 7, 2021. https://en.wikipedia.org/wiki/Opa-locka,_Florida.

———. "*This Is Not a Pipe*." Last modified September 30, 2021. https://en.wikipedia.org/wiki/The_Treachery_of_Images.

———. "*Village of Euclid v. Ambler Realty Co.*" Last modified July 30, 2021. https://en.wikipedia.org/wiki/Village_of_Euclid_v._Ambler_Realty_Co.

Wilkins, Craig L. *The Aesthetics of Equity: Notes on Race, Space, Architecture, and Music*. Minneapolis: The University of Minnesota Press, 2007.

Wittgenstein, Ludwig. *Culture and Value*. Edited by G. H. von Wright in collaboration with Heikki Nyman, translated by Peter Winch. Chicago: University of Chicago Press, 1980.

Wolf, Michael Allan. *The Zoning of America: 'Euclid v. Ambler.'* Lawrence: University Press of Kansas, 2008.

Wolfe, Tom. *From Bauhaus to Our House*. New York: Bantam Books, 1999.

Writers' Program (U.S.), Georgia. *Drums and Shadows: Survival Studies among the Georgia Coastal Negroes*. Savannah Unit, Georgia Writers' Project (U.S.), Works Progress Administration. Foreword by Guy B. Johnson, photographs by Muriel Bell and Malcolm Bell Jr. Athens: University of Georgia Press, 1940.

Young, Eugene B. "Duration." In *The Deleuze and Guattari Dictionary*, Bloomsbury Philosophical Dictionaries series, Eugene B. Young, with Gary Genosko and Janell Watson. New York, Bloomsbury, 2013.

———. "'Francis Bacon: The Logic of Sensation.'" In *The Deleuze and Guattari Dictionary*, Bloomsbury Philosophical Dictionaries series, Eugene B. Young, with Gary Genosko and Janell Watson. New York, Bloomsbury, 2013.

Index

Page references for figures are italicized. Words that appear in the glossary are indicated by "gl."

9/11:
    attacks, 11, 134–39, 149, 151;
    National 9/11 Memorial and Museum, 138

Abdul-Rauf, Muhammad, 104, 113
Adamson, Peter, 18–20
adhan, gl. *See also* prayer(s)
aesthetic(s):
    of contemporary mosques, 25, 39;
    and distance, 101;
    Ibero-Islamic aesthetic traditions, 47, 48, 49–50, 57, 60, 66–68, 70, 74, 176, 177;
    Ibero-Moorish aesthetics, 47, 176, 178. *See also* Islam;
    Islamic tradition of, 9–10, 22, 39, 47, 48, 66, 67, 92–93, 111, 176. *See also* Moorish style/architectural tradition;
    and the Middle East, 25, 71;
    of monotheism, 21, 83;
    and truth. *See* mimesis;
        resemblances and similitudes;
        simulacrum/a
Al-Andalus, 49, 56

al-Arabi, Ibn, 85, 92, 117n7
al-Azraqi, Muhammad ibn 'Abd Allah, 84, 90–91
Alexander, Christopher, 23
Alger, Richard W., 53
Al-Ghazali, 91–92
Alhambra, 21–22, *21*, 39, 47, *50*, 51, *52*, 55–57, 67, 68, 176
al-Harithy, Howayda, 97, 98
al-Maghrib, 49, 56, 87
al-Mursi, *111*
al-Rāzī, Fakhr al-Dīn, 18–20
Altria Theater, Richmond, VA, 61
aniconism, 56, 83, 87, 115
Anthemios of Tralles, 181
anti-Islamic sentiment, 134–35, 141, 143, 151, 153
antimosque rhetoric or sentiment, 124, 139, 141–45, 152–56, 159, 162;
appropriation:
    of architectural elements, 67–68, 71–72;
    of space, 2, 8, 32–33, 73
The Arabian Nights, 68, 69, 70, 72, 73
architect, the:
    burden of, 10, 84, 93–102, 178;

213

and volition, 53, 67, 83, 84, 92–93, 110, 114, 115–16;
and five ontological Qur'anic themes, 92;
and language, 74;
of pleasure, 48, 57;
and power, 5;
production of, 21, 22, 23, 180
Aristotle, 18, 19

Bachelard, Gaston, 142
Bacon, Francis, 72
Ballantine, Thomas, 176
Barthes, Roland, 5, 7
basilica, Christian, and mosque compared, 114–15;
Basilica of Saint Vincent of Córdoba, 3
Basking Ridge, NJ. *See* The Islamic Society of Basking Ridge (ISBR)
Baudrillard, Jean, 9, 16–17, 51, 66, 93–94, 97
Bauhaus, 23
Beckford, William, 53, *54*
Belsey, Catherine, 163
Bevan, Robert, 29, 31
Beydoun, Khaled A., 37
Bialasiewicz, Luiza, 34–35, 36
Bible Belt, 126, 132, 159, 162, 174
Biennale Architettura 2021, 35–36, 182
biopolitics/biopolitical:
    defined, 124, 134, 155, 158, 174, 177;
    and falsehood, 110, 111, 131, 158. *See also* "will to truth";
    and Islamophobia, surveillance, 36–37, 137, 159. *See also* Islamophobia;
    and place, 136–37;
    and power. *See* power;
    and public discourse. *See* discourse(s)
Black Americans/community, 77n19, 126, 132, 157, 175;
    Charleston Church Massacre, 157;
    enslaved Africans, 99–100, 132, 159–63, 166n52.
    See also discrimination; racism; segregation; slave trade/slavery; subjugation; zoning
body/space experience, 5, 6–7, 10, 20, 38, 76, 87;
    Muslim, 7, 13, 14, 17, 20, 28, 33, 76, 113, 115, 173
Bolaria, B. Singh, 27, 33
Bond, Max, Jr., 23
boundaries, 25, 68. 130, 142, 162, 175
Brabant, Jean-Michel, 174
Braga, Ariane Varela, 60
Bridge Initiative, Georgetown University, 37
Brown v. City of Richmond, 61, 126
Buchanan, Ian, 174
Büchel, Christoph, 34–36, 182
built environment, 14, 47, 56, 76, 146
Burckhardt, Titus, 89
Burnham, Daniel H., 101, 119n47
Burton, Sir Richard, 73–74

call to prayer. *See* prayer(s)
Cass, Jeffrey, 39–40
Cathedral of Our Lady of the Assumption debate, 1–8
Ceci n'est pas une mosquée, 65–66, 74–76, 177–78
Ceci n'est pas une pipe, 64–65, 74–75
Çelik, Zeynep, 179
Chao, Jenifer, 33
Chapel of Thanksgiving, Dallas, TX, 28
Charlemont, Eduard, 57
Charles V, Holy Roman Emperor, 4–5
Chicago World's Fair (1893), 84, 94–101, *96*, *98*, 102, 115, 179
Chittick, William C., 83
Christianity:
    and Islam, 5, 35, 139, 148. *See also* hybridity/hybrid spaces;
    and hegemony, 138–39. *See also* zoning

non-Christian faith communities, 128, 147, 148;
and sacred ground, 134, 138;
and slavery. *See* slave trade/slavery
Church of the Holy Wisdom, 180–81
Cisneros, Cardinal Francisco Ximenez de, 176–77
civil rights, 126, 132, 145–46, 162, 174–75
Clark, Gordon L., 145
Cobb, Henry Ives, 97
Cooper, Sam, 59
Corbett, Rosemary R., 182
Cordes, Mark W., 127, 140
Cordoba House, NYC, 133–37, 139, 174
Critical Race Theory, 38
culture:
cultural knowledge and architectural production, 23–25, 27–29;
cultural spaces, 23, 142.
See also tradition
Curtiss, Glenn H., 70, 72

D'Ascoli, Angela, xv, 12n12, 32
Delacroix, Eugène, 57, 59
Deleuze, Gilles, xiii, 75–76, 101–2, 173, 174
DeRose, Justin P., 139
diaspora:

aesthetics, 105–10;
Islamic, 105–10, 116, 139
Dickie, James, 110
discourse(s):
on aesthetics, 21, 47–48, 73, 111–12, 178–79;
on buildings, 101, 110;
discursive analysis, 8, 14, 34, 47, 75, 76, 83, 105, 163, 173, 177, 182, 184;

discursive formation(s), 8, 9, 10, 15, 16, 17, 24, 33, 35, 64, 67, 74, 75, 76, 99;
discursive knowledge/ geography, 67, 73;
discursive strategy, xiv, 9, 13, 149, 176;
genealogical discourse(s), xiii, 24, 40;
and Giedion's "space conception," 18–19, 73;
hermeneutic, 93;
juridico-discursive power, 133
micropolitical, 35, 140, 146;
ontological, 22, 91, 179;
and power relations, 34, 35, 37, 38, 123, 129, 131, 137, 142, 148, 157, 174, 181;
public, 123, 137, 138, 142, 153, 154;
on resemblances and similitudes.
See resemblances and similitudes
discrimination:
racial, 132, 139, 155–56, 175;
religious, 131–32, 132, 143–44, 146, 152–53, 156–57, 158–59, 175, 182;
societal, 127.
See also exclusion; racism; segregation
dislocation, 15, 33
distance and location,142, 147
Douglass, Frederick, 123, 132, 133, 159, *160*, 162
doxa, 59, 92, 139, gl.
due process, 127, 130–31, 133, 140

Eco, Umberto, 25
Eisenhower, Dwight D., 105
Elden, Stuart, 127
epigraphy, 21, 103, 109, 110, 111, 112, 115
Ertegun, Munir, 103
Escher, M. C., 56–57, 60, 65

Estes v. Rutherford County Regional Planning Commission, 144
Euclid v. Ambler, 124, 139–40
Evans, G. S., 64
exclusion:
    forms of, 35, 36, 38, 73, 163, 175;
    means of, 10, 37, 130, 138, 147, 152, 153, 155, 156.
    See also discrimination; segregation
experience-effect, 33
Exposition Universelle, Paris (1867), 102

Fathy, Hassan, 23, 105
fear, 36, 37, 137, 147, 154, 156–57. *See also* Islamophobia
The Feeling of Being Watched: Surveillance in a US-Arab Community, 34, 36
Felix J. Brown, et al. v. City of Richmond, et al., 61, 126
Ferdinand III, king of Castile and Leon, 4
First Amendment, 124, 128, 132, 133, 144, 145, 147, 156
Fleming, Walter Millard, 50
Fontana-Giusti, Gordana, 66, 69, 73, 173
Foucault, Michel, 8, 9, 13, 38, 67, 75–76, 111, 142, 157–58, 162–63;
    and effective history, 16;
    Eurocentrism of, 8–9;
    and the genealogical method, 13, 15–16;
    and government/discipline, 147;
    and heterotopias. *See* heterotopias/the heterotopic;
    and historicity, 3, 99;
    on meaning systems/subjugated discourse, 28;
    methodology of, 24;
    and "other spaces," 15, 105, 145–46, 179. *See also* space(s), "other";
    and phantasms, 75–76;
    on power, 126, 129, 151. *See also* power;
    and resemblances and similitudes, 47, 69, 71. *See also* resemblances and similitudes;
    and space/place, 17, 103, 173;
    and subjectivity, 148–49;
    triad of space, knowledge, and power, xiii–xv, 6, 9, 10, 14–15, 22, 24, 34, 39, 159, 184–85;
    on truth and power, 158, 181–82
Fox Theatre, Atlanta, GA, 9–10, 47–51, 53, 55, *55*, 57, 59, 60, 74–75, 83, 177, 178
Frampton, Kenneth, 13
Freund, Ernst, 155
Friday prayers, 88, 115, 128

Gadamer, Hans-Georg, 48, 51, 72
Gagnon, Julie Elizabeth, 175
Galland, Antoine, 73
Germain, Annick, 175
Giedion, Sigfried, 18–19, 73
Giese, Francine, 60
Gingrich, Newt, 135
Giuliani, Rudolph, 138
Glass, Philip, 92
God, 18, 20, 21
González, Bishop Demetrio, and the Great Mosque of Córdoba debate, 1, 2, 5
Gordillo, Gastón R., 14, 22, 27
Grafmeyer, Yves, 173, 177, 179
Gril, Denis, 85
Gropius, Walter, 23–25, *26*, 27, 28, 178
Guattari, Pierre-Félix, 173, 174
Gutterman, David S., 136
Gutting, Gary, 15, 31, 65–66

hadith, 88, 91, gl.
hajj, 84, 90, 115, 118n26, 180, gl.
Haskins, Ekaterina V., 139
hegemony, 16, 29, 67, 80n85, 138. *See also* Christianity

Hejduk, John, 72, 80n85
hermeneutics, 22, 47, 56, 83, 90, 93, 111, 113, 178–79;
Herz, Max, 84, 93, 95–97, 99, 101, 102, 115
heterotopias/the heterotopic, 9, 10, 48, 51, 53, 65, 66, 68, 142, 152, 178, 179
Hier, Sean, 27, 33
Hillenbrand, Robert, 21, 39, 48, 53, 76
Hillman, James, 177
Hirst, Paul, 10, 15, 24, 33, 34, 36, 38–39, 53, 55
Hispano-American world/art/architecture, 47–48, 49–50, 66, 176
historicity and effective history. *See* Foucault, Michel
historiography, 14, 16, 30–31, 65, 73
Hoeveler, Diane Long, 39–40
Holt, Jaan, 87
houses of worship. *See* Christianity; mosques; synagogues
Howar, A. Joseph, 103, 104
hybridity/hybrid spaces, 7, 35–36, 49–50, 74, 75;
    Christian/Islamic hybrid space, 35–36, 74, 75

Ibn al-Jayyāb, 21
Ibn al-Khatib, 21
Ibn Said, Omar, 100, 159–61, 162
Ibn Sīnā, 18
Ibn Zamrak, 21
ICM. *See* Islamic Center of Murfreesboro (ICM)
identity/ies:
    crisis. *See* place, decentering of;
    diaspora and, 105–10, 116, 139.
        See also diaspora;
    ethnic, 29, 163;
    Jewish, 133–34, 138;
    of mosques, 3–5, 8, 39, 183;
    nativist and protonational.
        See nativism;
    of place, 74, 75, 134–35;
    racial, 139, 163, 175;

    religious, xv, 2–3, 126, 139, 163.
        See also self
intergrist ideology, 29–30, 31
Iqbal, Sir Allama Muhammad, 5–7
Irving, Washington, 56, 67, 68
Irwin S. Porter and Sons, 106
Isidoros of Miletus, 181
Islam:
    aesthetic(s) of. *See* aesthetic(s)
    and architectural episteme, 47;
    as ideology vs. religion 143–44, 159
Islamic Center at Regent's Park, London, 39
Islamic Center of Manhattan, 39
Islamic Center of Mississippi. v. City of Starkville, 10, 124, 125, 127–29, 131
Islamic Center of Murfreesboro (ICM), 140–45, *141*, 146–47
Islamic Center of Murfreesboro v. Rutherford County, 124, 126, 140–45, 146, 147, 159
Islamic Center of Washington, DC (ICW):
    analysis of, 84, 102–3, 104–10, 116, 178;
    architectural details of, *103*, *106–109*, 112–13, 115
The Islamic Center v. The Boston Herald, 175
Islamic Cultural Center of New York, 105
The Islamic Society of Basking Ridge (ISBR), 150, 151–55, 156–57;
    Washington Tavern, Basking Ridge, NJ, *149*
The Islamic Society of Basking Ridge et al. v. Township of Bernards, 10, 124, 153, 154, 157;
    mosque location dispute, 149–57, 163;
    and power, 124,150–51, 155, 157, 163.
        See also antimosque rhetoric or sentiment

The Islamic Society of Boston v. Boston Herald, Inc., 151
Islamophobia, 37, 38, 134, 137, 140, 143, 151, 153–54, 159. *See also* fear

Jamaleddine, Ziad, 181
Jeffery, R. Brooks, 47, 48, 49–50, 66–67, 176
Jewish Community Center (JCC), NYC, 133–34
jihad, 159, 161
Jim Crow, 126, 132
Johnson, Philip, 28, 39
Jones, Owen, 55–56, 59–60, 61, 65, 68
Journal of the American Institute of Architects (1928), 70
justice/injustice, 132, 146, 157, 159, 161, 162, 174–75

Ka'ba, 86;
    facing the, 10, 83, 87, 88, 113–14, 179;
    history of, xiv, 89–90;
    meanings of, 84–85, 89, 91–92, 113–14, gl.
Kahera, Akel, 13
Kant, Immanuel, 6, 111
Kilde, Jeanne Halgren, 138
King, David A., 86–87
Kitab Akhbar Makkah (*Book of Reports about Makkah*), 89–90
Kivel, Paul, 138–39
knowledge:
    cultural, 23–25;
    discursive, 67, 73;
    forms of, 142, 151, 153, 179–80;
    and light, 91–92;
    and power. *See* power;
    public, 3, 10, 27, 33, 36, 74;
    subjective, 35, 159, 179;
    subjugated, 16, 142, 162, 175

Laborde, Alexandre de, 57
Lambert, Gregg, 174
Landmark Theater, Richmond, VA, 61

land use:
    controls, 124, 133, 145;
    disputes/court rulings, xiv, xv, 124, 125, 141, 150, 151;
    and location, 128–29, 141;
    by Muslim groups, 125, 140, 141, 152–53.
    and parking requirements, 125, 128–30, 152–56, 158, 163;
    permits. *See* permits;
    regulation, 131, 140, 154;
    religious. *See* Religious Land Use and Institutionalized Persons Act (RLUIPA, 2000).
    See also discrimination; segregation
Landy, Frédéric, 30
Larsonneur, Claire, 7, 36
law:
    equal treatment under, 125, 133. *See also* Jim Crow;
    shari'ah, 124, 142, 154, gl.
Leach, Neil, 15, 27
Lefebvre, Henri, xiii, 16, 25, 97, 98, 113, 115–16
Lévi-Strauss, Claude, 32
Leviter, Lee, 138
Little Mosque on the Prairie, 33
Llewellyn, Karl, 130
location:
    and the Islamic Center of Mississippi, 128–30;
    and the Islamic Center of Murfreesboro, 140–41, 142–43, 145;
    and the Islamic Center of Washington, DC, 107;
    and Liberty Corner/Basking Ridge, 151–53;
    in the Qur'an, 18.
    See also boundaries
Lugo, Karen, 124, 142, 153, 154
Lukermann, Fred, 16

Madinah (Medina), 88, 114

Maghrib of North Africa, 49, 56, 87
Magritte, René, 64, 65, 75, 178–79
Makkah (Mecca), 3, 10, 85–93, 101, 105, 114, 179–80
Malpas, Jeff, xiii, 17–18, 27
Mamluk architectural tradition, 84, 95, 97, 102, 110, 178
Marye, P. Thornton, 53
masjid, 61, 66, 85, 87–88, 92, 178, 183–84, gl.;
    American, 83;
    Islamic Center of Washington, DC (ICW), 84, 112, 173
memory:
    destruction of, 5, 31–32, 75;
    meaning, 3, 5, 89, 90, 105, 180;
    and place, 88;
    and symbolic locus, 114, 180
Mencken, H. L., 126
Mersch, Dieter, 178
micropolitics, 35, 140, 146
mihrab:
    in Great Mosque of Córdoba, 3, 5, *6;*
    meanings of, xiv, 25, 83, 87, 114, gl.;
    in Moschea della Misericordia, 35;
    placement of, 87–88, 105
mimesis:
    mimetic mosque reproductions, 66, 101–2;
    and Mosque Theater, Richmond, VA, 63–64, *64;*
    and Opa-Locka city hall, 71–72;
    Qaytbay complex. See Qaytbay complex, Chicago World's Fair.
    See also representation, mimetic
minaret, 28, 29, 51, 60, 63, 65, 71, 72, 109, 153, 181
modernism, 23, 25, 29
Moore, Kathleen, 140
Moorish Revival style, 47–48, 51, 53, 55, 57, 59, 62, 66, 67, 68, 75, 76

Moorish style/architectural traditions, 39, 47–48, 49, 51–56, 66, 176. *See also* aesthetic(s); Islam
mosques:
    American, 124, 142, 146, 153, 154, 182;
    destruction of, 29–32;
    identity. See identity/ies of mosques;
    mosque reproductions, 57, 98, 101–2;
    ontological meaning of. *See* ontology
    and permits. *See* permits;
    public support of bans on, 154, 175;
    Three British Mosques, 182;
    urban mosques, 10, 35, 39, 99, 100, 102–13, 179
mosques, specific examples of:
    al-Nuri Mosque, Mosul, Iraq, 31, *32, 33;*
    Babri mosque, Ayodhya, India, 30–31, *30;*
    Baghdad State Mosque, 27–28, *28;*
    Baghdad University mosque, 23–27, *26,* 28, 178;
    Brick Lane mosque, London, 182, *183;*
    Dar al-Islam Mosque, NM, vi, 105;
    Grande Mosquée de Paris, 8, 39;
    Grand Mosque of Rome and Islamic Center, 39;
    Great Mosque of Córdoba, 1–8, *3, 4,* 38, 56, 57, 176;
    Great Mosque of Damascus, 122n99;
    Ground Zero mosque, NYC, 10, 123, 124, 133–35, 137, 140, 174, 182. *See also* Cordoba House, NYC;
    Hagia Sophia, 180–81, *180;*

Harrow Central mosque,
UK, 182, *184;*
Islamic Center, Starkville,
MS, 158–59;
The Little white
Mosque, NM, *89;*
London Central Mosque,
39, 103–4;
Masjid al-Haram,
Makkah, 84, 179;
Masjid Farah mosque, NYC, 136;
Mezquita de Córdoba, 1–8, *3*, *4*,
38, 56, 57, 176;
Missiri (Mosque) of Frejus, 9;
Moschea della Misericordia,
Venice, 34–36, 174, 182;
Mosque of the Prophet (Masjid
al-Nabawī al-Sharīf),
Madinah, 87–88;
Old Kent Road mosque,
London, 182, *184;*
Qaytbay mosque complex, Cairo,
Egypt, 93–97, *94;*
Women's Mosque of America,
Los Angeles, 183.
See also Islamic Center of
Washington, DC (ICW)
Mosque Theater, Richmond, VA, 9, 10,
47, 48, 50, 60–68, *64*, 74–75, 83,
126, 176, 177, 178
Mudejar style, 47, 48
Mugerauer, Robert, 23, 48
Muller, Bernhardt E., 68, 69–70, 71, 73
Murphy, Andrew R., 137
Murphy, James Cavanah, 60
musalla, gl.:
in Cordoba House, 123,
134, 136–37;
for enslaved Africans, 99;
at Islamic Center of
Mississippi, 125.
See also prayer hall
Museum of Islamic Art, Doha, Qatar, 23
Muslim community:
and enslaved Africans, 99–100,
132, 159–62, 166n52;
obstacles facing, 146, 155–56
Mustafa, Sulaiman Ahmed, 24, 25, 27

Nasrid dynasty, 47
National Register of Historic Places
(US), 60, 149–50
nativism, 124, 140, 141, 146, 147, 153
Nat Turner's Rebellion, 159
Nietzsche, Friedrich, 13, 148, 150
"nonspace and nonplace," 174
Norberg-Schulz, Christian, 84
norms:
aesthetic, 67, 105. *See also*
aesthetic(s);
sociocultural, 59, 127, 163
North Jersey Vineyard Church v.
Township of South Hackensack
et al., 151

Olbermann, Keith, 137
ontology:
and architecture, 10, 21, 27, 76,
83, 84, 87, 115, 179;
of epigraphic inscriptions, 22;
of five ontological Qur'anic
themes, 92;
in Ibero-Moorish
traditions, 177–78;
of the *Ka'ba*, the *mihrab*, and the
qibla, xiv, 85, 87, 93, 179–80;
of the *masjid*/mosque, 20, 21,
27, 178, 184;
and ontological experience, 112;
of time, place, and space, 20,
70, 87, 182.
See also discourse(s), ontological
Opa-Locka city hall, 9, 10, 47, 48,
68–75, 83, 177, 178
ordinances. *See* zoning
Orientalism, 53, 56, 57–59, 63–64,
67–68, 70, 76
original, the, 48, 51
other, the, 7, 67, 68, 74, 147;

out-groups, 147, 152.
  See also space(s), "other"

palimpsests, 2, 14, 32–33, 90, 178
Pangalo, George, 97
Pareto criterion, 127
Park51 (Park Place), NYC, 10, 123, 133, 134, 137, 174
parking requirements. *See* land use
Pasha, Hassan Nachat, 104
Pasha, Mahmoud Hassan, 103
Paterson, William S., 50
Patriot Act, 136
Pei, I. M., 23
permits:
  denials, 128, 130, 152, 155;
  exceptions, 127–28, 130, 131, 132;
  in Liberty Corner/Basking Ridge, 151–53, 154, 155;
  in Starkville, 128–30
philosophy as theater (*theatrum philosopicum*), 75
Picasso, Pablo, 56, 72
place, 13, 19;
  control of, xiv, 10, 15, 23, 37, 127, 177;
  decentering of, xv, 15, 22–27, 28–29, 33–34;
  discursive analysis of, 137, 182;
  and the Great Mosque of Córdoba debate, 1–8;
  identity of. *See* identity/ies;
  and the Islamic Center of Washington, DC, 113;
  place/space-making, 9, 94, 138, 145;
  and space, 9, 38, 139
place of the mosque, the:
  challenges to, 147, 182;
  complexities of, 175, 177;
  genealogical analysis of, 13, 14, 15, 16.
  See also space(s), contested Muslim spaces

Plato, 18, 19
Ponce de Leon Hotel, FL, 50–51, 54
Powaqqatsi: Life in Transformation, 92
power:
  and biopolitics, xiv, 5, 8, 10–11, 34, 37, 123, 124, 142–46, 162
  exercise of, 127, 129, 158;
  government, 10, 147;
  in the Great Mosque of Córdoba debate, 8;
  holders, 126, 157, 165n17;
  juridical, 10, 11, 133, 147, 148;
  and knowledge, xiii, xiv;
  macro-, 124;
  micro-, 8, 34, 37, 116, 123–30, 133, 138, 147, 174, 175–76;
  police power, xiv, 36–38, 123, 125, 127, 131, 146–47, 150–57, 163, 174
  power/force, disciplinary, 10, 131
  power/knowledge nexus of Foucault, 34, 124, 142–46, 150, 151, 177, 181;
  relations (Foucauldian), 37, 129, 131, 137, 142, 148, 157, 158, 174, 181
Pragmatica of 1529, 177
prayer hall, 105, 107, *109*, 112, 151, 152. *See also musalla*; space(s), prayer space
prayer(s):
  call to, 4, 5, 7, 12n13, 92, 118n32, 181. *See also adhan*;
  five daily, 87, 88, 92;
  Friday, 88, 115, 128;
  and the Great Mosque of Córdoba, 7, 38
Prince Among Slaves, 100
Puritanism, 147–48

Qaytbay complex, Chicago World's Fair, 84, 93–100, *96*, *98*, 101–2, 115, 179
qibla, 83, 87, 88, *89*, gl.;
  qibla axis, 85, 92, 101, 105, 114, 179

Qur'an:
    and the Alhambra, 21–22;
    al-Rāzī's Qur'anic exegesis, 20;
    and devotional acts/Qur'anic
        injunctions, 86–88, 179–80;
    and *hajj* rites, 90;
    Qur'anic verse, epigraphy of,
        21–22, 109, 112–13, 115.
    See also ontlogy of five
        Qur'anic themes

racism, 162, 163, 174. *See also*
    discrimination; segregation
Ramadan, 93, 128
Rattansi, Ali, 158
religion:
    free exercise of, 128, 130,
        132, 146, 153;
    and race, 162. *See also* racism;
        white Christians
Religious Land Use and Institutionalized
    Persons Act (RLUIPA, 2000), 10,
    124, 125, 141, 143, 144, 145–46,
    154, 156, 162. *See also* land use
representation:
    as basis of Western
        culture, 66, 73;
    and *Ceci n'est pas une pipe*
        (painting, Magritte), 10,
        64, 74, 75;
    and *Ceci n'est pas une mosquée*,
        10, 65, 74–75, 177;
    mimetic, 66, 71–72, 97–98,
        99, 101–2.
    See also Orientalism
resemblances:
    and the construction of
        place, 177;
    East/West cultural merger and, 48;
    and the Fox Theater, 55, 60;
    and the Islamic Center of
        Washington, DC, 110;
    and the Missiri of Fréjus, 9;
    and Opa-Locka, 70–72;

    and similitudes, 9, 47–53, 55, 60,
        63–74, 83, 94, 101–2, 179
Rice, Andrew, 151
right-wing factions, 147, 154
Rizvi, Kishwar, 182
RLUIPA. *See* Religious Land Use
    and Institutionalized Persons Act
    (RLUIPA, 2000)
Robinson, Charles Custer, 62
Robinson, Charles M., 62
Rossi, Mario, 84, 102, 104–10, *111*,
    113, 115, 116
Rothstein, Richard, 155, 157
Rykwert, Joseph, 84

sacred:
    geography, 85–90, 88, 90;
    ground, 134–35, 138;
    presence of the, 103.
    See also space(s), sacred
Said, Edward, 40, 135
Salingaros, Nikos A., 148, 150, 157, 163
San Giorgio Maggiore, Venice, 20
Sani, Hanisah Binte Abdullah, 114
Santa Maria della Misericordia,
    Venice, 35–36
Schad v. Borough of Mount
    Ephraim, 131
Schwartz, Frederic, 28
segregation, 55, 61, 77n19, 126, 127,
    132, 165n17. *See also* discrimination;
    exclusion; zoning
self:
    self-determination, 124, 139;
    selfhood, 24, 33;
    self-understanding of
        society, 13, 30.
    See also identity/ies
shari'ah. *See* law
Sheller, Mimi, 146–47
simulacrum/a, 9, 10, 27, 47, 60, 65, 66,
    72, 73, 74, 148. *See also* Qaytbay
    complex, Chicago World's Fair
Sinding-Larsen, Staale, 114
Skidmore, Owings and Merrill, 105

slave trade/slavery, 99–100, 132,
    159–62, 166n52
Sørensen, Mathias Klitgård, 131
Sori, Abdul-Rahman ibn Ibrahim, 100,
    100, 161, 162
*Source Book of American
    Architecture*, 105
South, the, 126, 132, 159, 162, 174
space(s):
    contested Muslim spaces, xv, 2,
        125, 146, 174, 180;
    and gender,182–83
    and language, 22–23;
    non-Western, 13;
    "other," 8, 9, 10, 15, 17, 76,
        142, 146, 173;
    and place. *See* place and space;
    prayer space, 25, 35, 84, 99,
        105, 107, 112, 123, 137. *See
        also musalla;*
    production of, 8, 10, 14, 17,
        22, 27, 28, 36, 76, 104–
        107, 110, 136;
    public, xiii, 2, 32, 34–35,
        36, 37, 38, 73, 114, 116,
        146, 158, 176;
    space, knowledge, and power. *See*
        Foucault, Michel;
    spatial mobility, 11, 116,
        127, 146, 147;
    spatial transformation(s),
        122n99, 174, 182;
    and topographies, 85, 113–
        14, 138, 179
stabilitas loci, 2, 22, 27, 33,
    85–86, 92, 101
Starkville, MS:
    Board of Aldermen, 125, 129,
        130, 132, 158;
    permitting process, 128–30;
    zoning in, 127–28, 130, 133
Stevens, Justice John Paul, 137, 176
Street in Cairo exhibition. *See* Qaytbay
    complex, Chicago World's Fair
subjectivity, 23, 71, 92, 148–49

subjugation:
    of Black Americans, 126, 160;
    techniques of, 150, 151
sunnah, spatial, 88
surveillance. *See* power, police power
Sweetman, John, 48
synagogues, 125, 145, 154, 155, 156

terrorism, 124, 134, 143. *See also*
    Islamophobia
theophanic experience, 85, 92
Tillman, Benjamin, 157
time:
    architect's knowledge of, 83, 84;
    and Cordoba House,
        NYC, 135–36;
    in Fakhr al-Dīn al-Rāzī, 18–21;
    and the Great Mosque of Córdoba
        debate, xiv, 2, 5;
    and historical agency, 182;
    and the *Kaʿba/qibla* axis,
        85–86, 101;
    in Opa-Locka city hall, 73;
    and space, 15, 32, 35,
        93, 113, 115
Tocqueville, Alexis de, 147–48,
    156–57, 160
tradition:
    and culture, 23–24, 76;
    power of, 48, 53;
    uses of, 23–24, 39, 113, 182
Treene, Eric, 141
Twain, Mark, 23, 42n54, 56

Umayyad dynasty, 1
*United States v. Rutherford County,
    TN,* 10, 141
urban mosques. *See* mosques
US Department of Justice, 143, 144–45,
    147, 153, 156

Venice Biennale, 34–35, 182
Venturi, Robert, 27–28
Vienna World's Fair (1873), 102
Vinour, Ollivier J., 53–56, *55*, 57, 59, 60

Voting Rights Act, 162

Waldman, Amy, 139
Washington Mosque Foundation, 103, 104
Weeks, Edwin Lord, 57
white Christians, 126, 127, 148, 155
white community, 66, 156, 165n17
white supremacy, 132, 133, 157
Wilkins, Craig L., 29
"will to truth," 16, 31, 148, 149, 150, 155, 181
Williams, Clinton L., 61
Wittgenstein, Ludwig, 116
Wolf, Michael Allen, 124, 139–40, 143
World's Columbian Exposition, Chicago (1893), 84, 94–101, *96*, *98*, 102, 115, 179
Wright Sr., Marcellus E., 62, 63, 68

xenophobia, 11, 135, 140, 146, 147, 149, 175. *See also* Islamophobia

Yaarab Temple, Atlanta, GA, 53

zoning:
  and church ordinances, 125, 127–28, 130–33, 152, 155;
  as a discursive system, 152–53;
  exclusionary, xiv, 127, 140, 152, 155–56, 158, 174–75;
  in Liberty Corner/Basking Ridge, 151–52, 154, 155, 163;
  in Rutherford County, TN, 143–44, 145;
  in Starkville, MS, 127–28, 130, 133;

About the Author

Akel Isma'il Kahera, PhD, professor of architecture and sustainable urbanism at Hamad Bin Khalifa University, Doha, Qatar, is an architect and design critic with over twenty-five years of professional practice and experience in the international arena. He is author of over thirty peer-reviewed papers, book chapters, and encyclopedia entries, as well as three books: *Deconstructing the American Mosque: Space, Gender, and Aesthetics* (2002), *Design Criteria for Mosques and Islamic Centers: Art, Architecture, and Worship* (2009; with Latif Abdulmalik and Craig Anz), and *Reading the Islamic City: Discursive Practices and Legal Judgment* (Lexington Books, 2012).

www.ingramcontent.com/pod-product-compliance
Lightning Source LLC
Chambersburg PA
CBHW020116010526
44115CB00008B/851